CABOOL:

A

PERSONAL NARRATIVE

OF A

JOURNEY TO, AND RESIDENCE

IN THAT CITY,

IN THE YEARS 1836, 7, and 8.

BY THE LATE

LIEUT.-COL. SIR ALEXANDER BURNES, C.
OF THE INDIA COMPANY'S SERVICE.

SECOND EDITION

WITH NUMEROUS ILLUSTRATIONS.

LONDON:
JOHN MURRAY, ALBEMARLE STREET.
1843.

London:
Printed by WILLIAM CLOWES and SONS,
Stamford Street.

TO

JAMES BURNES, Esq.,

MONTROSE,

THIS VOLUME IS INSCRIBED,

As a proof of my affection to a father to whom I am indebted for all I enjoy in the world: who, besides cherishing me in youth, early associated me with himself, and taught me to think and to act as a man when most of my companions had not even acquired the rudiments of their education.

ALEXANDER BURNES.

Cabool, 16th May, 1841.

PREFACE.

Some time has now passed since the following pages were written. They contain my personal recollections of an interesting country through which I passed, and in which I resided whilst employed on a mission to Cabool, in the years 1836-7 and 1838. Subsequent events have not diminished, as it appears to me, the anxiety of the public for information regarding these regions: on the contrary, the great political events of which they have since become the arena have given importance to all that appertains to them. On political subjects, however, it is not, at present, my intention to enlarge. The time is yet distant when an accurate judgment can be passed on the line of policy which we have adopted; but the travellers through these countries will, in some degree, have paved the way for the political inquirer, if, in the mean while, they can portray something of the tone and spirit of the people among whom circumstances have now placed us. My esteemed friend, Lieutenant John Wood, of the Indian Navy, has already, in his valuable work, laid before the public the stirring incidents of his journey to the lofty regions of Pamere, which was undertaken while associated with myself on this mission to Cabool. I had long and fondly hoped that the easier task of giving the minor details, which I have now imposed on myself, would have fallen to the share of Dr. P. B. Lord, a dear and much-valued friend; but his bright and short career has since abruptly terminated on the field of battle.

The reader must not expect of me a connected series of incidents. I have already carried him over part of the ground in my published travels; and I hope he will now be content to accept the gleanings which subsequent opportunity and inquiry have enabled me to present to him.

Cabool, 1841.

CONTENTS.

CHAPTER I.

Objects of the Mission—Departure from Bombay—Arrival in Sinde—Instructions—Embedded ship—Changes in the Indus—Reminiscences—Tame otter—Vikkur—Pelican—Fish—The Boolun, or porpoise—Singular ceremony—Peer Putta—Tattá—Chief of the Jokeeas—Superstition—Ramazán—Condition of the Hindoos—Kulan Cote—Ruins—Sumovee Nuggur—Kinjore—Presentation to the Ameers of Sinde—Conference—Hydrábád—Old acquaintances . . . Page 1

CHAPTER II.

Hunting excursion with the Ameers—Camel-riding—Costumes—Accident—Mode of hunting—Murderous sport—Lakat—Amusements—Hawking—Sehwun—Moral degradation—Geology—Natural history—New companions—Larkhanu—Dr. Lord—Ameer of Khyrpoor—Sindian dance—Ghoolam Nubee Khan—Deejee—Maraschino, a new medicine—Antelope-hunting—Sindian falcons—Bukkur . . . . p. 26

CHAPTER III.

Sukkur—Shikarpoor—Its commercial communications, population, bazars, &c.—River festival—Beauties—Character of the people—Wild tribes—Muzarees—A chief—Native song—Crocodile-steaks—Alligators—Mittuncote—Bhawul Khan, chief of Bhawulpoor—A French adventurer, Mons. Argoud—Mohammedan convert—Don José Gonsalvez, our artist—Runjeet Sing's officers—Kind reception—The Indus at Mittun—Dera

CONTENTS.

Ghazee Khan—District of Deerajat—Its great importance—Lohanee Afghans—Their routes—The "Gates of Khorasan"—Traffic of Dera Ghazee Khan—Vicinity—Bazars   Page 53

CHAPTER IV.

Battle between the Afghans and Sikhs—Departure from Dera Ghazee—Baber's routes—Voyage upwards—Sungur—Gurung—Dera Ismael Khan—Bazars, &c.—Corps de ballet—Donna of the Indus—Voyage to Kala Bagh—Romantic country—Kussooree hills—Singular formation—Villages—Sooleeman range . . . . p. 87

CHAPTER V.

Our critical position—State of the country—Influence of the Sikhs—The Euzoofzyes and their Chief—Plain of Peshawur—Futtihghur—The Khuttuks—Kala Bagh—Eesá Khyl Afghans—The Wuzarees—Ascent of the Indus—Coal deposits—Excessive heat—Duncote—Husn Abdal—Dr. Falconer—Arrival at Attock . . . . p. 99

CHAPTER VI.

Cross the Attock—Khyrabad and fort—Bridge of the Indus—Inscriptions at Hund—Arrival at Peshawur—Reception by General Avitabile—Prince Kurruck Sing—Review of his troops—A Peshawuree's story—Changes by the Sikhs—Curious incident—Arrival at Jumrood—Enter the Khyber Pass—Ali Musjid—Duka—Visit from the chiefs—Customs of the Khyberees—Bassoul—Kuju—Its pomegranates—Gundamuk—Anecdote of Nadir Shah—Hyat—An old friend—A facetious Mooftee—Meet Mr. Masson—Arrival at Cabool—Cordial reception . . . . . . p. 118

CHAPTER VII.

Interview with Dost Mahomed Khan—Gracious reception by the Ameer—Nawab Jubar Khan—State of affairs at Cabool—Siege of Herat—A Russian agent—Fears and hopes of the Ameer—Alchymy—Famous swords—Visit Koh-damun and Kohistan—Istalif—Its fine scenery—Wild inhabitants—Blood feuds and customs—Chareekar—Pass of Hindoo Koosh—Mines of Fureenjal—Ghorbund and Purwan rivers—Value of irrigation—Expenses of farming—Reg Ruwan—Frequency of earthquakes—Objects of our tour—Begram—Topes—Water-fowl and animals—Return to Cabool . . . Page 141

CHAPTER VIII.

Cabool—Agent from Moorad Beg of Koondooz—Letter from the Chief—His change of policy—Answer given to it—The Envoy's character of his Chief—Dr. Lord's journey to Koondooz—Extracts from his letters—Arrival and reception—Conversation with Moorad Beg—The invalid's a hopeless case—The Chief's friendship—Lieutenant Wood's journey—Syud of Talikhan, the friend of Moorcroft—Atalik Beg—Moorcroft's books, &c.—Date of his death—Mr. Trebeck's character—Customs of Uzbeks—Marriages—Man-selling—Traffic in wives—Mode of salaam—Circumcision—Enormous eating—Horse-racing and prizes—Amusements . . p. 167

CHAPTER IX.

The Siah-poosh Kaffirs—Character and customs—Mode of life—Language—Inscriptions at Bajour—Idols—Cashgar—Commerce—Climate—Clouds of red dust—The hot sand of Aksoo—Khoten—Kokan—Maimanu—Andkho—Shibbergam—Siripool—Akchu—Huzara Country—Population and descent—Customs—Curious tradition . . . . p. 206

CHAPTER X.

Our occupations at Cabool—Visit to "a Country Gentleman"—His estate—Our party—A Moollah—His ingenuity—Visit to the Mirza—Peculiar science—Summary marriage—Riches a proof of ability—Ladies of Cabool—Employments—Ameer's sisters—A murder and punishment — Courageous female—The Winter season—Lohanee merchants—Cruelty of the King of Bokhara—Horrid dungeons—Acquaintance of Mr. Elphinstone—The Ramazán—Opinions on death—Belief in dreams—Traditions—A Persian envoy—His adventures—Rejoicings—A Bokhara merchant's tea-party . . . Page 234

CHAPTER XI.

Russian Agent, Lieutenant Vilkievitch—Distribution of our party—Vicinity of Cabool—Pillars of Chukreea—Mr. Masson's researches—Ancient history of Cabool—Idols and Hindoo remains — Gurdez—Geographical memoirs—Dialects—Herat—Major Pottinger—Delay in Indian Courts—Kuzzilbash secretaries—A Moollah's tenets—Mode of lighting houses—Mild Winter—Early Spring—Idle habits—The Ameer's position—Change of policy—My departure from Cabool—Arrival at Jelálábád—River of Cabool—Our rafts—The Shutee Gurdun—Peshawur—Arrival at Lahore—Runjeet Sing—Join the Governor-General at Simla . . . . . p. 261

APPENDICES.

APPENDIX I.

REPORT OF THE ESTABLISHMENT OF AN ENTREPÔT, OR FAIR, FOR THE INDUS TRADE.

Fairs common in Asia—Lohanee Afghan merchants—Their routes—Positions on the Indus—Kala Bagh not adapted—Dera Ismael Khan—Mooltan—Bhawulpoor—Mittuncote—Dera Ghazee Khan preferable to all—January the best season—Site to be neutral—A small military force—A British superintendent necessary—Booths and warehouses—Duties to be levied—Remission of tolls on vessels returning—Rock salt of the Punjaub—Grain, probable exports—Articles of traffic—Russian fairs—Banking establishments at Shikarpoor—Effects of the Mission to Cabool . . . . . . Page 283

APPENDIX II.

REPORT ON THE RIVER INDUS, BY LIEUT. JOHN WOOD, INDIAN NAVY.

General view of the Indus—The navigable character of the river—The soundings in Indian rivers—The mode of navigating the Indus—The winds and weather in the valley of the Indus—The boats upon the Indus—Steam-vessels—Remarks on the steam-boats of the Ganges—The fuel for steam-boats—Report by Captain Johnston on the relative value of wood and coal—The inundations of the Indus—Its fords, and sites for the proposed fair—The Indus and Punjaub rivers—Concluding remarks—Tables :—1. Comparison of Chronometers—2, 3, 4. Longitudes and Latitudes of places in the line of the Indus—5, 6. On the soundings of the river—Tonnage—8, 9. Cost and hire of boats . . . . p. 304

APPENDIX III.

NOTES ON CABOOL.

Cabool favourable for commerce—Its extent—Division of government—The Ameer's army—His position powerful—Relations with Koondooz, Bokhara, Candahar, Persia—The Sikhs—Internal affairs of Cabool—Character and policy of Dost Mahomed—Prices and supplies of the country—Value of land—Crippled resources—Amount of revenue—Moderate duties—Profit on English goods—Tribes of Cabool—Ghiljees   p. 369

APPENDIX IV.

Vocabulary of the Kaffir Language . . . p. 381

APPENDIX V.

Description of the wild sheep and goats of Cabool, extracted from Dr. Lord's "Rough Notes on Natural History," now in the Library of the Asiatic Society of Calcutta . Page 384

APPENDIX VI.

An Eastern Essay on Physiognomy, &c. . . p. 389

LIST OF PLATES.

Portrait of the Author	*Frontispiece.*
Raos Palace at Mandivee	*To face page* 2
A Jokeea Soldier	12
Beelooches professionally employed	63
Son of the Governor of Dera	96
Inscriptions near Hund	121
Hyat Cafila-Bashee	137
Dost Mahomed Khan, the Ex-Chief of Cabool	141
Bactrian Coins from Koondooz, and Ancient Pateræ from Budukshan	204
A Siah-poosh Kaffir	208
Cabool	234
Umritzir	279

N. B. The original large Map, by Mr. John Arrowsmith, which accompanied the "TRAVELS TO BOKHARA," may be referred to.

CHAPTER I.

Objects of the Mission—Departure from Bombay—Arrival in Sinde—Instructions—Embedded ship—Changes in the Indus—Reminiscences—Tame Otter—Vikkur—Pelican—Fish—The Boolun, or porpoise—Singular ceremony—Peer Putta—Tattá—Chief of the Jokeeas—Superstition—Ramazán—Condition of the Hindoos—Kulan Cote—Ruins—Sumovee Nuggur—Kinjore—Presentation to the Ameers of Sinde—Conference—Hydrábád—Old acquaintances.

IN the latter end of November, 1836, I was directed by the Governor-General of India, the Earl of Auckland, to undertake a mission to Cábool. Lieutenant (now Major) Robert Leech of the Bombay Engineers, Lieutenant John Wood of the Indian Navy, and Percival B. Lord, Esq., M.B., were associated with me in the undertaking. The objects of Government were to work out its policy of opening the river Indus to commerce, and establishing on its banks, and in the countries beyond it, such relations as should contribute to the desired end. On the 26th of November we sailed from Bombay, and, sighting the fine palace at Mándivee on the 6th of December, we finally landed in Sinde on the 13th of the month. Dr. Lord did not join our party till March.

On entering the river Indus I drew up such instructions as seemed necessary to guide Lieutenants Leech and Wood. To the former I pointed out the advisability of noting all the military features of the country, and recording all the information which he could collect; to the latter I intrusted entirely the survey of the river, and to both I gave instructions to combine the advancement of general knowledge with a correct discharge of the specific duties on which they were employed. To Dr. Lord the branches of natural history and geology were subsequently assigned; but, as the published reports of this mission serve to show, the abilities of this much-lamented public servant were likewise enlisted on subjects certainly not more important, but of more immediate and pressing interest. I must refer to the printed papers before Parliament, and those reports to which I have already alluded, for the nature of the duties which devolved upon myself. With the dry diplomatic details which they contain I have no intention of fatiguing the reader. It is sufficient for me to have the satisfaction of believing that I kept open, for a time, the door of inquiry through which others entered. The object of the present volume is to give the personal and miscellaneous details of our journey.

Shortly after disembarking on the coast of Sinde

an opportunity was presented us of examining a square-rigged vessel, which had been imbedded in the Deltá of the Indus, and left, by the caprice of the river, on dry land, about twenty miles from the sea, near the fort of Vikkur, where it has lain since the time of the Calorás, the dynasty preceding that which now reigns in Sinde. This vessel, called "Armat" by the Sindians, is about 70 feet long and 28 in breadth: she seems to have been a brig of war, pierced for fourteen guns, and capable of carrying not more than 200 tons English; her greatest draft of water, marked on the stern-post, being only 9 feet, which is less than is drawn by some of the present country-boats of 40 tons (160 candies). It is, however, obvious that the Indus was at one time entered by vessels of a different description from those now in use, as this *half-fossilized* ship, if I can so call her, amply proves. The word "Armat" suggests the idea that the vessel was Portuguese, and that it is a corruption of Armada. There was also a Roman Catholic cross on the figure-head, and we know that the Portuguese burned Tattá in 1555, though this vessel, I imagine, belongs to a much later period of the history of that nation. We dug up from her hold six small brass guns, about twenty gun-barrels, and four hundred balls and shells, the latter filled with powder. These implements of war

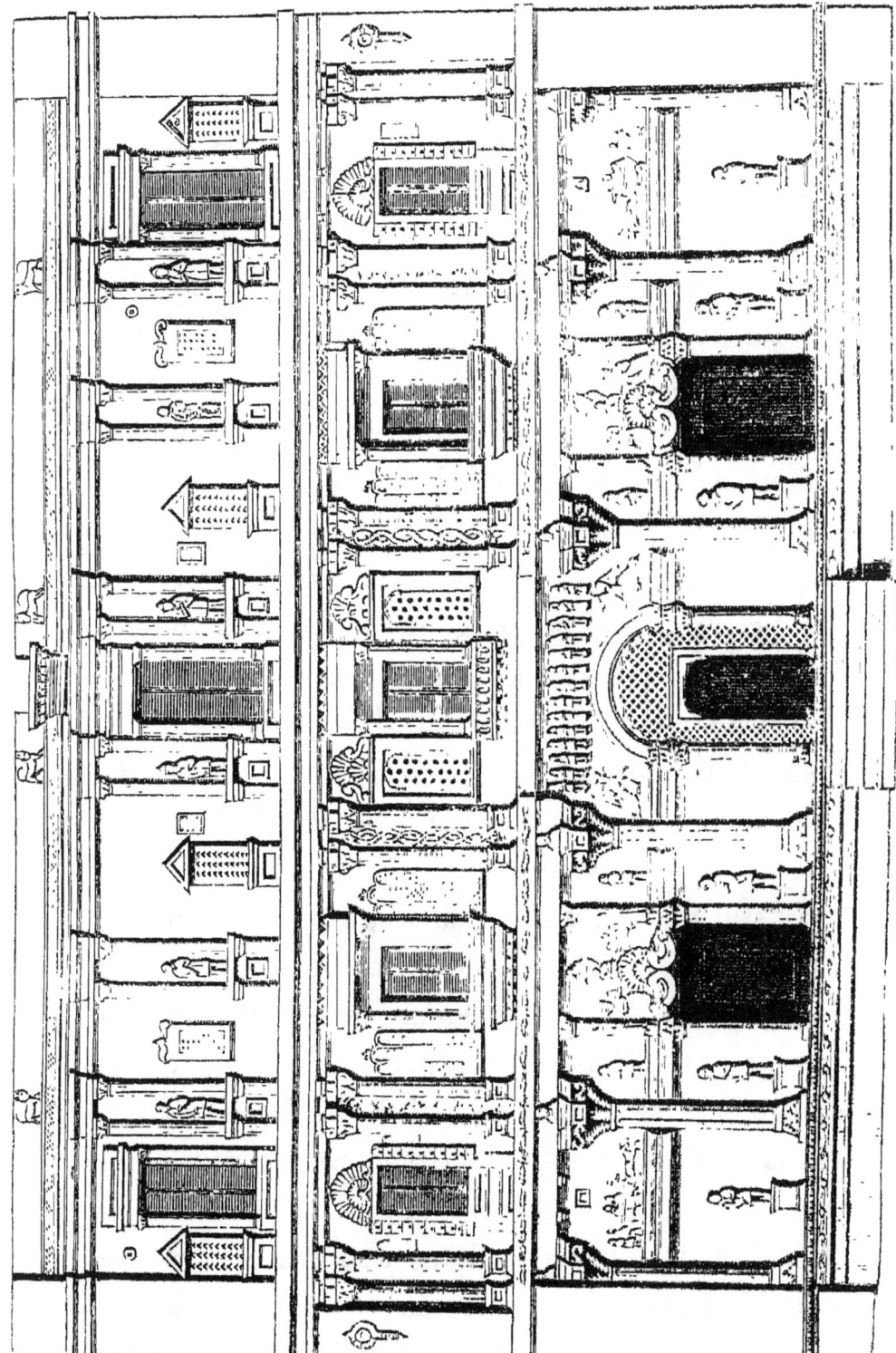

J. M. Gonsalves, del.

FRONT OF THE RAOS PALACE AT MANDIVI.

were found near the stern in the armoury, so that it is probable the vessel foundered: her position is now erect; and a large tamarisk-tree grows out of her deck. The sailors call her " Nou Khureed," or the new purchase, and state her to have been left last century in her present site, where she remains a singular object.

Since my former visit to Sinde much of the jealousy of its Government had disappeared, though enough still existed to render some degree of caution necessary. We however conversed freely with the people at the seaports, and some of them were old enough to remember the names of the English which they had heard from their fathers. They mentioned those of Calender, Baker, Erskine, and Smith, as near as I can approximate Sindian pronunciation to English; and they told us that there were still the remains of an Englishman's tomb at Dehra. The records of Government state that Mr. Calender was the gentleman who withdrew the factory from Sinde in 1775, " as we had before experienced some instances of the arbitrary disposition of the prince"—so that the present generation had not mistaken the traditions handed down to them. They seemed willing and ready again to welcome us as rulers; nor has the gratification of their wishes been long delayed, Sinde being no longer connected with Britain by a commercial factory only, but having become one of the tributary states of our mighty Indian empire.

The Indus had undergone various alterations since I saw it in 1831: but, from all that I can gather, I have doubts whether any of the vast changes surmised by Captain Macmurdo have taken place in this river. That the water has shifted from one mouth to another is certain: but the number of its mouths must long have been much the same as at present, since, in a chart published by Captain Dalrymple in 1783, I can distinguish eleven or twelve of the embouchures by the names they yet bear. It is also very questionable if the Indus were ever entered by such ships as navigate the Hoogly branch of the Ganges. Still there is ample depth in its estuaries to give encouragement to the merchant to seek, by this line, with properly-constructed vessels, a new channel for the exports of our country.

Among our earliest visitors on the river was one Cassim, who had been permitted to stop on board our boats in the Pittee, in January, 1831, and now begged to remain in our service. The sight of this man brought to my remembrance the unpleasant feelings of that night, when we were hurried down the river by ignorant men shouting and yelling: nevertheless I was glad to see Cassim again. We were visited also by the owners of three or four boats (Doondees), who had sailed with us to Bukkur, and again sought to be employed by us: one of them, Ibraheem by name, son of one of the owners, had grown up a fine young man; and as I stepped on shore he greeted me with a laughing welcome, and placed some Indian corn at my feet in renewal of our acquaintance. Self-interest may sway these people, still it is agreeable to meet with such expressions of kindly feeling.

In the evening I went out to look for some of the "raræ aves" of Sinde, and on the banks of the Gora presented my gun at a singular-looking creature; but, fortunately, curiosity held me, and I discovered it to be a tame otter searching for his evening meal, and devouring a fish which he had caught. The owner of this animal presented it to us, and it became as domesticated as a dog, and made the voyage with us as far as Bukkur; but it suffered from the change of diet, as we were unable to catch fish for it in the large river. It had also been so constantly tormented by the sailors and servants that its temper was spoiled, and we were obliged to get rid of it. In following up this river, the Gora, I found myself about two miles from Vikkur at its termination; and, entering its bed on horseback, I rode for two miles farther, when I reached the main Indus.

This fact deserves notice, for by this very branch I sailed into the river in 1831, since which time layers of mud, deposited by each succeeding inundation, have worked this change.

On the 24th of December we quitted Vikkur, and, entering the Sceam, now the favoured branch, had a pleasant sail for two days between its well-wooded banks. There, in the morning, the larks sang as clearly and loudly as in Europe, and their notes, with the slow hollow sounds of the bells hanging from the necks of the buffaloes, as we wandered among the tamarisk-shrubs, were soothing to our ear. It was here that we added the pelican to our small collection of natural history. This bird is often tamed in the Deltá of the Indus. It stood 4 feet high, measured 9 feet 8 inches from tip to tip of its wings, and was the largest bird, except the ostrich, which I had ever seen. The pelican of the Gulf of Persia and the Red Sea is white, but on the Indus it is of a greyish brown. This bird swallows with difficulty, and only when the fish is so placed that it will descend endways into the stomach.

In our wanderings on shore we always visited the "rajs," or villages of the inhabitants, and every one left his occupations on our approach to greet us with a good-humoured smile. If any of us killed a crow on the wing, no difficult task assuredly, we were pronounced " Hakim and bád sháh," ruler and king. The round flat turban of the Juts, and their peculiar expression of countenance, calm and placid, present a study for the pencil. They are industrious, and very expert in reed or basket work, which they weave from the twigs of the tamarisk, and fit into all their vessels, thus rendering them dry and comfortable. At one of these villages we purchased for our boatmen two loads of fish, about eighty in number, for one rupee. The distribution was made with great pains: the fish were first divided into two lots; an indifferent person then took two bits of clay of different sizes, the parties guessed, and they were delivered accordingly. Each lot was again subdivided into three more shares, and much the same ceremony gone through; after which the fishes were with all haste transferred to the cooking-pot, the men chopping off the scales with an axe—a formidable instrument for so delicate an affair. The fish were chiefly what are called " dumbree."

Our entrance into the great river was first distinguished by the rolling of the " boolun," a kind of porpoise, by far the most remarkable inhabitant of the Indus, and which I have only once had an opportunity of catching alive. It is well described by the Emperor Báber as the " water-hog," which it much resembles while playing in its element. It is evidently of the order Cetacea. The temperature of the Indus was 58°, whilst that of the small branch we had left was 62°.

The solemnity with which the Sindians navigate their mighty river never ceases to amuse the voyager. In any part of it where it is necessary to give the boat an extra pull, the "meerbur" or master calls out "Sháh bash puhleewán!" "Bravo, my heroes!" and gravely promises to have their beards dyed fresh on the termination of the voyage; and there is as much zeal and industry displayed as if an enemy instead of a river were to be opposed. In turning a corner of the stream one vessel grounded about fifty yards from the shore, and threw up a wave five or six inches high, which moved steadily along until it met the bank. Lower down this becomes the "bore," which is so formidable; only there the causes spring from nature, and not accident. It is curious to notice the boats of Sinde, made of foreign wood, as in Egypt: the latter country is supplied from Syria, and the former from India—another point of resemblance between the two countries, in addition to the many that have been remarked.

On the 31st of December we passed Noora Kanode, and halted near a sugar-plantation about seven miles from Peer Putta. They water the cane day and night by two sets of Persian wheels, one above the other. A camel turned the first, and two bullocks the other, while one man attended both. If the animals, which were blinded, could have seen, they would assuredly have expected more attention. In Sinde they never advance further in the preparation of the cane than molasses. We passed inland to visit the shrines at Peer Putta, a vast collection of whitened tombs on a ridge of hillocks, overlooking the Buggaur branch of the Indus, on which they stand, and the neighbouring country, which is a dense jungle of tamarisk. This place of pilgrimage is stated to be 800 years old, and is frequented by Hindoo and Mahomedan. On taking off our shoes we were readily admitted, and civilly treated. On the walls of one of the principal shrines we saw the name of "Henry Ellis, 1809," one of Mr. Hankey Smith's assistants, and lately our ambassador at the court of Persia. Under Peer Putta the Buggaur lay before us in a fine and deep expanse of water—a clear proof of its communication with the Indus a few months before; though, at this season, the water was stagnant, and the sand-banks at its mouth prevented the further ingress of the stream, yet this year boats from Hala have passed down it to the sea laden with chaunia (alkali).

On New Year's Day we reached Tattá, to which the river was now tending, and will probably adjoin before this century closes. My old political antagonist, Zoolfkár Sháh, whom I had expected to meet, had paid the debt of nature but seven days before we arrived. I had brought, at his request, some candlesticks for him from Bombay; but, poor man! he requires no more the light of sun or torch in this darkened world. I wished much to have seen this accomplished Asiatic under the altered circumstances of our present visit, and hoped for his aid in gathering information of this once great but ruined emporium. The Nuwáb of Tattá and a confidential servant of the rulers received us instead of the poor Syud, and showed the way to the city. We entered without pomp or suite; the inhabitants shouted out welcomes to us, and besought us to "come and people this desert:" one man said, "What is there to look at in this wilderness? Come, and it will flourish under the English." Others said, but more softly, that the rulers were blind; and a perfumer called out to us to purchase his rose-water, as there were no buyers left. They facetiously tell you that from Curáchee to Hydrábád, by land or by sea, there is nothing left to the poor man, and but half to the rich. Since 1831 the cholera has desolated Tattá, but it is deemed throughout Sinde one of the lowest and most unhealthy sites: the wells and water are generally fetid: there is also much stagnant water; and even in the winter the mists of the morning are disagreeable.

One of our first visitors was the chief of the Jokeeas, Jam Mihr Alee, who had come from the hills west of Tattá, where his tribe leads a nomade life, to provide us with a guard. The Jam was a stout man of advanced age, with a beard dyed with henna—an uncouth being, who seemed mightily delighted at hearing from me a few words in bad Sindee. Although this was a Jokeea of rank, it will be seen he retained the Hindoo title of Jam. On his taking leave some medicines were given to him, which secured his good offices; and he shortly sent a dozen of his tribe to escort us. Wild and uncouth-looking and long-haired as they are, they are famed for their fidelity. In the portrait of Peroz I shall present the tribe better to my readers than by description. With his men the Jam sent a fine buck, slung across the saddle of one of his horsemen, and in return we gave him powder to continue his sporting avocations. The specimen which these Jokeeas shortly gave us of their ball practice left no favourable opinion of their skill. At ninety yards every one of them missed a bottle: the distance was lessened, but the result was the same; and then it was gravely discovered that the shots had been fired in the direction of Mecca, which rendered success impossible. The practice was continued from an opposite point of the compass, but with equally bad success. We were vastly amused at this trait of superstition, and at the crestfallen looks of the mountaineers, who had been boasting loudly of their skill; but all Sindians are given to gasconade: if a dozen people live together, they call their dwelling a city (shuhur); and if eight or ten of our party moved about anywhere, they were designated an army (lushkur). Besides these Jokeeas, our only escort in this lengthened journey consisted of a dozen Arabs, and six Myánás or plunderers from Cutch. Accompanied by these children of the desert and the mountaineers of Sinde, we saw no foes. The constitution of such a guard affords some subject for reflection as to the state of British influence in India.

At Tattá many Moollás visited us, and brought, on our inquiring for them, various books for sale. Among the volumes I found the "Chuch-namu," and "Toohfut aol Kiramee," both histories of Sinde: but the major part of their stores consisted of commentaries on the Korán, prayer-books, and poetry, though I doubt not that a diligent search here would be well rewarded. Our principal guide was

PEEROZ, A JOKEEA SOLDIER.

one Mirzá Gool Mahomed, a scion of the great Mirzá Eesá Toorkhanee, and who, though poverty-stricken, yet possessed "furmáns" of Sháh Jehán. Literature in this region has decayed with commerce and population. During our stay the "eed," or festival at the termination of Ramazán, occurred; and the whole assemblage at the place of public prayers did not exceed 2000 souls. No Hindoo ventures out on such an occasion in Sinde; and this exhibition, as well as subsequent inquiries, led me to fix the present population of this city at from 8000 to 10,000 people, but the town is gradually going to decay.

Assoomul, the brother of Gundá, a Hindoo, and one of the most intelligent of his tribe, is the first merchant in Tattá. He visited us, and was very communicative: he deplored the decay of his native city, and said, metaphorically, that the merchant and the cultivator were but the soil of a country—that the soil could not flourish unless it was watered by commerce.

The condition of the Hindoos is best illustrated by statements of their own. While we were at Tattá a half-witted person died: the Moslems claimed the body, that it might be buried: the Hindoos waited on the Governor to remonstrate. Some Mahomedans declared that the deceased had, on more than one occasion when he was uttering curses, used certain of their holy names, and they supported their arguments by the Korán: so the corpse was borne in triumph to the hill of Mukklee, and consigned to the earth in the consecrated ground of Islám. A month before our arrival a mother and two children became voluntary converts to Mahomedanism. Eighteen months previous a Hindoo, at a neighbouring village, was seized and forcibly converted because of the offences of a brother who had absconded. At the same time it is said that most of the converts become so voluntarily, and I state this on Hindoo authority. The Hindoos avoid with scrupulous care all mention of the names held sacred by their masters. The mercantile town of Ulláh yár Ká Tandá they simply designate Tandá, to avoid saying Ulláh, which means God. Not a Hindoo shows himself in a procession; while in India the "eed" is celebrated by a far greater number of them than of Mahomedans. Within these five or six years a very outrageous instance of conversion by force happened in Sinde, in the person of Hotchund, one of the first merchants of Curáchee. He subsequently fled to Cutch, and now resides at Lucput with a numerous family; but his sons decline to eat with their parent. The unhappy man has wealth and property, but no outlay of it can restore him to the lost privileges of his tribe.

The antiquities of Tattá have ever excited a lively interest, nor were we idle in our inquiries. We paid an early visit to Kulan Cote, which lies about four miles to the south-west, on the same ridge of hills as that on which the fine tombs of Mukklee stand. It at once struck me as the site of ancient Tattá. "Kulan Cote" literally means the large fort; and here, in fact, we found a fortified hill, about three-quarters of a mile long and 500 yards of average breadth. Its shape is that of a parallelogram, excepting on the south-west angle, where it juts out. The whole surface of the hill has been fortified with a mud wall, faced with kiln-burnt bricks. In the space I have described, the ruins of streets are to be traced; and there is a mosque of rather large dimensions, with a fountain in front of it. In treading on these remains we often heard a sound as if the ground beneath us were hollow. At one end we found a large store of burned or charred wheat: many of the bricks, too, were vitrified. Kulan Cote is considered, and called, the old fort of Tattá. To the west are the remains of a suburb, but on all the other sides it is surrounded by a lake of spacious dimensions, supplied by a cut from the Indus east of Tattá. At one end of this lake there are various places of Hindoo worship, formed in the grottoes or natural fissures of the rock, a conglomerate honeycombed limestone, full of shells, and often separating, in a very remarkable manner, into caverns. The fish of this lake are preserved, because of its being a place of pilgrimage for the Hindoos of Tattá, who offer up their devotions here twice a month. Is this the " Dewul Sindee," of which antiquarians are in search? There is certainly not a temple (dewul), but there are no temples in Sinde; besides, this country is often called Dewul, even in modern times. When last I was in Bombay, the native agent at Muscat, in Arabia, wrote as a matter of news that the Imam was about to attack Zanguebar, and had sent to *Dewul* to hire soldiers; he had applied to Sinde for mercenaries. Kulan Cote, as it now stands, is not given to an age prior to that of Islam, but it stands on ground peculiarly adapted for the site of a fort, and one which the founders of Tattá would of course have selected. There are no ruins between it and modern Tattá, and a circumference of three miles encloses all the mounds of the latter. On the northern side of the town the remains differ from those in the other parts, and a wall may be traced. This is said to have been the fort of the Soomrás and Sumas. Tattá is yet called, *par excellence*, " Bulda," or " Nuggur," both of which mean *the* city; and in its site, as I have elsewhere stated, we have little doubt of having found the ancient Minagur.

Four miles N.W. of Tattá, and due north of Kulan Cote, we have the remains of Sumovee-nuggur, which is said to have been peopled before the present city. There are now but eight or nine huts, which are inhabited by those who protect the shrine of Sháh Jeendá hard by. A small branch of the Indus, the Kulairee, lies beyond, and is the first offshoot of the river on its right bank: if full it would insulate Tattá, but now its waters are wasted. The hill of Mukklee terminates at Sumovee-ṅuggur. Sumovee was a town of the Jams, or Sumas, and their tombs still remain near it. Bumboorá, on the road to Tattá from Curáchee, is said to be coeval with Sumovee. Between Tattá and this ancient place is another ruin called Sida, also marked by a shrine; with it a fable is coupled of a Hindoo converting paper into money, and, on being found out, sinking into the earth. It is yet a place of pilgrimage. Brahminábád I cannot find under that name, although some Sindians tell you its bricks were used in the modern houses of Roree, and others that it stood near Khodábád or Hala. There is a place of antiquity called Bamina, in the Thurr; and another, named Kake, near Omercote. There is however much in modern Tattá to mark its antiquity. The fossil shells of the Mukklee hills are made into beads for rosaries: a seed of the palm, I believe, from Lus, called "pees," is also bored for the same purpose, and looks very like agate. The Hindoo pilgrims encourage this trade on their road to Hinglaj. The "teeruts" at Kulan Cote, and Kalka on Mukklee hill, with the residence of five hundred Brahmin families even now in this decayed city, all point to its Hindoo sanctity; and if they do not supply sufficient data to enable us to discover Dewul Sindee and Brahminábád, they at least furnish scope for surmise and conjecture.

But antiquity has detained me too long, and I must dismiss the tombs of the Suma-Jams, Nunda, and Tumachee, with an expression of admiration at their chaste beauty, and continue my account of our voyage.

The Ameers announced, through the Governor of Tattá, their anxiety for our advance, as the hunting season would soon be concluded, and they wished us to join them in their sports. I was at first disposed to give them less credit for their sincerity than the result proved them to deserve. They could not imagine it possible that we should have found anything to interest us in Tattá, as not one of the reigning family had ever deigned to visit the place, though it is but 56 miles from their capital. We quitted Tattá on the 11th of January, and proceeded on our voyage.

On reaching Hiláya we disembarked, and proceeded for about three miles inland to the lake of Kinjore, one of three sheets of water which extend north and south for about 20 miles, and during the inundation communicate with the Indus. Here we were promised much sport, nor were we disappointed. We embarked in skiffs on the lake, a large and beautiful expanse of water, for the purpose of seeing a new mode of ensnaring fish. Nets were stretched across the lake at a point where it was about 600 yards wide, and four circular receiving nets were fixed at intervals along the line in such a manner as that the fish, their progress being stopped by the long nets, might be tempted to leap into the circular ones. The fishermen conducted us to the end of the lagoon, where they commenced beating the water, jumping in their boats, striking their cooking utensils, shouting and yelling, and making all sorts of imaginable noises; at the same time they gradually advanced. The fish, frightened, fled before them, and, finding no other exit, leaped into the circular nets, and became an easy prey to their pursuers. Upwards of a hundred were caught, and the fishermen seemed to enjoy the sport as much as ourselves. They are a tall and handsome race, and claim to be aborigines and descended of Rhátore Rajpoots. They refer with exultation to the days of Jam Tumáchee, when one of their females, famed for her beauty, fixed the affections of that prince, and secured privileges for her tribe which they yet possess. After a day's enjoyment of fishing and shooting we proceeded onwards, passing many decayed tombs, with which, in this region, most of the hillocks are crowned, and directed our course towards the river at Sonda, to which place our boats had advanced. The country was saline, and as usual little of it was cultivated. The capparis, asclepidias, and tamarisk had been our companions throughout the route; and before nightfall we reached a "shikárgáh," or hunting-thicket of the Ameers, and were delighted with the perfume of the babool as we sauntered along the banks of the river. Our boats were on the opposite side, and when the boatmen shouted to our party their cries resounded through the thickets, and were re-echoed by the rocky hillocks. We had no sooner reached the boats than one of our Jokeeás commenced playing upon his "tumachee," a kind of rude guitar, much to the amusement of his companions. After enduring his inharmonious strains for some time, we opposed him with some fine musical boxes, and from this day the vanquished performer fairly admitted that his instrument had lost its power. A Swiss mountaineer would not have been so easily turned aside from the airs of his native hills; nor perhaps was our Jokeeá friend in his inmost heart.

From Tattá to Hydrábád the western bank of the Indus presents to the eye a maze of hills, of sand and lime formation, and destitute of herbage. The lower hills bear the name of Gara or Kara, and it is difficult to discover in them any continuous range; the Hala mountains lie beyond and tower over them. There are roads through the hills from Curáchee to Sehwun, and also to Jurruk and Hydrábád. We passed these bleak scenes rapidly, and reached the capital on the 18th of January.

On the following day we were presented to the Ameers, when I delivered my credentials from the Governor-General of India. The interview was a protracted one, and the chiefs were cordial and kind. We first saw the two Ameers Noor and Nusseer Khán, and then accompanied them to Meer Mahomed, who was sick and confined to his apartments. Sobdar, the fourth Ameer, was, as usual, absent, but his son appeared in the assemblage. Noor Mahomed said that "his father had firmly planted the tree of friendship between the states." "Yes, my lord," said I, "it is true he did so, but your highness has watered it." "It has grown into a large tree," rejoined the Ameer. "It is true, my lord," I replied, "and the fruit is now visible." In this complimentary style, to which I had been familiarized during my former visit, all our conversation was carried on. After some general topics had been discussed, I was questioned as to Runjeet Sing's designs on Northern Sinde. I answered that a friend's country was not to be invaded by a friend's friend. I then explained the objects of the Governor-General in sending me on the present expedition,—the line of my proposed journey, —our intention of examining and measuring the Indus, even as far as to Attock,—my ultimate destination to Cábool and Candahár, for the purpose of explaining to the rulers and merchants there our policy in opening the Indus, and,—finally, the most important point of all, the instructions which I had received to endeavour to infuse confidence into all classes, by a declaration of the happy and close friendship which subsisted between the British and the Powers on the Indus. To all this statement a profound attention was given. When I had concluded the Ameer said, "Your journey is a long one; you shall be welcome whilst you continue in Sinde, and when you return to it." Before separating, the Ameers, as usual, caused me to speak the few sentences in Sindee which I had picked up by the roadside, and expressed their delight; but I now told them that I had a grammar of their language, prepared by Mr. Wathen, the Chief Secretary to Government; and with a promise to give them a copy of it the interview terminated.

The Ameers proceeded next day to enjoy the sports of the field, and left us to examine the bazárs of Hydrábád. No one could more heartily appreciate than I did the change of tone in this court, or more sincerely rejoice at the prosperous consequences which had flowed from my former voyage by the Indus to Lahore.

At Hydrábád I found a cássid or courier from Cábool, a relative of my old acquaintance Hyát the Cáfila-báshee, and who had accompanied me to Khooloom and Koondooz. I recognised the man at once, and inquired after my friends. "Moorád Beg," said he in a very significant tone; "was *that* Moorád Beg?" "Atmá Dewán Begee, his minister," continued the cássid, "had been in Cábool to get a wife, and had often blessed himself for having treated you so well." I gave the old courier, by name Massoom, as much flesh as he could eat, and he exclaimed, "Who could tell that you were the man who wore a pelisse with two robes? but we always knew you!" This wanderer offered to carry my despatches to Cábool, and I readily accepted his services. Molláh Nanuk also came to tell me the news of Bokhárá, and that he knew Ulláh Dád,

Sirwur Khán, and many of my old *compagnons de voyage*. He asked me if I had seen any Islám like that of Bokhárá. But I must get nearer these scenes ere I enlarge upon them.

It is not my design to enter into any detail of the arrangements which I made with the rulers of Sinde. I had frequent and friendly intercourse with them: one day Noor Mahomed said to me, "You had not even a beard when I first knew you." I replied that "one now covered my chin with black, in mourning for my departed youth,"—an idea which I had stolen from Sady, and which was loudly applauded. He next asked me what books I had read: I replied, chiefly historical; when his brother inquired if I had finished the Goolistán and Bostán? They asked me why we objected to the slave-trade? Upon which I explained the enormities of a slave-ship, and the compact which the powers of Europe had entered into to suppress the traffic. On taking leave of Noor Mahomed, he said, "It is pleasant to converse with intelligent men, as it makes one learned;"—a specimen of Sindian adulation which must stand in place of further details; and I shall now transfer the scene beyond Hydrábád.

CHAPTER II.

Hunting excursion with the Ameers—Camel-riding—Costumes, —Accident—Mode of hunting—Murderous sport—Lakat— Amusements—Hawking—Sehwun—Moral degradation—Geology—Natural history—New companions—Larkhanu—Dr. Lord—Ameer of Khyrpoor—Sindian dance—Ghoolam Nubee Khán—Deejee—Maraschino, a new medicine—Antelope-hunting—Sindian falcons—Bukkur.

THE Ameers of Hydrábád gave us a pressing invitation to accompany them on one of their hunting excursions north of their capital, which we readily accepted. We left the city in the evening of the 5th of February, and the next morning joined their highnesses at the ferry of Khaupootra, ten miles distant. All ceremony seemed now laid aside. Meer Shahdad, the eldest son of Noor Mahomed, visited us at our breakfast-hour, and the Ameers pulled up at our tent-doors, and asked after us as they passed.

Shahdad is about 22 years old. He looks worn, and is said to be dissipated; he struck me as better educated than his father or uncles. He asked me what was the religion of China; and, after receiving some explanation on the subject, said it must then be that of Jengis Khán. A number of the 'Edinburgh Review' lay on the table, and in reply to his inquiries I explained, as well as I could to a Sindian, what a review was. He listened very attentively, and said that "Two-thirds of all nations were fools, but he supposed we had reduced the number to one-fifth." He seemed uneasy at thinking that he was interrupting our meal; and, saying his father would be wondering at his absence, took his leave. He had been praying at the tomb of his grandfather, Moorad Ali, and is a rigid Shiah.

Before mid-day a messenger came running to our tents and informed us that the Ameers were waiting for us. Our party, consisting of Lieutenants Wood and Leech and myself, immediately set out to join them, mounted on splendidly-caparisoned riding-camels, which had been sent for our use. We found Noor and Nusseer Mahomed in "mafras," a kind of conveyance like a native palanqueen, carried by two strong mules, one in front and the other in the rear. They alighted on our joining them, and mounted camels. I expressed a hope that this new arrangement, by which they exchanged a comfortable conveyance, sheltered from a hot sun, for the back of a camel, was not made on our account. The Ameers replied with great kindness, declaring that it was perfectly agreeable to them, and we all trotted along together on camels, which, when trained, are certainly a pleasant means of conveyance. When prayer-time arrived we dismounted, and, sheltering ourselves under a tree, sent a message requesting the Ameers to proceed without us, which, as they had had rather too much sunning, they accordingly did, and we joined them in the evening. The Ameers, on this occasion, affected no state; they conversed very familiarly with all their attendants, and the men who guided their camels were as well dressed as themselves. They wore common yellow shirts, made like a blouze, with large loongees round their waists. Noor Mahomed asked why we had no kummerbunds, or waist-sashes, and I replied that we wore tight clothes instead. He said that the sash was a great ornament. The Sindians of the party were as noisy as their countrymen are in general, and the number of "bismillas" (in the name of God), and "Ya Ali" (Oh Ali), as the camels climbed the side of an aqueduct, or as they shuffled along the road, was highly amusing. The cortège was very scattered: there seldom were more than thirty people in all with the Ameers, the falconers and the physicians following as they pleased; but, by the evening, we were all gathered together at Mesa, a mean village, which has a garden and a hunting-box, where the chiefs alighted. At night they sent to us, requesting a sight of the caps we had worn, and which they perceived had shaded us from the sun, by which they themselves had suffered so much. Lieutenant Leech's cap in particular, a large white *broad brimmer*, turned up inside and out with green, had drawn forth great laudations during the march. As for mine, it was a "*shocking bad hat*," and I was absolutely ashamed to submit it to the inspection of these potentates, its days of service had been so many. I sent it nevertheless, convinced that anything which taught a Talpoor to screen himself from the sun would be of important service to him. At dinner we enjoyed the roast meat of our entertainers, and all our people, as well as their own, shared the hospitality of the Ameers, not only on this evening, but throughout the excursion.

The Sindians are very expert in putting their horses in and out of boats, but at the ferry this morning one of the horses dislocated his shoulder, and his terrified groom brought him to us for our advice. After examining the poor animal, I ordered him to be thrown down, and all our horse-keepers to pull and tug at the limb. The struggles of the animal, probably more than the skill of the operators, set all to rights, for to our great surprise, and to the decided increase of our reputation for universal science, he sprung up as well as ever. The Ameers soon heard of the affair, and the owner of the horse was far more delighted at the honour done to his steed than he had previously been when I presented him with a lithographed copy of the Goolistan. He was Ali Khán, the brother of Ahmed Khán, the Lagharee chief.

On the afternoon of the 7th we set out on camels and followed the Ameers to Majindu. The distance was about 20 miles through an open and arid country, very near the outlying hills, and the Lukkee range was in sight. We found the chiefs in another of their hunting-boxes, examining their weapons and talking over their expectations of sport. They received us without any ceremony, and placed Lieutenant Leech and myself on a cot opposite to them. Lieutenant Wood was unavoidably absent. Noor Mahomed made me a present of a small Sindian rifle, and taught me the manner of using it, he and his brother adjusting my hands. At last the Ameer got up and fired at a jar as a mark which was placed so near that he could not well miss it. I followed him and shivered the vessel twice; no great feat, but which fixed my character as a " topchee." A dagger was then given to Lieutenant Leech, and another was sent to Lieutenant Wood. We promised to join the party next day in the Sindian dresses with which their highnesses had provided us; it having been decided *nem. con.* that the game in the hunting-grounds could not but be frightened at so novel a sight as the tight habiliments of a Firingee.

We started at sunrise, as usual, on camels, and after proceeding about three miles entered the preserve. The Sindians, usually so noisy, became at once quite silent. Meer Nusseer Khán, near whom I was riding, dismounted, and, desiring me to do the same, took me by the hand and led me to a grass hut, in which was a raised platform, where he seated himself, and me beside him. The front of the hut was open, and here we remained in anxious expectation till the game should be driven down towards us by men and packs of ferocious-looking dogs, which we soon heard yelling and barking from the opposite side of the thicket. One solitary hog came, but he did not give us an opportunity to fire, though the Ameer had passed to me one of his fine guns, and insisted upon my taking the first shot. After the lapse of half an hour the arrival of the dogs, bloody and almost breathless, showed that this preserve at least was cleared. We therefore mounted our camels and joined Noor Mahomed Khán, who led the way to other ground. Here the same arrangements were made; and I sat by the side of the principal Ameer, with the gun which he had given me the preceding evening. The game was here more abundant, and some eight or ten hogs soon showed themselves. The Ameer, like a true sportsman, exclaimed, "That is your side, this is mine." I fired first, and killed a hog,—nor could I well miss, since the animal was not more than 25 or 30 yards off, and I fired with a rifle and a rest. The Ameer, however, was greatly delighted, seized me by the hand, and shouted his applause; and I, knowing myself to be but a poor representative of the British sportsman, was glad that at least I had not disgraced my nation. After a short interval up bounded a hog-deer (Kotah-pachir, or para—*Cervus Porcinus*), and, as he sprung past the box, and while in the air, was shot dead by the hands of the Ameer. It was a clever quick shot, but the sport would be considered as pure murder by the initiated; for in this instance the distance between the muzzle of the rifle and the game did not exceed three or four yards; but Noor Mahomed is a keen and good sportsman, and there was much both of pleasure and excitement in the whole affair. Covers of young tamarisk generally surround the hunting-boxes, and narrow alleys are cut through these in different directions, but all converging to the hut where the Ameer is seated. It was amusing to notice the poor animals pause as they crossed these paths, and gaze deliberately down them, as if consulting with themselves what course to pursue:

then ever and anon frightened at the yells of the dogs behind them, they would rush onwards in despair, and generally to certain death. After this the party broke up; and, bidding farewell to our kind entertainer, Nusseer Khan, who proceeded from hence to enjoy the sport in his own preserves, we trotted on for a dozen miles until we reached the Indus. On our way we overtook Noor Mahomed Khan in his palanqueen, and rode with him for some distance. He and his brother wore plain suits of grey woollen cloth—the only visible indication of their rank consisted in their sleeve-buttons of emeralds, and their jewelled daggers. Their rifles also were richly ornamented, and of these each had three or four loaded by him. The locks were English. but the other parts of the piece of native manufacture. They only used English powder in priming. We crossed the river in the state barge of the Ameer, and now found ourselves in the district of Lakat. Next morning we rode along the river for about ten miles to Nihaya, which is considered the best sporting-ground in Sinde.

The pleasures of the field were for a few days interrupted by a southerly wind, which is considered unfavourable to the sport, but on the 12th a change of wind again drew us forth, and there was a slight hoar-frost on the ground and bushes, but on the boughs of the tamarisk it was soon converted into tear-drops. Noor Mahomed Khan was in great spirits, and laughed heartily when one of the grass huts in which we were sitting came down with us, and we all rolled over each other. On this day we had good sport, and I began to question the opinion I had first formed regarding their mode of killing game; for so densely thick are the covers in this region, that, without some such arrangement as that which they adopt, I doubt the possibility of their killing anything. These parks, or " Moharees " as they are called, seem to be planned with care. A large tract of ground, shaped as a square or parallelogram, is staked off, and wattled all round so as to prevent the egress of the game. This again is subdivided into many triangular divisions, and at each of the angles so formed a shooting-box, or " Koodunee," is placed, and the animals which escape at one point are constrained to pass to another. The plan of these parks seemed to me as follows.

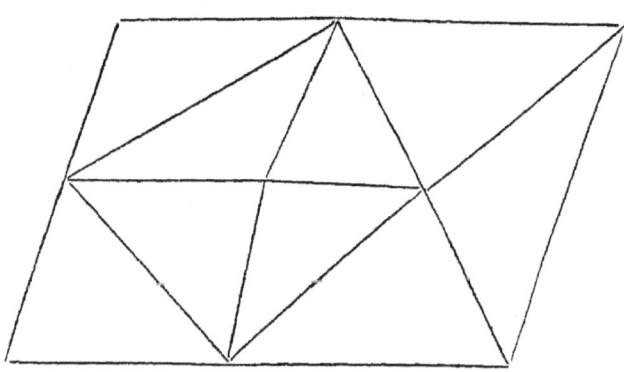

During the whole of the sport the Ameers were the only persons, with the exception of myself, who fired a shot. Innumerable sons and nephews were present, but were not allowed to pull a trigger.

We passed several days in this manner, hunting and fishing. The venison from the hog-deer is most delicious, but the society we were in prevented our eating the wild hog: we had, however, roasted partridges and Beloochee kabobs daily sent to us, and fared extremely well. Some mornings we went out hawking with the Ameers' falcons. This is a spirited sport, and I should say there was as much certainty of the game being killed by a hawk well managed as by a gun in the hands of a good shot. With a couple of hawks we generally returned, after two hours, with six brace or more in our bag. The birds were of two sorts—the " baz," or grey falcon, with large yellow eyes, from Khorasan, and the " bashu," a native of Sinde, a kind of sparrow-hawk. The mode of training seems much the same as in Persia—the eyes being sewn up for many days, and the creatures denied all sleep till subdued.

We received many friendly visits from the Ameer, and had frequent and familiar conversations with him. He was evidently anxious to impress upon us that he had no higher way of marking his favour than by bringing us with him through his own country to his preserves, since it showed to the people that we were "as one." We cordially acknowledged the justice of the observation and our full appreciation of his kindness. "A better understanding," said I, " has lately arisen between the Governments, and this friendly intercourse will cement it." Foreseeing, I suppose, the inevitable departure of independent greatness, Noor Mahomed asked much about the treatment shown by us to the native princes of India. He inquired as to the pension granted to the Great Moghul. This information I gave him, at the same time claiming credit to England for her liberality in not only releasing that personage from the Mahrattas, but assigning to him an annual stipend of fifteen lacs of rupees. He expressed surprise that the Guicwar, the Mahratta ruler of Baroda in Guzerat, should have an income of nearly a crore of rupees, and asked how the resident at his court was paid. He enlarged on the wealth of Guzerat; inquired into the cause of Girnar having fallen into decay, also whether there was still a place named Champaneer, and what was the state of Ahmedabad, as all these had been noted places in the time of Mahomed Begra. He asked if I had ever seen any river which could be compared with the Indus? I replied that I had seen the Ganges, the Oxus, and the Nile; but never any river so favourable for the ruler, the subject, and the merchant, as the Indus. "Most other countries," added I, "require rain, but Sinde can do without it." He said Sinde was a fine country, particularly the lower part of it; that rain always brought with it disease, and that they were better without it. The Ameer also told me that he had five histories of Sinde which he would give me—a promise, by the by, which he never fulfilled. He seemed tolerably conversant with the annals of his country, of the Soomras and Sumas, and quoted the tradition of the Sund Rajas having captured Cutch by concealing themselves under grass and entering one of the principal forts. These subjects drew him on to speak of his own ancestors, and their connexion with the British government. He asked after Mr. Ellis, whom he said he remembered, adding that his abilities were great, and that a saying of his was often repeated by his father and uncles. When a native agent was to be stationed in Sinde, the Ameers wished to fix him at Tattá. Mr. Ellis replied, "No; let him be under the shade of the Ameers;" and Hydrábád became his residence. I give the foregoing as a specimen of the general tone of his conversation. We bade farewell to his Highness on the 16th at

Nasree, and proceeded to join our boats near Sehwun, the Ameer departing the same day for his capital; both parties, if protestations could be relied upon, delighted with the expedition, and with all its incidents and adventures.

Now that I had made the journey from the sea to near Sehwun by land, and had acquired a more extensive knowledge of the country, I perceived how liable we are to be mistaken as to its wealth and fertility. Nothing can be more tiresome to the eye than the monotonous plains of tamarisk which bound the view in every direction; but it is quite certain that a great portion of these plains might be irrigated. The tamarisk is easily hewn down, and the Ameers never proceed to hunt but a broad road is cut through it with little labour. The rich part of Sinde is not to be found on the banks of the Indus, but at some miles inland, where the water is conducted by canals. Often too, in the interior of the country, there are large " dunds " or stagnant lakes left by the inundation, and these are also used for irrigation. I have already mentioned those of Kinjore, and in Lakat also we met with several. They abound in fish, and innumerable fresh-water shells are found round the banks of all these pools: some of these are transparent and delicate. It was remarked that, though we were in low countries, we had not seen a frog, a scorpion, or a snake; the cast-off skins of the latter had, however, been found.

On our way to the river we were met by many of the inhabitants, and it was curious to see the interest which even the poorest of them took in the late sport. They invariably asked us if the Ameer had killed much game. I expected such questions from the higher orders, but was not prepared to find the peasants equally interested in the matter. Near Tattá one of them brought to me the head of a wolf, which he had killed in one of the preserves, and demanded a gift, not because he had destroyed the enemy of man, but because wolves injured the Ameers' sport. Laws very similar to the old forest-laws of England seem to obtain here. Any trespass on the hunting-thickets is severely punished; and a stray bullock or buffalo which enters them is confiscated. Our presence among the Sindians had evidently made no little impression upon them, for they asked if they would still be allowed to kill beef and say their prayers aloud, the interdiction of these privileges being the proofs of conquest which their neighbours, subdued by the Sikhs, have had imposed upon them. The Sindian, however, whether his station be high or low, has attained but an humble place in the scale of civilization. Throughout this journey we found all parties dissipated and indifferent to almost everything but sensuality. The tamarisk, their native shrub, is a type of the country —weeds overgrow the soil, physical and moral.

Before passing on to Sehwun we visited the mineral springs at Lukkee, which flow from a fissure of the rock under a perpendicular precipice of about 600 feet, which, in its nakedness, put me in mind of Hindoo Koosh. The temperature of the water was 102°, the air being at 70°, and the odour sent forth was sulphureous and unpleasant. The spring flows unintermittingly, and deposits near its source some caky substance, or silica. The rock is entirely formed of shells and limestone, and the rents and fissures present a singular chaos, as if nature had been convulsed. The organic remains of former ages are innumerable; the asteroid, the cockle, the oyster, the nummulite, and almost all kinds of sea-shells, may be collected on the Lukkee range. In the clefts I found bones, but these were modern, and had evidently been dragged there by hyænas and jackals. A more minute search would, however, reward the geologist in this interesting range. I have also little doubt that the loftier mountains of Hala, seen to the west, are similar in their conformation to those at Sehwun: both are destitute of vegetation.

On the 20th we moored in the Arul; and proceeded to revisit the singular mound or castle of Sehwun, on which so much discussion has been expended. I felt still as much puzzled and pleased with these curious remains as I had formerly been. I however avoided the tomb of Lal Shah Baz, for a visit once in a man's life to such a scene of noise and importunate begging seemed to me sufficient. The town of Sehwun did not now appear to contain one-half the number of people which I had formerly assigned to it, viz. five thousand souls: the inhabitants were chiefly beggars and fishermen. The fish here are very numerous, and a favourable opportunity was presented to us of largely increasing our drawings of them. In the end these formed a valuable portfolio of every specimen to be found in the Indus, 36 in number. The water-fowl of Lake Munchur, which Lieutenant Leech went to visit, were also figured with care. Some of them were very curious, particularly the "aree," with three joints to its web-foot, which overlapped each other like armour. Of these, and others of the feathered tribe, the drawings at length amounted to 191, those of quadrupeds to 20, and those of reptiles to 11. The whole of these were presented by Government to the Asiatic Society of Calcutta, together with about 200 specimens of natural history, and the extensive geological collections which we made throughout the journey.

The trip to Munchur gave us an insight into that singular tract. As the water retires, cultivation is resumed, while the lake itself is covered with small fishing-boats not overrated at a thousand in number. They are in the custom of spearing the fish, the weeds rendering it impossible for them to spread their nets.

On quitting Sehwun, my former fellow-traveller, Mohun Lal, met me from Bhawulpore. He had been placed at my disposal, and I was glad to see him after a lapse of five years. I had been previously joined by another protégé, Nourozjee Furdoonjee, a young Parsee educated at the Elphinstone college in Bombay. I was very anxious to give an opportunity to the youth of that presidency to distinguish themselves on so important an occasion as the present journey afforded them; and young Nourozjee had volunteered to accompany me. Besides the recommendation which he possessed from promising talents, he had been educated under the care of a respected and venerated friend of my own, now no more, the Honourable James Sutherland, than whom no one was ever more beloved, or commanded more universal esteem; and thus I took a double interest in the welfare of the young man. The absence however from his country-men pressed heavily on Nourozjee, and he ultimately returned to Bombay, after giving me, throughout the journey, the highest satisfaction. He is at present an assistant professor in the Elphinstone college—an institution which bids fair to do honour to the name it bears.

On the 1st of March we reached Meetanee, the frontier of my old friend Meer Roostum Khan, and were received as well as old friends could wish to be: I need say no more. Our entrance into this chief's territory was marked by a very successful operation on the part of our native doctor Mahomed Ali. A boy about nine years old presented himself with a capsular cataract in both eyes: he had been born blind. One of these cataracts the operator broke; and we kept the patient in our boats for several days till he could distinctly see, count numbers on his fingers, and move about without a guide. It was an interesting occupation to note the progress which he made, and with it the gratitude of his relatives. They did not wait for the second eye being cured, but were anxious to return home with their present success. This was not the only work of the native doctor: he removed with celerity and success a cataract from the eye of an old woman who had had it for six years. The woman saw at once; and prayed aloud for joy. This practitioner had acquired his experience in India under Dr. Richmond, whose pupil he had been for a considerable time. There is nothing in which European surgery produces a stronger impression on the minds of Asiatics than in operations on the eye, a branch of the science of which they are altogether ignorant.

After some very squally and rainy weather, in which we nearly lost one of our boats, we passed Chandkoh, and, disembarking, proceeded to visit Larkhanu, a town of about 12,000 inhabitants, fourteen miles from the Indus. Half way we crossed the Nara river, which was about three feet deep, with a current of a mile an hour. Up to this point the soil was saline, and entirely covered with a salt efflorescence, but after crossing this river we entered a rich and well-cultivated country. Larkhanu is pleasantly situated among date-trees, and is a place of note, having a bazar of 370 shops and some manufactures of coarse cloth. It lies also on the road between Curachee and Shikarpoor. We found a few Hindostanee soldiers here under Moosa Khan, an Armenian, who sent us very civil messages, but was afraid to visit us. Larkhanu cannot boast of the morality of its population, and its intoxicating liquors were too great a temptation for our people, some of whom had, I am sorry to say, become decided drunkards since our entering Sinde. A Sindee proverb runs "Jeehoo nano, goom Larkano" (If you have money, go to Larkhanu and get rid of it); but the same may be said of many other places.

After a day's residence we quitted Larkhanu, and joined our boats at the ferry of Keree, where we were received by a deputation from Ali Moorad, who had sent his brother-in-law, and Simon Michael, an Armenian, the commander of his troops, to welcome us. They brought dogs with them, and a civil invitation to us to go to their hunting-grounds, but political circumstances obliged me to decline the offer. We passed up the river to Buttee ferry ("putung") twenty miles from Khyrpoor, where we were joined by the minister, Futteh Khan, who with the usual ceremonies escorted us next morning to Khyrpoor, passing on our route through the large village of Peer-gote. One of the commanders of the boats accompanied us, and, sailor-like, seemed uneasy on shore: I asked him why he did not enjoy himself? "Enjoy myself!" exclaimed he; "why, what is this to a boat? In a boat we are kings, and go ten cosses a-day, but here we are nothing better than tired mortals!" I differed widely in opinion from this man; for it was always with pleasure that I exchanged the boat for the shore. We were joined at Khyrpoor by Dr. Lord, who had been escorted from

Hydrábád by a young Englishman, named Howell, in the employ of the Ameers, and who was distinguished by the title of "Chota Khan," or the little lord.

On the 16th we all paid our respects to the Ameer, who received us even more kindly than his relative had done at Hydrábád. He seated me on the same cushion with himself, and said that I had founded the friendship between him and the British, and that I was his dearest friend, with many other obliging speeches which I leave untold; but it is only justice to him to remark that, in the day of need, nearly two years after, his Highness proved by his conduct towards the British the sincerity of his professions, and, when all Sinde was hostile to us, he separated himself from the local confederacies and surrendered to us the fort of Bukkur for a dépôt, which, as he justly styled it, was "the heart of his country." I, however, found myself not altogether pleasantly situated with this good chief, for the Hydrábád family were at this time exerting themselves to secure the supremacy in Sinde, in which they in the end failed, but which retarded that cordiality between our Government and Khyrpoor which subsequent events have happily established.

The second "eed," or festival, happened while we were at Khyrpoor, and it gave us an opportunity of seeing the national dance of the aboriginal Sindees of the Mai or Myauee tribe, who subsist by fishing. The women of the tribe all came dressed in holiday clothes, and, forming a circle round the musicians, moved in slow time, beating the ground and clapping their hands, which they raised above their heads. In marriages and festivals men and women join in the dance together. All these women were on a very large scale, thick-set, and dark; few were handsome, and their ear and neck ornaments were so large as to be unseemly.

After this the prima donna of Khyrpoor, Jewun Bukhsh, entertained us with a "natch." This girl is a religious courtesan, who builds mosques and gives away large sums in charity; her features were melancholy but handsome, and the shape of her feet peculiarly elegant. She and her sisters, beautiful girls also, exerted themselves to amuse us. They danced with naked swords and guns, personifying jealous husbands and ardent lovers, and fell at last, as it appeared to us, more from the effect of *ardent spirits* than from fatigue.

There was at this time, at Khyrpoor, a mission from the Brahooee chief of Kelat, and through it we opened a communication with the ruler of that country, Mehrab Khan, and his young son, who reside at Gundava; and for a time this negotiation gave promise of being useful to us. The Vakeel, or agent, by name Ghoolam Nubee Khan, visited us in our camp, and we derived from him and his people much information. I showed him some drawings of Asiatic costumes, which so delighted him that he actually leaped for joy. On seeing the portrait of Runjeet Sing he ejaculated, " Are you then so little and so blind, and yet trouble the world so much?" On turning over to a Eusoophzye of Peshawur he exclaimed, " And you, you wretch! why don't you cut out the Sikh's heart?" And then, placing the one picture before the other, he continued, " Look at the diminutive infidel,—look at him,—kill him! Would you not like to be as near him as you are now?" All this was said with an energy that made it amusingly ridiculous.

The chief of Deejee, Ali Moorad Khan, finding he could not tempt us to hunt, got politically sick, and requested me to send Dr. Lord to him, which I did. The day following Roostum Khan paid that chief a visit of condolence on the loss of an infant child; and we, having received an invitation, went also, and joined Dr. Lord. Deejee is about fourteen miles from Khyrpoor. It is a neat mud fort, built on one of the flat hills of flint, lime, and sand, which occur in this part of the country. It is a showy castellated work of some little strength, and contains the riches of this scion of the Talpoors, who has the credit of being the wealthiest chief in Sinde. The town near it is small, and chiefly occupied by retainers. The desert, which stretches towards Jaysulmeer, begins at Deejee. The chief received us well, housed us in his fort, and, soon forgetting all his ailments, proposed a hunting excursion for the next day. He pronounced himself cured by Doctor Lord's medicines, who, however, had only given him a glass of maraschino, which was discovered in Sinde to have effects unknown to us. The medicine was so highly appreciated, that we were not only constrained to part with the little stock which we had with us, but to send an order for three dozen of it, for the special consumption of the invalid.

In the morning we set out on our excursion to hunt the antelope on the skirts of the desert. The Ameer mounted me with himself on his own camel, and Doctor Lord was driven by the chief's brother-in-law, which greatly surprised the people. Ali Moorad is about 25 years old, and a clever sharp man, with some energy of character. He put many questions to me on political matters, and it was very evident that sport was not the only object he had in view in arranging the party. We rode in among the antelopes; then dismounted, and advanced under the cover of a camel near enough to fire. I essayed twice, but was unsuccessful. At length Ali Moorad killed a fine buck; and great was my surprise to hear him shout out to his people in praise of my firing, and declare that the successful shot was mine! I laughed outright on receiving gratulations so undeserved; but I could undeceive no one except the gentlemen of my own party. There is more sport in antelope-shooting than in the preserve and hut affairs in which we had been engaged lower down. It a good deal resembles what we call in India deer-stalking. After some hours of exertion, we sat down under the bushes and enjoyed some camel's milk, which we got fresh from the herds grazing on the ground; when drunk thus it is palatable. We returned to Deejee, where we partook of a splendid entertainment; and in the evening returned to Khyrpoor, the Ameer again mounting me on his own camel, and driving me himself. The whole affair was got over in the most amicable manner, without giving offence even to Meer Roostum, which was a delicate point. Before parting, the Ameer gave permission to Lieutenant Leech to visit the manufacturing districts of Raneepoor and Gumbut, which lie in his territories, and that officer accordingly proceeded thither direct from Deejee. Lieutenant Wood was absent on the river during these festivities, and his unremitting zeal had already enabled him to send me very perfect nautical information regarding the lower Indus.

This Ameer, Ali Moorad, had some very fine hawks, which amused us on our way to and from the hunting-grounds; and as I have heard sportsmen express much curiosity on the subject of these birds, I give the list of falcons, &c., known to the Sindians:—

Luggur, female, Juggur, male.	Native of Sinde; a large sparrowhawk, with dark eye, trained for the season and then let loose.
Baz, female, Zorru, male.	Native of Khorasan; goolab (yellow) eye: a noble bird.
Bashu, female, Bisheen, male.	Native of Khorasan; goolab eye: small.
Churgh, female, Churghela, male.	Native of Cuthee; black-eyed: fastens on the antelope, and kills the "tuloor."
Bahree, female, Bahree buchu, male.	Native of Sinde; found near the Indus, and not prized.
Kohee, female, Koheela, male.	Also called Shaheen; native of Sinde; black-eyed.
Tooruratee, female, Chatway, male.	Native of Sinde; black-eyed: let loose after the season.
Shikra, female, Chipuk, male,	Native of Sinde; goolab eye.

The Ookab, or vulture of Sinde, attacks all these hawks; and it is a curious fact that the domesticated hawk, when let loose, is frequently set upon by all the wild birds of its own species.

On the 30th of March we took leave of Khyrpoor and proceeded to Roree Bukkur. So great a change had taken place in the feelings of the inhabitants towards us, that we had now only to express the wish, and we were at once ferried across, by the Vizier himself, to the celebrated fortress of Bukkur. He chose this singular time to renew some requests that had been previously made to me, with a view of cementing more closely our alliance; but I asked him, and I did so with perfect sincerity, what he could wish for more, since our mutual confidence was already so great, that we stood together as friends in Bukkur? Little at this time could I have ventured to hope that on Christmas-day of the ensuing year I should have been the envoy to negotiate a treaty placing Khyrpoor under British protection. Such, however, was the case; and on the 29th of January, 1839, in company with my respected friend, General Sir Willoughby Cotton, I saw the British ensign peaceably planted on this important fortress, and waving over the waters of the Indus.

CHAPTER III.

Sukkur—Shikarpoor—Its commercial communications, population, bazars, &c.—River festival—Beauties—Character of the people—Wild tribes—Muzarees—A chief—Native song—Crocodile-steaks—Alligators—Mittuncote—Bhawul Khan, chief of Bhawulpoor—A French adventurer, Mons. Argoud—Mohammedan convent—Don José Gonsalvez, our artist—Runjeet Sing's officers—Kind reception—The Indus at Mittun—Dera Ghazee Khan—District of Deerajat—Its great importance—Lohanee Afghans—Their routes—The "Gates of Khorasan"—Traffic of Dera Ghazee Khan—Vicinity—Bazars.

From Bukkur we crossed to Sukkur, and marched next day for Shikarpoor, then a *terra incognita*. We were conducted through its dirty but extensive bazars by representatives from Hydrábád and Khyrpoor: the governor shortly after waited upon us; and the whole host of merchants, bankers, and money-changers soon besieged our camp. From them we gathered intelligence of the designs of Persia on Herat and Candahar, and altogether found our attention transferred, in consequence of their communications, from the Indus and Sinde to matters of more stirring interest, and which, in the end, brought about unlooked-for changes. The chief of

Bhawulpoor had been keeping up an active correspondence with us since we had entered the Indus, and now begged me " to quicken my steps and withdraw from between us the screen of separation." Runjeet Sing, although not over-pleased at our stepping between him and the wide region of Sinde, which he looked upon as his prey, was nevertheless most kind in his invitations; and his rival, Dost Mahommed Khan, of Cabool, likewise sent his messengers to urge us to visit him. We continued at Shikarpoor for ten days, engaged in inquiries regarding its commerce, which, as is well known, extends over all Asia, China and Turkey excepted. Shikarpoor is a town of the first importance to the trade of the Indus. This does not result from any superiority in its home manufactures, but from its extensive money transactions, which establish a commercial connection between it and many remote marts. It stands near the northern frontier of the Sinde territories, 28 miles directly west of the Indus, and about the same distance from the fort of Bukkur. Towards the north the Sinde boundary extends to Rozan, on the road to Candahar and Kelat, by the well-known pass of Bolan: so that the merchants always speak of Shikarpoor and Dera Ghazee Khan, a town higher up, as the " Gates of Khorasan;" by which name they here distinguish the kingdom of Cabool. In every direction commercial roads conduct the trade to Shikarpoor; but the communication is entirely carried on by land, although all the merchants of the town, great and small, agree in the opinion that their profits would be much increased, and their interests promoted, were a communication by water established.

Shikarpoor is not a town of any antiquity, though there has always been a place of note in its neighbourhood. Alore, Sukkur, Bukkur, and Roree have all followed each other, and the present town has succeeded Lukkee, a place eight miles south of it, which was held by the ancestors of the present chief of Bhawulpoor, who were expelled by Nadir Shah. It appears to have been built A.D. 1617, since its date is preserved in the Arabic word ghouk, غوک or frog, the numeral letters of which give the year of the Hegira 1026; the word likewise conveying some idea of the neighbourhood, which lies low. The slope of the country favours its easy irrigation; and in consequence of the Emperors of Delhi having caused extensive canals to be cut from the Indus, Shikarpoor is supplied with abundance of food, and cheaper than any part of Sinde. The obscure term of "nou Lakkee Sinde" has reference, I am informed, to this part of the country, that being the amount of revenue above Sinde Proper derived from the province called Moghulee. Natives of Shikarpoor who have seen British India assert that their own town is capable of being made a second Bengal. Nadir Shah visited Shikarpoor in his conquests; but its vicinity to countries so much disturbed prevented its becoming a commercial mart, till the Suddozye princes established their authority in it; and its prosperity may be dated from the year 1786, in the reign of Timour Shah, who first located Hindoos in the town, after he had conferred the government of Sinde on the family of the present Ameers. Shikarpoor is the only place in Sinde where that tribe have established a paramount influence, and the Ameers have hitherto had the good sense not to seek to deprive them of it, although Shikarpoor has been subject to Sinde for the last 16 years. The revenues collected in it are divided between the Hydrábád and Khyrpoor chiefs, the latter having three shares and the former four, and the expenses incurred in defending it are borne by them in the same proportions. The population of the town exceeds 30,000 souls; but it is to be remembered that, in addition to the actual residents, there are a considerable number of Hindoos belonging to the place, who are scattered all over Asia in commercial pursuits, and who return to their families in after-life. The inhabitants consist of Hindoos of the Bunya, Lohanu, and Bhattea tribes; but Baba Nanuk Sikhs compose more than half the number. About one-tenth of the population is Mahommedan; most of these are Afghans, who received grants of land, or "puttas," as they are called from the name of the deed, and settled around Shikarpoor, in the time of the Dooranees. The town, though surrounded by gardens and trees, is quite open; for a mud wall, which has been allowed to fall into decay, can scarcely be called a defence. There are, however, eight gates. The bazar is extensive, having 884 different shops. It is covered with mats as a shade from the sun, but has no architectural beauty. The houses are built of sun-dried bricks: they are lofty and comfortable, but destitute of elegance. The climate is said to be very hot and oppressive in the summer, and there are so many stagnant pools around the walls, that it is surprising the people do not find the place insalubrious. The thermometer had a range of 26° in the middle of April, falling to 59° in the night, and rising to 82° in the day; but we were informed that the temperature this year was unusually moderate, and that across the Indus, at Khyrpoor, the thermometer had already stood at 96°. Water is found at 12 or 15 feet from the surface, but the river has for three or four years past flooded large tracts in the neighbourhood. The land revenues, exclusive of expenses in collection, &c., now average two lacs and a half of rupees per annum; and the customs and town-duties are farmed for 64,000 rupees, the currency being inferior by 5½ per cent. to the Company's rupee. This statement, however, does not include the whole of the districts which were held by the Afghans, Noushera being under Larkhanu, and several rich jagheers having been bestowed on religious persons. The inundation, having lately inclined towards Shikarpoor, has also increased its revenues, probably to half a lac of rupees, but the addition cannot be considered as likely to be permanent. It will only be necessary to name the towns at which the Shikarpoor merchants have agents, to judge of their widely extended influence. Beginning from the west, every place of note from Astracan to Calcutta seems to have a Shikarpooree stationed in it. Thus they are found at Muscat, Bunder, Abbass, Heeman, Yezd, Meshid, Astracan, Bokhara, Samarcand, Kokan, Yarkund, Koondooz, Khooloom, Sulzwar, Candahar, Ghuzni, Cabool, Peshawur, Dera Ghazee Khan, Dera Ismael Khan, Bukkur, Leia, Mooltan, Ooch, Bhawulpoor, Umritsir, Jeypoor, Beecaneer, Jaysulmeer, Palee, Mandivee, Bombay, Hydrábád (Deccan), Hydrábád (Sinde), Kurachee, Kelat, Mirzapoor, and Calcutta. In all these places bills may be negotiated, and at most of them there is a direct trade either from Shikarpoor or one of its subordinate agencies. The business seems, however, to be more of a banking nature than a commerce in goods; but still there is not any great quantity of ready money at Shikarpoor, for there is no mint to which gold or bullion may be carried, and consequently a loss ensues upon its import. The Hindoos of Astracan, I am informed, have lately been converted to Islam; and within these two years those of Bokhara have been molested, for the first time, on account of their creed.

On the 6th of April we had a good opportunity of seeing the people of Shikarpoor, there being on that day a great festival in honour of the river, which is held at the new moon, and happened this year to be also the beginning of the Moohurrum, or great Shiah holiday. Shikarpoor was quite deserted on the occasion, for nearly the whole of its population betook themselves to the banks of the Sinde canal, where there was a fair under some lofty trees. I think that two-thirds of the assemblage were composed of women and children. They prostrated themselves in the canal and prayed; then shook each other by the hand, with a good hearty European shake; and mothers and brothers bought toys, and suitable English whirligigs, for their children and sisters. Confections and meats were in great demand. We threaded the crowd; and not the least remarkable feature of the scene was a couple of grey-bearded men, more fit to personate Moollahs than anything else, dancing like girls, with bells at their feet, striving to personate two lovers and to look bewitching. Shikarpoor can certainly boast of the bright eyes of its daughters; and this day gave us an excellent opportunity of judging of them. The Shikarpoorees are an astute, shrewd body of men, with no literature, however, and little education beyond accounts and reading. I doubt if I could describe them in language so graphic and true as that used by the inimitable author of 'Anastasius,' in speaking of their brethren of Smyrna: "Their whole hearts are wrapped up in cotton and broadcloths: they suppose men created for nothing but to buy and to sell; and whoever makes not these occupations the sole business of his life seems to them to neglect the end of his existence; and I verily believe that they marry for no other purpose but to keep up the race of merchants and bankers."

On the 10th we returned to the Indus at Moulanu Chacher, about twenty miles above Bukkur, where we found our boats. The country was a perfect thicket for half the distance: near Shikarpoor it was more open, and the cultivators of the ground were now cleaning out the small aqueducts which run from the Sinde canal, and on which the prosperity of the land depends. A few days after this time the water will enter the canal. At this season the country was overgrown with a shrub of a purple colour, like heather. I never saw in any country a greater profusion of roses than in Upper Sinde, but they are destitute of fragrance. This was also the season of the mulberries, which are large and of good flavour. They ripen well under the great heat, which was now above 95° of Fahrenheit.

The wild tribes who occupy the western bank of the Indus, the Boordees, Boogtees, and Muzarees, now flocked about us full of promises of obedience and good behaviour. The plundering disposition of the Muzarees had for some time engaged the attention of our Government, and we had made it a point of express stipulation with the authorities in Sinde that they should suppress it, in order that peace might be maintained on the river. This had become the more necessary as the Sikhs had marched troops into their country, and now held two of their villages—an event which was to all parties a subject of alarm and regret. The chief of the Muzarees, Behram Khan, had taken an early opportunity of showing his submission to the British, and had met me at Khyrpoor, with some sixty persons of his tribe from the plains and hills, "to seize," as he said, "the hem of the garment of the British nation." This chief attended us with his bards, who, as he entered the camp, sang his praises and deeds of valour, accompanying their voices by a kind of "siringee," or guitar, which sent forth softer sounds than could have been expected from the instrumental music of the *pirates* of the Indus. These barbarians, for they are little better, were astonished and enchanted when we produced our musical snuff-boxes: their chief, however, Behram, was evidently a man of sense and judgment. They all rode mares, which they said were more docile than horses, and capable of enduring greater fatigue on their "Chupaos," or forays; and that, when it was necessary to dismount, one man could hold half a dozen of them. They illustrated this by a curious proverb: "A man with a saddle on a mare has his saddle on a horse;—a man with his saddle on a horse has his saddle on his head." Whilst the musicians were singing I requested to be informed what was the subject they had selected, and found it to be, as I have stated, the praises of their chief. The following is a free translation :—

MUZAREE SONG.

"Thanks be to God for destroying the fort!
It will smooth away the difficulties of the poor.
Lend an ear to the supplications of Behram,
A generous chief, and the lord of castles.
His forces are like the waves of the sea;
Kurman, Dildar are his experienced commanders.
Aid him, oh the Ghilanee saint!
Aid him, oh the Ooch saint!
He slew one hundred men of the enemy;
His fame as a hero is spread afar;
Those at a distance will find what they fear.
There are twelve thousand chosen Muzarees.
His court is like Mitta the Great.
Ali has given him power.
The light of God shines upon him.
The ears of his mare are like a pen.
His saddle is worth a thousand rupees.
The world knows that the Lagharees came against him;
He relied on God, and went to fight.
Ghoolam Mahomed Baum, the general of his army,
Roostum Maseed defeated the enemy:
Five hundred of them were slain;
All their property was plundered.
Behram Muzaree conquered the enemy."

The country of these people is rich in wool, but their garments were all of the coarsest cotton cloth. The accompanying spirited sketch of these Beeloochees, for which I am indebted to my friend Captain Hart, very correctly delineates the appearance of

these men. Of their boldness of character we had ample opportunities of judging in the army of the Indus.

Eight days carried us beyond the Sinde frontiers, as we had a fair wind, and in fact a little too much of it, for it carried away a mast and some spars, and nearly killed our barber, who was knocked into the river; but he was a Hajee, and had made four pilgrimages to Mecca, to which circumstance he of course attributed his escape. One day, as we were proceeding rapidly through the water, we were followed by a man, and the extreme anxiety which he evinced induced me to stop the boat and listen to him. His request was, that, as we had now become masters of the country, we should restore to him certain lands which had been wrested from his family in the time of Nadir Shah, and of which he still possessed the title-deeds; and, as statutes of limitation are unknown here, he assured us, again and again, that we had the power to do this if we had but the will. We found it impossible to persuade this man, and many others at different times, that we had no intention to interfere in domestic arrangements in this country more than in any of the others with which we had treaties. It was in vain that I frequently explained the objects of my mission: some loudly expressed their astonishment; others, particularly the chiefs, listened to my declaration in silence, but almost all evidently disbelieved it.

Near the ferry of Bara we found the fishermen actively engaged in sharing amongst themselves an immense alligator (seesar) which they had just caught. The monster had been cut up into joints and bits, some of which they were about to eat, assuring us that the steaks were delicious. I asked if these animals did not eat men, but the fishermen boldly got rid of this objection by assuring me that alligators and crocodiles lived entirely on fish! Having partaken of frog, horse, shark, and camel, I resolved to add a new item to my list of gastronomic experiences, and to try my hand at crocodile-steaks; but I found the food to be poor, close-grained, dry, and deficient in flavour, and I was very soon satisfied. Probably the art of cooking crocodiles may be yet in its infancy. The gall-bladder of the animal is carefully preserved, and used as a medicine in cases of obstinate wounds and defluxions. We had an opportunity not long after this of verifying the truth of the statement made by the fishermen, that these creatures live on fish. We had employed above a hundred men to try and catch the "boolun," or water-hog, and in their unsuccessful attempts to do so they caught a large crocodile (gurial) some thirteen or fourteen feet long, which they pinioned and bound in such a way, that Mr. Waterton's feat of mounting on his back for a hunt might have been performed without danger.* When the monster was killed, his stomach was found to contain four pulla, or sable-fish, showing, at least, that his taste in fish was refined, and disproving the assertion of the Sindians, that these fish do not ascend the Indus higher than Bukkur. On the authority of the crocodile we caused search to be made for this fish, upon which a waterman naïvely observed, "Why should not that animal have the best of the river, seeing he is the governor of it?" Wherever the current was slack, we found the alligators in great numbers, and could approach them within pistol-shot: I have seen as many as a hundred on one bank, and innumerable young ones, which were always easily captured.

On the 22nd of April we reached Mittuncote and found ourselves on new ground; but previously to ascending the Indus we disembarked a few miles up the Chenab, and proceeded to visit my old and respected friend Bhawul Khan, at his residence of Ahmedpoor. From thence we passed to Bhawulpoor; and, descending the Gara, as the Sutledge is

* This specimen may now be seen in the museum of the Bombay branch of the Asiatic Society.

here called, passed by Ooch, and returned to Mittun after nearly a month's absence, which period, however, had not been uselessly employed. We found Bhawul Khan, as Englishmen have ever found him, a true friend and a princely host. He erected "landees," or wicker-work cottages, at each of the stages where we had to alight on our route to join him; and, not satisfied with his usual display of cooked meats, he had kindly been making inquiries as to what we would most relish. Some wag had assured him we were immoderately fond of frogs: whereupon all the pools and ditches were searched and cleared, and the frogs cherished and fattened up in ponds; but, alas! the worthy Khan on our arrival found out that he had been imposed upon: so the frogs were again let loose, and we had much fun and no death, contrary to the well-known fable. At Bhawulpoor we met a respectable officer in the Khan's service, Captain M'Pherson, and an Englishman named Crawford, a singular character, who had nearly forgotten his native language.

At Bhawulpoor we heard of an European being in a caravanserai, and immediately sent him an invitation to join us. He proved to be Monsieur Benoir Argoud, Capitaine d'Infanterie, who had arrived here from Lahore: he was a red-hot republican; and, after we had risen from table, the good things of which had a little overtaken him, continued half the night shouting out "Liberty!" "Equality! and Saint Simonianism!" Early the next morning he broke into my apartment and exclaimed "it was seven o'clock, and that I must instantly rise, as the battle of Wagram had been fought, and his father killed at it, before that hour!" To crown all, Monsieur announced himself to be *en route* for Cabool to join Dost Mahommed Khan, and constrain him to raise the green shirt of the Prophet, and attack these canaille the Sikhs; being determined, as a preliminary part of his plan, to plant potatoes for the subsistence of the troops. We concluded Monsieur to be mad; but, as Fanny Kemble says of the Americans, "it might be otherwise;" and the question of "How comed you so?" would in this instance also have led to the explanation of the whole affair. Monsieur Argoud too had method in his madness, for he made out his journey safely to Cabool by the Bolan Pass and Candahar, not a very easy thing; and afterwards, when I had the honour of again meeting him, he told me that he had "saved himself from death, *with the sword over his head!*" by ejaculating the Mahommedan "Kuluma," or creed, of there being but one God, and that Mahommed was his prophet.

We were however witnesses, shortly after these

amusing scenes, of a real conversion, in the person of one of Dr. Lord's grooms; who, becoming dissatisfied with Hindooism and its dogmas, resolved to become a Mahommedan. This happened at Chacher, opposite Mittuncote, where the Peer, a sleek but burly Moollah, named Khodah Bukhsh, has the reputation of working miracles, and the more certain merit of keeping a school for children. Sundry messages and interviews passed between the parties: but the priest stood in awe of us, and declined to officiate without our sanction. On our interrogating the man as to his reasons, he affirmed that it was a voluntary act on which he had resolved for some time; and as we felt that we had no right to oppose his intention, Lieutenant Leech and myself determined to be present at the ceremony. We found an assemblage of about 150 persons, sitting in great solemnity and quietness under a grass shed, the ground being laid with mats. Here, after a few complimentary words, we saw the Hindoo Mankoo admitted into the bosom of Islam; and his name changed to the more euphonious one of "Shekh Deen Mahomed." Before the ceremony, the priest, bringing him to the front, repeated, in three distinct sentences, the Mahommedan creed; and the quondam Hindoo followed him, word by word, without a trip: whereupon the assembly shouted out their "Moobahik," or congratulations; and the affair ended with a feast. This conversion will not satisfy a Christian; nevertheless, it is no small step to advance from Hindooism, its superstitions and abominations, to Mahommedanism, even with all its imperfections and absurdities. From that day this man became one of the "people of the book," and was exalted in worldly station and religious truth. The priest at Chacher is a man of influence in these parts, and I believe of respectability; his family once held Mittun, in which place are the tombs of his ancestors. Lately, when the Sikhs were descending the Indus, the Ameers sent to implore his blessing. He replied, "It is unnecesssry, they will not advance,"—a guess founded on a knowledge of circumstances, and which, as it proved true, has vastly increased the saint's reputation. He however rebuked the Sindians for their neglect of their own interests; and told them that, although the world was governed by fate (tukdeer), it was governed also by arrangement (tudbeer), and that they should not have lost sight of this, but should have prepared their troops.

On the 22nd we set sail from Mittuncote, and took leave of Bhawul Khan's officers. The Khan promised to send me the history of his tribe, and this promise he fulfilled by transmitting a long and elaborate account of it, concluding with an enumeration of *all his own successes in hunting*. In return for this production he requested me to give him an orrery, which at a subsequent period I forwarded to him, and in the mean time I sent him a splendid drawing of Medina, executed by our draftsman, Mr. Gonsalvez, to match one which he had of Mecca. I have hitherto omitted to introduce to my readers this very useful member of our party, and to whom I am indebted for several of the drawings by which this work is illustrated. Don José, for I must give him titles which, if not inherited, were readily accorded to him by every one, was a Portuguese, a native of Goa, and educated at the Propaganda of that city. His forte was music, to which he added the sister accomplishment of drawing. Besides his own language he knew some Latin, a little French, and spoke tolerable English: in fact he did high honour to the city of Albuquerque, and could sympathize with his illustrious countryman Camöens, when far from home. His heart he had left behind him, but not his good spirits, and his gay disposition and musical talents often enlivened us whilst on the Indus, and when the snows of Hindoo Koosh were frowning over us. The guitar was the Don's favourite instrument, but sometimes he played on the accordion, and would give us "Home, sweet Home" in our own native tongue, a "Ça ira" in French, a loyal air in Portuguese, or the merrier accompaniment to his own fandango. Altogether Don José Gonsalvez was a very original character, and a vast favourite with us all: during the day he laboured with industry and attention at his proper calling of draftsman; and, when invited to join us after dinner, never failed to enliven the evening. He is, I believe, still in Bombay; and, if this page meets his eye, I hope he will consider it as written with sincere good wishes for his future success, and accept my congratulations at his safe return to his senhora.

At Mittun we were joined by the officers of Runjeet Sing, and were received by them with all that pomp and distinction which he is accustomed to bestow on his visitors. Money, confections, &c., were brought to us, and Hurree Sing, an old acquaintance, was appointed our Mihmandar. This functionary's first present to us was a ram with six horns, which I at first thought he meant should be typical of something or other, but it appeared that he merely brought it as a *lusus naturæ* which he had no doubt would be highly prized. We did not find Mittuncote, although so favourably situated in a geographical point of view, at all suited for an emporium of trade. The country was low, and liable to be flooded. There is a place of some antiquity west of this, called Aguee, and the mound on which Mittuncote stands has the appearance of great age. Hurund, near Dajel, which stands inland from this point, is believed to derive its name from Huree, one of the slaves of Alexander.

From Mittun upwards all was novelty to us: we were on an unexplored river, which had never been navigated by Greeks or Britons, and it was problematical how far we could ascend. The inundation had now fairly set in, and the river consequently was somewhat rapid and looked large; but I am satisfied, after careful observation, that the Indus is a much fuller river in its upper than in its lower course; as in the latter it is diminished by drainage for cultivation, as well as by evaporation. Above the confluence of the Indus and Chenab the country was already in part under water, and the sedgy plants show that the soil is very humid. In the inundation the waters tend towards the west. The subject of the discharge of the Punjab rivers, as well as the Indus, was carefully attended to by Lieutenant Wood, whilst Doctor Lord bestowed a good deal of care in ascertaining the quantity of silt held in solution in the water of these rivers, and the nature of it. It was found to be composed of silex, alumine, carbonate of lime, and a small proportion of vegetable matter. The result is thus given by Doctor Lord in his "Memoir on the Plain of the Indus:—"

"To make the quantity of water discharged round numbers, let us assume 300,000 cubic feet as the mean discharge per second. Let us take $\frac{1}{500}$, which is less than the experiments warrant, as the proportion of silt. This being a proportion by weight, let us take the specific gravity of silt at 2; which, being that of silica, is probably not far from the truth. The proportion by measure then will be $\frac{1}{1000}$; and from these premises it will follow that, for the seven months specified, the river discharges 300 cubic feet of mud in every second of time; or a quantity which, in that time, would suffice to form an island 42 miles long, 27 miles broad, and 40 feet deep; which (the mean depth of the sea on the coast being 5 fathoms) would consequently be elevated 10 feet above the surface of the water. Any person who chooses to run out this calculation to hundreds and thousands of years will be able to satisfy himself that much may be done by causes at present in action towards manufacturing deltas."

A run of eight days brought us to Dera Ghazee Khan, for the southerly winds continued strong and favourable. It is said that Amrou wrote to the

Caliph Omar that Egypt presented in succession the appearance of a field of dust, a fresh-water sea, and a flower-garden. Dust we had in Lower Sinde in abundance; a fresh-water sea we now encountered, as we often could not see from bank to bank; but, as we had as yet beheld nothing but high grass and tamarisk, we presumed that we had to look forward to Cabool for the flower-garden. On our voyage we passed Noushera Raik, the ferry of Juttooee, and Sheroo; but these are inland, and can only be seen from the mast-head, their position being marked by the trees which are near them. The river is divided into many channels, but we made our way without a pilot through a scene of wearisome monotony. At two P.M. the river had a temperature of 84°, whilst that of the air was 108°. On the evening of our arrival the wind blew from the south long after sunset, and was oppressively sultry. We could not dine without tatties (cooled screens), nor did they reduce the temperature below 94°. The climate, as may be imagined, was oppressive. The sun rose like a globe of intense fire, and threw forth a scorching heat as long as it remained above the horizon. Sickness, chiefly fever, overtook many of our people, but their complaints were no doubt aggravated by the state of inactivity in which they were compelled to remain whilst in the boats, and by the over-feeding to which the liberality of the chiefs had given occasion.

It will be necessery to give a brief description of the tract we had now entered, as, from many considerations, it is one of considerable interest. The country on the right bank of the Indus, below the salt range and to the point where that river is joined by the waters of the Punjab, is known by the name of Derajat. It is so designated from the two principal towns in the tract, Dera Ghazee Khan and Dera Ismael Khan; Derajat being the Arabic plural of the word Dera. The lower part bears the local name of Sinde, and the upper that of Damun (or border), from its bordering on the mountains of Soleeman. The country itself is flat, and in many places fertile, particularly in the vicinity of the two Deras; but to the westward of the river, even at the distance of only a few miles, there are no wells, and the soil is entirely dependent on rain, and on the water from the hills, without which there is no crop. On the opposite bank of the river, in Leia, the Indus overflows to the east, and the land, which is exceedingly rich, yields heavy crops, and is known by the name of "Cuchee." From Leia the great ferry of Kaheeree conducts the traveller beyond the Indus into Derajat, where the mountains are crossed by caravan routes which lead to Cabool and Candahar; and as it is here that the greatest of the Indian caravans assemble before passing to the west, the Derajat is invested with a high degree of commercial importance.

From Calcutta by Lucknow, Delhi, Hansee, and Bhawulpoor—from Bombay by Pallee, Becaneer, Bhawulpoor, and Mooltan—from Umritsir by Jung and Leia—and from Dera Ghazee Khan itself on the south by Bhawulpoor—all these routes join at the small town of Derabund, about 30 miles west of Dera Ismael Khan. At this point commences the well-known road by the Goomul river to the pass of Goolairee, which is always traversed by the Lohanee Afghans. Some of these people enter the mountains higher up, west of Tak, and also by an inferior pass, named "Cheree," lower down; but all these routes eventually unite about 45 miles from Derabund. The Lohanee Afghans are a pastoral and migratory people, and many of them proceed annually into India, to purchase merchandize; and assembling here towards the end of April, and being joined by their families who have wintered on the banks of the Indus, they pass into Khorasan, where they remain during the summer. They effect this change of residence in a fixed order by three divisions, or "kirees," which term, I believe, simply means migrations; and these kirees bear the respective names of Nusseer, Kharoutee, and Meeankhyl, which are also the names of the branches of the tribes conducting them. The first is the most numerous, and with it go from 50,000 to 60,000 head of sheep; but it is with the last that the Hindoo merchants and foreigners generally travel. The extensive nature of the traffic is proved by the custom-house books, which show that 5140 camels laden with merchandize passed up this year, exclusive of those carrying the tents and baggage of the people, which are rated at the enormous number of 24,000 camels; the Nusseer having 17,000, the Meeankhyl 4000, and the Kharoutee 3000. The tract which they pass leads by broken, rugged roads, or rather by the water-courses of the Goomul, through the wild and mountainous country of the Wuzeerees; but the Lohanees have arms and numbers to protect their own property and that of the strangers who accompany them. They all reach Cabool and Candahar by the middle of June, in sufficient time to despatch their investments to Bokhara and Herat; and at the end of October, as winter approaches, they again descend, with the same arrangement, into the plain of the Indus, bringing horses, dyes, fruits, and the productions of Cabool, in return for the goods of India and Britain. This channel of trade is ancient; for we find that in A.D. 1505 the Emperor Baber states that, when campaigning in the Derajat, he had fallen in with Lohanee merchants and plundered them of "a great quantity of white cloth, aromatic drugs, sugar (both candied and in powder), and horses," which are the self-same articles in which the trade is now carried on. It is due to the Emperor to state that if, during his own difficulties, he plundered these Lohanee merchants, he afterwards, when firmly established on the throne of Cabool, clothed them in dresses of honour.

Having given the routes of the Lohanee caravan, I ought to note also the whole of the other roads leading from India to Cabool; but it would be difficult to do so clearly by a mere verbal description. There are three great roads leading from India: the first, by Lahore and Attock, the second from the Derajat (already described), and the third by the Bolan Pass, from Shikarpoor to Candahar. Intermediate to these lines there are also various routes, some of which have been used even by large bodies of armed men; but they are not at present traversed by merchants. The one leading from Dera Ghazee Khan, across the Sukhee Surwur Pass, by Boree to Candahar, has been used in modern times by the kings of Cabool, to obtain the luxury of mangoes; and I met persons who had seen the fruit arrive by it at Candahar from the Indus in eight or nine days. The climate of Boree is described in very favourable terms, not only by Mr. Elphinstone, but by all the natives I have interrogated on the subject; and it was by this route that Baber passed up to Ghuzni with his army after the campaign of 1505, already alluded to. His horse suffered from the want of grain; but, as a caravan route, this seems not to be inferior to the Golairee Pass, and to have been deserted only of late years; indeed at the present time it is used by couriers (cassids) to bring speedy information to and from India. From Dera Ismael Khan, north to Peshawur, there is no direct traffic. The roads are bad and the people predatory. To Cabool, however, there is a good road by the Koorum river. From Dera Ghazee Khan, south to Dajel and Hurrund, there are roads leading over low hills to Bagh, Dadur, and the Bolan Pass: these have been used by large caravans within the last twenty-five years. Dera Ghazee Khan, indeed, and Shikarpoor, as I have already stated, are always spoken of by the people as the two "Gates of Khorasan."

From a neighbourhood so advantageously situated the merchant exports the native productions of the soil with profit; and the manufacturer converts them and the imports from other countries into cloth, which accompanies the foreign goods that pass through for consumption in the interior. Dera Ghazee Khan itself is a manufacturing town, but it is surpassed by Mooltan and Bhawulpoor, which are in its neighbourhood. At one time its trade with the west, and even with the east, was brisk; and though, from the great influx of British goods, it does not now exhibit it former prosperity, its native manufactures are still healthy and thriving. It is celebrated for its goolbuddens and durriees, or striped and plain silken cloths, which, being much sought for and admired, are annually exported to Lahore and Sinde, and are there considered to surpass those of every other country. To the east it sends its silks, the raw material being obtained from Bokhara and the west. To the west it sends its cotton and a coarse white cloth, which is the most important of its exported manufactures, and is sought after in Khorasan, where it yet stands its ground in competition with English cloth, as far at least as demand goes, for it is much inferior in quality. The demand for British calicoes has decreased this year by one-half; last year the sales effected amounted to 50,000 rupees, and this year it is under 24,000. Chintzes of different descriptions, with soosees, bafta, and some coarse loongees, complete the list of manufactured cloths: there are none made of wool. The value of all the cloths made here may amount to about one and a half or two lacs of rupees; and the greater part is exported. A coarse kind of cutlery, swords, scissors, and knives, such as are used by sailors, is also made at Dera Ghazee Khan, and exported. The bazar consists of about 1600 shops, 530 of which are engaged in weaving and selling cloth. The town has a prosperous appearance, which is altogether attributable to the protection afforded it by Monsieur Ventura, who was lately in charge of the district. The population is about 25,000. It is said to have been built by a Beloochee about 300 years ago; and its name long fluctuated between "Ghazee Khan" and "Hajee Khan." It was formerly subject to the crown of Cabool, but fell into the hands of the Sikhs about twenty-five years ago. They farmed it to Bhawul Khan, who had no interest in protecting it, and his officers were guilty of the grossest extortions; but since 1832, when it was resumed by the Sikhs, it has greatly recovered itself.

The land around Dera Ghazee Khan is very rich: the town is pleasantly situated in a flat country about four miles from the Indus, and is surrounded by gardens and lofty trees, among which the date predominates. It is said, indeed, that around Dera there are no less than 80,000 date-trees. By far the most valuable production of the place is indigo, 2000 maunds of which were this year exported to the west; and I am informed that this is about as much as the district can produce. The best sort now sells for sixty-five rupees per maund, that of medium quality for fifty, and the worst for thirty-two: this export alone amounts to about one lac of rupees in value. The dye is inferior to that procured in Bhawul Khan's country; but it is cheaper, and has a ready sale in Cabool and Bokhara, besides being nearer at hand. The cotton of Dera Ghazee Khan is of a superior quality, being soft in staple; 25,000 maunds are procurable: it is at present exported. Sugar is cultivated, but in small quantities, and only of late years. The place is rich in grain; the wheat and barley are excellent, but the rice is red, and of a poor quality. The price of grain in June, 1837, was as follows, the currency being that of Shooja-ool-Moolk, and much the same as that of Shikarpoor already detailed:—

	Rupees.
Rice, per maund of 40 seers, 80 rupees to a seer	3
Rice, 2nd sort, 1½ maund	2 to 1¾
Wheat, 1½ maund	1
Grain, 70 seers	1
Dale, or mohree, 2 maunds	1
Moong, or mash, 50 seers	1
Ghee, per maund	8½
Oil, per maund	4

		Rupees.
Salt, per ruja, or piece of 1 maund, 25	.	3¾
Native salt, 2 maunds	. . . .	1
Goor, or molasses	. . . . .	3½
Sugar-candy, per maund	. . . .	16

Under Cabool, Dera Ghazee Khan yielded a yearly revenue of about twelve lacs of rupees; it now produces eight and a half or nine lacs, and that only within the two or three last years. The country which gives this income includes the district of Sungur on the north, and Hurund Dajel on the south; also Cuchee, across the Indus. The revenue is farmed to the same person who is now Governor of Mooltan, and is improving daily. The villages around Dera Ghazee Khan are exceedingly numerous: they are nearly all peopled by Mahommedans; and in the town of Dera Ghazee Khan itself the two tribes are about equal, there being in it 125 Hindoo temples, and 110 mosques, great and small, every description of religious buildings being included in that number. Dera Ghazee Khan communicates with all the countries around it by good roads, except those to the west, which have no claim to commendation. A list of the marts or places of note to which they lead may not be useless:—Asnee, Hurund, Cutch Gundava, Mittun, Shikarpoor, Bhawulpoor, Khyrpoor, Ullah, Yan, Hydrábád, Mooltan, Lahore, and Umritsir.

I will conclude my account of this place by an enumeration of the different classes of shops in the bazar, which I deem to be somewhat curious as a statistical document.

List of the Shops in the Bazar of Dera Ghazee Khan, on the Indus.

	No. of Shops.
Sellers of cloth	115
Sellers of silk	25
Weavers of white cloth	128
Weavers of silk	112
Cleaners of cotton	25
Sellers of cotton	17
Dealers in grain	219
Boot and shoe makers	55
Do. Hindoo	25
Cap-makers	15
Tailors	50
Butchers	15
Dealers in vegetables	40
„ in fruit	32
„ in milk	30
Confectioners	75
Cooks	40
Hukeems	10
Grocers—passaree	30
Dealers in ivory, glass, &c.—mamgur	30
Blacksmiths	45
Coppersmiths	25
Jewellers	60
Cutlers	12

	No. of Shops.
Turners	9
Shroffs	30
Saddlers	20
Washermen	50
Painters	15
Dealers in tobacco and bang . . .	30
Dealers in salt and "maté" . . .	12
Pipe-sellers	18
Paper-sellers	18
Shops shut up, and consequently unknown .	165
Total	1597

CHAPTER IV.

Battle between the Afghans and Sikhs—Departure from Dera Ghazee—Baber's routes—Voyage upwards—Sungur—Gurung—Dera Ismael Khan—Bazars, &c.—Corps de ballet—Donna of the Indus—Voyage to Kala Bagh—Romantic country—Kussooree hills—Singular formation—Villages—Sooleeman range.

On the 1st of June, and whilst at Dera Ghazee Khan, despatches of a late date, and of an important nature, reached me from our ambassador in Persia, Sir John Macneil; and on the following day further intelligence arrived from Peshawur, by which we learned that a battle had taken place between the chief of Cabool and the Sikhs, at the mouth of the Khyber Pass, in which the Sikh general was slain. There appeared, therefore, every reason to fear that these countries would shortly be in a very disturbed state; and, weighing deliberately the instructions under which I was acting, I did not deem it advisable to tarry much longer at Dera Ghazee. I accordingly sailed from that place on the 5th of June; and at the same time Dr. Lord and Lieutenant Leech passed over to Mooltan, where they gathered much important information; and, although they experienced some difficulties, their stay there was by no means disagreeable. The difficulties which they met at Mooltan, and the neglect which we had to complain of at Dera Ghazee, all arose from the same cause. It had been arranged that Captain (now Colonel) Wade should meet us at Mittun: this he had not been enabled to do, the Lion of Lahore, who did not altogether relish our political measures on the Indus, having detained him at his capital.

Observing that Baber states that, after his campaigns in Bungush and Bunnoo, he passed up to Ghuzni by Choteealee, it appeared to me certain that he must have taken the road of Sukhee Surwur, and I therefore sent Lieutenant Leech to explore it. He proceeded to the mountains called "Kala roh," and found the road a mere pathway, and much molested by robbers; and from subsequent information we learned that these routes to the west of the Indus are rendered impracticable, even more from the poverty of the country than from the badness of the roads. It would also appear to be imprudent to use them for the passage of armies, after Baber's statement that he lost many of his horses in the attempt.

In the neighbourhood of Sukhee Surwur, a kind

of argillaceous earth, called "maté," is found and exported to India, where it is used in baths and to cleanse the hair.

On the 8th we anchored above Deradeen Punna; we passed Leia on the 9th, Gurung on the 11th, Kaheeree ferry on the 13th, and moored off Dera Ismael Khan on the 16th: thus performing a voyage of about 200 miles in eleven days, the wind being fair all the way, although the weather was squally, with rain, thunder, and lightning. We frequently sailed at the rate of four and five miles an hour against the stream, and at a time when the inundation was at its height. If we were enabled to do this by the force of the wind alone, what could not steam achieve? The birds—a kind of tern—which hover in flocks over the banks of the river, are a good guide to the navigator. These birds are always to be seen near spots where the river is washing away its banks, and where they pick up slugs; and thus the rapid parts of the stream may be descried from a distance and avoided.

The first district in ascending this portion of the Indus is Sungur. It is a fertile tract, lying under the hills about fifty miles north of Dera Ghazee. Water runs down upon it by a rivulet from the hills, and the harvest is so plentiful that a part of the produce is exported. Manglote is the name of the fort in Sungur, and Täosa is a village in it. We found nine boats loading at the ferry, and about ten miles higher up we halted on a bank which had all the appearance of an English park. The trees, it must be confessed, were babool, but they were lofty and clear of underwood, so that we could see far through them over a green sward. They would afford abundance of firewood, which may some day prove of use. At Gurung, which succeeds Sungur, and is within four miles of the river, the cultivators of the land came in crowds to see us. They were Beloochees of the Kolaichee tribe, but I found that the rest of the population were chiefly Mahommedan Juts. There were also some Koreeshee Mahommedans, and a few Hindoos. Their subjection to the Sikhs is complete, and newly-built Sikh temples are to be seen in several places, which testify their power. The people complained bitterly of the want of money, the collectors having sent out of the country all that they possessed. Their rulers would not consent to take the revenue in kind, but insisted on payment in cash, and this formed the grand subject-ground of grievance. I have heard similar complaints in the British provinces, and indeed the deterioration of our revenue may be traced to this cause. These people informed me that their crops were for the most part obtained by irrigation; the water being drawn, not from the Indus, but from the hills. This is also the case at Sungur, as I have already mentioned. Gurung is watered by the Vahova; the Rumal irrigates the country near Dera Ismael; and, higher up, the Goomul serves the same purpose, the whole of it being expended before it reaches the Indus. The crops consist of wheat, barley, and juwaree: rice is not produced.

Our camp was soon pitched at the ferry of Dera Ismael, and the Governor invited us to proceed to the town, which is about three miles inland. It was at this ferry that we first noticed a description of boat called "dugga," differing from the rounded "zohruk," and which we were informed was the only craft suited to the rocky part of the river above Kala-Bagh. They have a large prow and stern, which protect them when driven on shore with violence, as they frequently are. A zohruk exposed to the same danger would, to use the phrase of the natives, be certain to "split her breast." In the evening, whilst loitering near the ferry, I watched the lights floating down the river—offerings made by the people to the stream—pleasing emblems of devotion, which twinkled for a while and were lost for ever. I saw here also a strong instance of devotion of another kind in the behaviour of a deer belonging to one of our own people. The animal was so thoroughly tamed, that it even followed its owner into the river, and swam after him. It was strange to witness in a creature so timid, and in general so afraid of water, nature thus conquered by affection. The ferry presented a bustling scene—the whole town crowded to it, and the Hindoos swam about on red skins in their forbidden river with great dexterity. I had never seen the race *take to the water* so readily before. They have benefited by the change of masters, and have therefore become cheerful and elated.

Of all the towns in this district Dera Ismael Khan ranks next in importance to Dera Ghazee; but it is only a third of its size, and, from its position, labours under many disadvantages. About twelve years ago the town was washed into the Indus, and on a new site, about three miles from the river, the inhabitants have again fixed themselves. Until lately the place was held by an Afghan chief, to whom the Sikhs assigned it in *perpetuity*, after a brave and memorable resistance. A year ago they forcibly repossessed themselves of it on the fictitious plea of strengthening Peshawur; whereas, in reality, the places have no connexion with one another, being separated by the Khuttuk country, which is strong and mountainous, and only pervious to a large force, although there is a gun-road through it. The new town of Dera Ismael is laid out with order and regularity, having wide streets and a good bazar; but it is unfinished, and the present rulers are not likely to carry out the plans of its founder. The houses are of sun-burnt brick. The town when we saw it had a deserted look, but it is said to be a place of much life and bustle in the winter, when the Afghans return to its neighbourhood from Khorasan. There is a large caravanserai in it, where they transact business and dispose of their goods, as this is their bazar-town. The fruits of Cabool were to be had in abundance, and were excellent. The bazar contains 518 shops; but there are no native manufactures here as in the Lower Dera. The transit of coarse white cloth from the Punjab is great, the annual quantity sometimes amounting to 1,800,000 yards, or 3000 camel-loads. The revenues of Dera Ismael exceed four and a half lacs of rupees, and are derived from the town itself, and from the country extending to Puharpoor north, and Derabund west, including Koye, Kolaichee, and the tributary district of the Eesa Khyl. Grain and the necessaries of life are more expensive than in Dera Ghazee, although supplies are received by the river from Marwut, which is a grain country to the north-west.

On the 20th of June I was joined by Captain

Mackeson, the British agent for the navigation of the Indus, with whom I had much conversation on the commercial prospects by the river, and as to the advantages of establishing a fair on its banks. I give, in an appendix (*vide* Appendix No. 1), the result of the inquiries which I made, together with my own views on this very important subject, which appears to me to demand much more attention than has hitherto been accorded to it. Had a more active part been taken some years ago in extending our commercial relations in this quarter, we might, perhaps, by means of our manufactures, have successfully coped with our rivals, and been spared the necessity of using our arms beyond the Indus. That great geographer, D'Anville, however, used to congratulate himself on the certainty of distant wars adding to our geographical knowledge; and there can be no doubt that foreign conquest tends to produce this effect more rapidly than the slow progress of commerce.

A messenger here reached us, bearing an extremely kind letter from Runjeet Sing. It was full of his usual professions, and was accompanied by some half-dozen orders (purwanus) which would insure us attentions we had not hitherto received from some of his subordinates. Everything now went on merrily; but his Highness's parade of the extent of his kingdom, which he stated in his letter to extend from Ladak to Omercote, showed his fears that the British Government had some intention of clipping his wings. These fears were, however, totally without foundation.

On the 2nd of July Doctor Lord and Lieutenant Leech rejoined us from Mooltan; and the corps de ballet, from Dera Ismael, came down to do us honour and show their accomplishments to the five Firingees. The number of these young ladies was very considerable, and they displayed a profusion of ornaments which I had not before seen, and which we all agreed were in bad taste. These women use antimony in the eye, the effect of which extends beyond the organ, and gives to it the shape of an almond: indeed, it is called "badam-chusm," or almond-eye; and, strange as the assertion may appear, the effect produced is certainly good. Some of them wore necklaces of cloves, and one young lady had adorned her neck with a pod of musk, the scent of the deer. She was the Hebe of Dera, and bore the name of Mulam Bukhsh: although dark, she was extremely handsome, and elicited loud applauses from the citizens of Dera Ismael, who pronounced her to be "the Donna of all the Indus." Among the company present was the young son of the Governor, whose intelligent and beautiful countenance, faithfully given in the accompanying plate, interested us all greatly.

From this place I addressed a letter to the chief of Cabool, enlarging on the advantages of peace; and on the 3rd of July we again embarked on the Indus, and reached Kala Bagh at three P.M. on the 13th, not without adventures on our route. On the third day after our departure from Mooltan we closed with the hills of Khussooree below Beloote, on the right bank, and had a romantic sail along their base to Keree, where we halted. A sheet of verdure, covered with palms and other trees, now and then separated us from these hills. The landscape was striking—bare, brown, and bleak rocks overlooked the plain; their summits crowned with the ruins of infidel forts (Kaffir Killa); intermixed with which were some Hindoo pagodas, blackened by age, and now deserted. We landed to examine these buildings, and thought the locality well suited to the taste of sequestered men. The formation of the hills was limestone, with flints and fossil shells thickly embedded in it, some of which were very curious, as sea-weed could be distinctly traced upon them. On the next day, the 7th of July, we passed Sheenee, sailing literally among date-trees: for many of them had been, by the invasion of the stream, detached from the land; and the labour and difficulty of tracking was, in consequence of this, extremely great. The heat was most oppressive during the day, the reflection from the bare hills augmenting the effects of a sultry atmosphere; and even during the night the temperature was so high that not one of us could sleep. At dawn of the 8th the thermometer stood at 90°. We pushed off at once, and crossed, during the day, to the opposite shore; as the Khussooree hills, which are here very steep, and in some places almost perpendicular, pressed in close upon the river. Lieutenant Wood, however, subsequently surmounted these difficulties by the aid of the Eesá Khyl Afghans, who were most friendly towards us. From the eastern side of the river the view of these mountains was very imposing, the absence of ruggedness in their outlines giving them the appearance of a vast fortress formed by nature, with the Indus as its ditch. On the right side of the river we found a secure and permanent bank, some forty feet high, with fixed villages on it, and small forts differing from the reed houses, lower down. Herds and flocks were numerous, and the sheep appeared to thrive on the furze of the thull, or dry country. We got into a still branch of the Indus, called Bumberwah, and made rapid progress, passing the villages of Kolla, Koondee, Rokree, Moje, and Daöd Khyl, and at length arrived at Kala Bagh. Long before we

reached it we saw the crevice through which the Indus issued. The salt range to our right, which is here called "Soa-Roh," looked well, and stood out with a bold, well-defined outline in the transparent sky, which had been cleared by the recent rains. The Takht, or throne, of Sooleeman, with its table summit, was also a grand object in our rear. The people flocked about us; and the women—stout, sturdy dames, unveiled—begged us to buy their melons and vegetables. The men were also on a large scale, bony and muscular. The dress, too, had changed—the females wearing loose trousers falling down in folds that were becoming, and which reminded us of the garb of the Kattees of Kattywar. We became objects of special curiosity, for a dozen boats had never been seen here; and the appearance of a Firingee camp, with its novel paraphernalia, I doubt not, yet marks an era in the annals of these people. They all took to the water like amphibious beings, and swam about our boats on inflated skins, coming down to see us always skin in hand. As we approached Kala Bagh the water of the river became much clearer, and ere we crossed to that town we could see the rounded pebbles at the bottom: an agreeable contrast to the muddy Indus of the lower countries.*

* Lieutenant Wood's extremely valuable report on the River Indus is given at the end of the volume, Appendix ii.

CHAPTER V.

Our critical position—State of the country—Influence of the Sikhs—The Euzoofzyes and their Chief—Plain of Peshawur—Futtihghur—The Khuttuks—Kala Bagh—Eesá Khyl Afghans—The Wuzarees—Ascent of the Indus—Coal deposits—Excessive heat—Duncote—Husn Abdal—Dr. Falconer—Arrival at Attock.

WE now found ourselves in the theatre of war, and in a somewhat critical situation. The Sikh garrison at Puharpoor had, shortly before our arrival, been massacred, and the Eesá Khyl Chief, Ahmed Khan, having refused to pay his tribute and do homage, a force of 3000 men and ten guns had arrived from Lahore to reduce him to submission, and was now on the other bank of the river, under the command of Futteh Sing Mán. From neither party had we any danger to fear, but it might be difficult to steer a medium course that should not give offence to one or the other. The Eesá Khyl had acted throughout a most friendly part towards us, and some of them were now in our camp, while the drums and fifes, gongs and bugles, of the Sikhs echoed among the mountains within our hearing, and their troops were often in sight. On the 19th the Sikhs began to cross the river, and as the

"Ghazees," or champions, were assembled hard by, we thought it advisable to change our quarters to the right bank, and thus escape all chance of molestation. That the reader may understand the state of parties here and higher up the Indus, it becomes necessary that I should give, once for all, a rapid sketch of the power which the Sikhs possess on its western bank.

Their legitimate influence beyond the river may be said to be confined to the plain country, as their authority can only be enforced in the mountains by the presence of an army; and in some of the hilly tracts, even those bordering on the river, as has been seen, the Mahommedans can successfully resist it. It is, however, the strength of their country, and not their military power, which enables them to cope with the Sikhs. The low country, on the other hand, is under complete subjection to Lahore: the Derajat is without the presence of a regular force, which is, however, necessary in the plain of Peshawur. For six degrees of latitude, from 34° 30′ north down to 28° 30′, on the frontiers of Sinde, the Sikhs have either actual possession of the country west of the river, or exercise some degree of influence over it. An enumeration of the condition of the different petty states will best illustrate these observations.

The most northern territory is that of Poyndu

Khan, a Turnowlee or Moghul by descent. This state consisted of a small but rich tract of country eastward of the Moo-seen, as the Indus is here called, in Puklee, yielding yearly about a lac of rupees. Of this the Sikhs have deprived him; but he yet holds the fort of Chuttoorlye, on an island in the Indus about 10 miles north of Derbund, and also a country of about 240 square miles on the west bank. From this tract the Sikhs draw no tribute; and even on the eastern bank they hold their possession with difficulty, Poyndu Khan making continual forays across the river, and carrying off prisoners, on whose ransom he supports himself and his people. He has about 500 horse and 2000 infantry, most of whom are natives of Hindoostan, and wandered into this country during the crusade of Syud Ahmed, who was slain by the Sikhs in 1831.

Next to Poyndu Khan's country, and below Derbund, lies the district of Sittanu, about fifteen miles north of Torbaila. It is held, with a very small river tract, by Syud Akbar, a holy man who is much revered by the Mahommedans in this country: he has no tribute to pay to the Sikhs, nor are he or his few subjects molested by them.*

* Lieutenant Leech ascended the right bank of the Indus opposite to Derbund, and it is to him that I am indebted for these particulars.

Below these petty districts, and less immediately on the Indus, lie the territories of the Euzoofzyes, a numerous and powerful tribe of Afghans, whom the Sikhs control by retaining a regular force cantoned in the plain country north of Attock, between the Indus and river of Cabool. This body of troops is protected from surprise by a fort of some strength, called Jangura, built on the north bank of the river of Cabool, about five miles from the place where it falls into the Indus. The Euzoofzyes are the tribe from which the ruler of Lahore experienced so much opposition in his approaches on Peshawur, and with whom some of his most sanguinary battles were fought. The late Sirdar Huree Sing, who fell in the recent battle of Jumrood, was in the habit of making yearly incursions among the Euzoofzyes, burning their villages and crops, and seizing horses, &c., as tribute. At different times he destroyed the villages of Topee, Minee, Kota, Moonara, and Buree, which belong to the Otmanzye Euzoofzye. From these he used to exact about sixty horses: but, two years since, by mutual agreement, a tax of four rupees per house was fixed in lieu of every demand; and this would not be paid were it not for the presence of a force which overawes them. The sum realized sometimes amounts to sixty thousand rupees. The principal personage among the Euzoofzyes is

Futteh Khan, chief of Punjtar, whose territories to the west are bounded by Swat and Hushtnuggur. He has about 1500 foot and 200 horse, besides village (Ooloosee) troops. He occasionally sends presents of horses and hawks, but pays no regular tribute to the Sikhs,* nor will he allow their agent to enter his country. This chieftain has greater means of resisting than his more southern neighbours.

The plain of Peshawur is the most northern of all the actual conquests of the Sikhs west of the Indus. For many years it paid to Lahore an annual tribute of horses and rice; but, in 1834, when Shah Shooja Ool Moolk made the attempt to recover his kingdom by an attack on Candahar, the Sikhs seized upon Peshawur, and have since retained it. It is stated that the Maharajah's design in possessing himself of Peshawur was to counteract the power of the Shah, should he re-establish himself on his throne; but there is reason to believe that his foresight did not extend so far, and that Sirdar Huree Sing, who

* An agent of this chief waited upon me with a letter, tendering his master's allegiance to the British Government, and offering to pay us the usual tribute. Finding his country adjoined Kaffiristan, I made some inquiries regarding it, and the agent immediately offered to commute the tribute of horses into one of an equal number of young Kaffirs, thinking the change of terms would be more acceptable.

had long been stationed on the Attock and engaged in incessant wars with the Mahommedans, persuaded him to take the step, against his own better judgment. The policy of the conquest was always dubious: from first to last it has proved a source of much anxiety; and, latterly, a cause of serious disaster. Previous to its conquest Peshawur was held by a branch of the Barukzye family, under Sooltan Mahommed Khan and his brothers, who realized a yearly revenue of upwards of eight lacs of rupees. The assessment under Lahore amounted to ten lacs, and this sum has since been realized by the Maharajah's officer, Monsieur Avitabile, who fixed it. Only a small portion, however, now reaches the coffers of the Sikhs; for, at the present time, Sooltan Mahommed Khan and his brothers possess jaghires to the amount of four lacs and a half of rupees, and hold Cohat, Hushtnuggur, and the Doaba, the richest portion of the plain. The country of the Khuleels, which yielded about a lac of rupees, is now entirely deserted; and that of the Momunds, which was nearly as valuable, is only half cultivated. Six out of ten lacs are thus abstracted; and besides all this, extensive lands are alienated to religious persons, a large garrison is kept up, and much additional expense is incurred: so that Peshawur is a drain on the finances of the Lahore state, with the additional disadvantage of being so situated as to lead the Sikhs into constant collision with fierce and desperate tribes, who, were it not for their poverty, would be formidable antagonists. In the city of Peshawur the Sikhs have built a fort on the site of Bala Hissar.—It is strong, and, in the late war, afforded protection to the wealthier inhabitants. They have also strengthened their position by erecting another fort, called Futtihghur, near Jumrood, opposite the Khyber Pass.—It is a square of about 300 yards, protecting an octagonal fort, in the centre of which is a lofty mass of building which commands the surrounding country. This fort is dependent on the mountain streams for its water, which the Afghans can and do dam up. At the time of our visit they were sinking a well, which they had carried to the depth of 170 feet without coming to water; but, from indications in the soil, it was expected to be soon reached, and has since, I am informed, been obtained, but not in abundance. Even with these defences the position will be a troublesome one, as both the Afreedes and Khyberees consider it meritorious to injure the Sikhs.

Between the plain of Peshawur and the salt range at Kala Bagh lies the country of the Khuttuks and Sagree Afghans. The Khuttuks are divided into the petty chieftainships of Acora and Teree. Acora is situated east of the plain of Peshawur, on the river of Cabool; and as its chief, Hussun Khan, serves the Sikhs, he is permitted to retain his country. Those Khuttuks of Acora, however, who live in the hills, are not subject to Runjeet Sing. The southern division, under the chief of Teree, maintains its independence, in so far, at least, as refusing to pay a direct tribute; although it acknowledges the supremacy of Sooltan Mahommed Khan, who is but a servant of the Sikhs. When Peshawur was first captured, a Sikh officer was stationed at Cohat and Bungush; but he found it impossible to keep the country in order, and it has since been wisely confided to the intermediate government of the ex-chief of Peshawur: by this means a small tribute of about 1000 rupees per annum is drawn from Teree, in the plain of Bungush, which lies westward of the Khuttuk country. Below the Khuttuks are the Sagree Patans, a tribe entirely independent of the Sikhs: they hold the country on the west bank for nearly thirty miles above Kala Bagh; and also on the opposite shore as high as the plain which commences at Husn Abdal: they are shepherds, and their flocks are numerous. It will therefore be seen that from Attock to Kala Bagh the Sikhs have little or no power along the line of the Indus. The inhabitants, during the last campaign, resisted the ascent from Kala Bagh of the boats which were required for the construction of a bridge, till Sooltan Mahommed Khan interceded; and had the Sikhs met with further reverses at Jumrood, the Khuttuks were ready to have attacked them on their retreat to Attock, as they passed the defile of Geedur Gullee. The number of the Khuttuk tribe is variously stated at from 6000 to 8000 armed men.*

The town of Kala Bagh, so famous for its rock-salt, is subject to Lahore, but is held by a native malik, or chief, who pays only 10,000 rupees yearly, though he collects 32,000. The situation of the malik is one of uncertainty and peril; for he is surrounded on all sides by the enemies of the Maharajah, with all of whom he is obliged to live on friendly terms, lest they should injure him when the Lahore troops are withdrawn. Kala Bagh is an important position to the Sikhs, as it is here that their armies cross the river to make inroads and levy tribute upon the tribes of which we shall presently have occasion to speak. The subjection of Kala Bagh is complete.

Following the course of the Indus is the country of the Eesá Khyl Afghans, which extends to within

---

* Lieutenant Wood passed through the country of the Khuttuks and Sagrees, and it is on his authority that I am enabled to state the precise condition of this tract.

thirty miles of the province of Dera Ismael Khan. It is a strong and mountainous strip of land, and its valley abounds in water, and is well peopled. The Sikhs have, however, approached it from Puharpoor, on the south, and also from Kala Bagh, and exact, pretty regularly, a tribute of 34,000 rupees per annum. To enforce their authority, a detachment was last year stationed in the country: but the whole party were massacred, as I have already stated, during a popular insurrection; and the present chief, Ahmed Khan, who has the character of a humane and good man, has resisted all attempts to replace the detachment, though he acknowledges allegiance to Lahore and agrees to pay tribute. The mountains of Eesá Khyl and Khussoor rise so abruptly from the Indus, that, were not the country accessible on other sides, it might make successful resistance; and, in fact, the Eesá Khyls have been lately left to govern themselves without a garrison.

On the other side of Eesá Khyl lies the district of Bunnoo, intersected by the Koorum river, which renders it rich and fertile. It consequently excites the cupidity of the Sikhs; and the Lahore troops have frequently entered the district, and did so last year, exacting from it a tribute of a lac of rupees. They can, however, obtain nothing from it without a large force, and troops are generally sent into it every second year. In the times of the kings, Bunnoo paid a yearly tribute of one lac and 40,000 rupees; and the level and defenceless nature of the country will always enable the most powerful chief in its vicinity to exact something from it. The Sikhs enter Bunnoo by the village of Lukhee, but retain no permanent force in it.

South of Bunnoo lies Murunt. A tribute of 28,000 rupees is exacted from this district; but, as in Bunnoo, an armed force is necessary. It is a country rich in grain, which is sent down the Indus to Dera Ismael Khan.

The district of Tak adjoins the province of Dera Ismael Khan, and, being partly in the plains, has become subject to Lahore. At present, it forms part of the jaghire of the prince, and is farmed for one lac and 20,000 rupees; but the amount realized varies from year to year, although some payment is certain, as a Sikh force is located in the country. The chiefs, for some years, paid a tribute of 100 camels and 25,000 rupees, but they have now left the country and fled to Cabool. The only enemies of which the Sikhs here stand in awe are the Wuzarees, a barbarous tribe of Afghans; who inhabit the mountains to the westward, and sometimes descend into the low country and plunder the inhabitants.

Descending the Indus and passing by Dera Ismael and Dera Ghazee Khan, already described, we next come to Mittun; beyond which lie Hurund and Dajel, which, being late acquisitions from the Brahooees, require a watchful eye. In other respects the Sikh rule is paramount in this country; their Grinth, or holy book, is placed in mosques, and sometimes in temples built expressly for its reception; the cow is a sacred animal; and no Mahommedan raises his voice in praying to his God,—the clearest proofs of conquest, but, at the same time, an interference so impolitic, that, should a reverse occur westward of the Indus, the subdued and sullen population would, at once, rise *en masse* upon the invaders of their soil, whose position, during a portion of the year, is further endangered by the inundation of the Indus, as, at that time, it cannot be bridged, and is, therefore, with difficulty passed by an army.

From the political I will now pass to the physical geography of these countries. Our object, as I have already stated, had been to ascend the Indus to Attock, and even to Peshawur, but the information which we had lately received held out but little encouragement to us to attempt to do so at this season of the year: nevertheless, on the 16th of July we embarked with a southerly wind, and, passing Kala Bagh and its romantic cliffs, stemmed the river merrily to Maree, where, losing the wind, we found the stream too rapid for the track-rope, and were obliged to return. The river was smooth, and, at its narrowest part, about 400 yards in breadth. The water, although the thermometer proved that its temperature was 72°, produced so strong a sensation of cold, that the boatmen who were tracking complained much of it; and, the rope having pulled some of them into the river, one man was picked up benumbed and exhausted. Our failure, however, did not daunt a British sailor like Lieutenant Wood; and, although it now seemed advisable that the mission should prosecute its journey by land, he resolved to stand by his own element as long as there was any prospect of success: accordingly, he set out with a well-manned boat, and reached Sharkee, about one-third of the distance to Attock, when some of his crew left him, and he was obliged to return. He found the river running in a channel of rock, while detached cliffs stood up in the middle of the stream like basaltic pillars, having marks upon them which indicated a rise of the river of 50 and 60 feet above its bed. It is, however, for three or four months only that the upward navigation of the Indus is here interrupted; and the downward passage is open all the year: for Lieutenant Wood, having proceeded by land to Attock, descended the river from that point. In the beginning of May, the Sikhs, having occasion for boats to complete their bridge at Attock, dragged them up from Kala Bagh in twenty-two days, with only fifteen or twenty men in excess of their crews: since then, however, the strength of the current had increased, and the Indus was now rapid, noisy, and dangerous. From Attock we navigated the river of Cabool to Peshawur and Muchnee; and Lieutenant Wood ultimately descended from Jellalabad to the sea, as he has stated at large in his very interesting and able work.

The mineral riches of Kala Bagh—its rock-salt, alum, and sulphur—require no further mention from me; but it is important that I should state that we here commenced a series of inquiries for coal, and that our search was crowned with complete success. It was found close to the town at Shukurdura and Muckud, and, ultimately, in no less than twelve localities, stretching in the direction of Cohat towards Ghuzni, along the salt-range after it has crossed the Indus, and lower down at Kaneegoorum. Lieutenant Wood was also fortunate enough to discover it at three places on the eastern bank,—Joa, Meealee, and Nummul, between Pind Dadun Khan and Kala Bagh, and at distances from 25 to 50 miles of the river. On both banks the localities in which the coal is found were similar, viz., in deep, dry water-courses, and the channels of winter torrents. Anthracite was also brought by my messengers from Jummoo, high up the Chenab; and Dr. Lord procured coal at Kobal, on the north bank of the Oxus. I have not by me the analysis of the coal discovered by Lieutenant Wood; but Mr. James Prinsep, in reporting to Government on that found on the western bank, stated that " four of the specimens were, in fact, of the very finest form of mineral coal, that in which all vegetable appearance is lost:" of one of the specimens, a kind of jet, he remarked, " that, if found in sufficient quantities, it would not only answer well as a fuel, but be superior to all other coals for the particular object in getting up steam, from the large proportion of inflammable gas it disengaged under combustion." It is to be hoped that the time is not distant when these discoveries will be turned to good account by the British Government; and it is satisfactory to find, even at the present time, the enterprising Parsee merchants of Bombay navigating the Indus by steam as high as Kala Bagh, from which point, by means of land conveyance, they are enabled to supply the wants of Cabool.

Our stay at Kala Bagh now drew to a close, and as the road to Peshawur by Cohat had been already traversed by Mr. Elphinstone, and, moreover, was infested by robbers, we determined to proceed to Attock, up the eastern bank of the river; and accordingly commenced our march on the 22nd, heartily glad to get away from Kala Bagh, the heat of which can only be compared to that of an oven. So intense is it, that all the population leave their houses and live under trees on the banks of the river, in which they are perpetually to be seen spinning and amusing themselves. A quarter of the population suffer from goître. We found, however, that as far as related to temperature we had not bettered our condition by leaving the Indus; for at Musan, our first halting-place, the thermometer rose to 115° in a single-poled tent, and in the smaller tents, occupied by our people, it reached to 135°. We lay gasping all day, stretched out beneath tables as a protection, and at sunset the mercury did not sink below 100°! A week's suffering was, at length, terminated by a violent thunder-storm, which cooled the atmosphere.

Our halting-grounds were at the hamlets of Neekee, Jubbee, and Toote, and thence to Pindee Nurlik Oulia, according to the name given on the maps, but which is more properly called Pindee-Gaib-ne. We had made but little northing in a distance of 51 miles, for all the maps of this district are erroneous, and we had only, as yet, reached the latitude of 33° 10'. Steep ravines and execrable roads brought us, at length, to the Swan river, which we crossed, stirrup deep, at a point near Toote: it was rapid, red, and swollen. Nature seems to have been sportive in this neighbourhood, for the strata run in all directions—soft, red sand lies under hard sandstones, and time has furrowed the hills into peaks of singular irregularity. As we approached Pindee the face of the country changed. We had now an undulating upland moor, nearly destitute of vegetation, and, as I suppose, forming part of the "Chool-i-Julalee," or desert of Julal-e-deen, thus called from the hero of that name who so nobly swam the Indus when pursued by his enemies. Pindee was a cheerful-looking village, and, at the time of our arrival, was enlivened by the presence of Sikh soldiers, who were passing through it to join the force at Kala Bagh. Their commander, Soojet Sing, waited on us and was very civil: we had previously met a regiment of cavalry in the ravines of the Swan river, commanded by Captain Foulkes, an Englishman of high character in the Sikh service. These military movements disconcerted the people, and were considered as proofs of some ulterior designs beyond the Indus.

While in this neighbourhood I ascertained the position of Duncote, the village at which, according to Rennell, Timour crossed the Indus. The correct name is Dingote. It is a small hamlet on the west bank, marked by a bluff mountain, six miles above Kala Bagh. The route from Bunnoo leads own upon it, and not upon Kala Bagh, which circumstance settles the question as to the place of passage.

After remaining an entire day at Gaib-ne, in consequence of the rain, we prosecuted our journey; and, passing Tattee, Kote, and Futtih-jung, at each of which places we halted, and near the last sighted the snowy mountains, we found ourselves once again on beaten ground at Husn-Abdal, where we arrived on the 1st of August, the distance being 52 miles. Until we reached Futtih-jung we had the same sandstone formation as before; but the country was less broken and the road excellent. As we approached Husn-Abdal the vegetation became more abundant, the formation being limestone; and we at last found ourselves among the beautiful but decayed and neglected gardens of this celebrated spot: we pitched our camp by the crystal rivulet, filled our glasses with Burgundy, and drank to the memory of Noor Muhal and to the fame of her immortal poet, Thomas Moore. We were joined here by Dr. Falconer, the superintendent of the botanic garden, who accompanied us to Peshawur, and afterwards proceeded on a scientific tour to Cashmere. The researches of Dr. Falconer, and his able coadjutor Captain Cautley, in the lower Himalaya, and their success in unravelling the mysteries of fossil remains, afford good proof that their time was not wasted in the " happy valley ;" and the public may hope, ere long, to profit by their labours.

The intelligence which reached me at Husn-Abdal induced me to quicken our advance to Attock, for which place we set out on the 4th, and arrived on the following day, under a salute from the fortress.

On the banks of the Hurroo, where we halted the first day, we experienced a smart shock of an earthquake, about three P.M., or, in Greenwich time, at six minutes past ten A.M. It was accompanied by a loud rumbling noise, and the ground vibrated under us. The shock was from the east or northeast, and was succeeded by heavy rain and wind, under which my tent fell upon me, but I scrambled out unhurt.

CHAPTER VI.

Cross the Attock—Khyrabad and fort—Bridge of the Indus—Inscriptions at Hund—Arrival at Peshawur—Reception by General Avitabile—Prince Kurruck Sing—Review of his troops—A Peshawuree's story—Changes by the Sikhs—Curious incident—Arrival at Jumrood—Enter the Khyber Pass—Ali Musjid—Duka—Visit from the chiefs—Customs of the Khyberees—Bassoul—Kuju—Its pomegranates—Gundamuk—Anecdote of Nadir Shah—Hyat—An old friend—A facetious Mooftee—Meet Mr. Masson—Arrival at Cabool—Cordial reception.

WE crossed the Attock on the 7th of August, and encamped at Khyrabad, on the opposite side: in making the transit the boat rolled and pitched with violence, and one man began to blow into a skin with which he had provided himself, and to invoke his saints. When we had got safely over one of the watermen exclaimed, "The Firingees do not change colour in danger!" Of danger, however, there was more in appearance than in reality. Whilst at Khyrabad we experienced much civility from Runjeet Sing's son, who was stationed at Peshawur. He sent to us ice and fruit, and freely permitted us to examine the fortress, which, in spite of many defects, I found to be a much stronger place than I had expected. I made a trigonometrical admeasurement of the river from the "ab doozd," or sunken sluice, which supplies the garrison with water, to the rock of Kumalia, and found it to be exactly 800 feet wide; afterwards, however, I saw the stream bridged below the fort, and, upon crossing and measuring it, I found that it was only 537 feet broad in that part. The bridge was formed by thirty boats, and the water where it was placed was twelve fathoms deep; but, between that point and Kala Bagh, Lieutenant Wood found it in some places thirty fathoms deep. I sent Lieutenant Leech to Torbaila to examine the fords across the Indus at that place, of which we had heard much; but he found that, although there are fords there, they are not practicable at this season: at an earlier period of the year they are constantly used. Lieutenant Leech ascended higher up the Indus to Drabund, where it is but 100 yards wide, and he returned from thence to Attock on a raft, much pleased with the treatment he received from the Mahommedans. By way of an experiment I sent our heavy baggage up the river of Cabool to Peshawur, under the charge of Mr. Nock, a European surveyor. He found the river rocky near its confluence with the Indus, but quite navigable throughout.

The interesting nature of the district in which we now found ourselves led us to use every possible exertion to obtain information. I had learned from my friend General Court that there were some inscriptions between the Indus and Cabool rivers, and the messengers whom I despatched in that direction soon returned with the fac-simile of a very valuable one from Hund; and a few days afterwards the marbles themselves were sent to me, and have now finally been transferred to the museum of the Asiatic Society of Bengal. The inscription proved to be Sanscrit, and did not long elude the skill of James Prinsep, who lithographed the facsimile; and, although the marbles had been mutilated, was enabled to translate the most important of the inscriptions. He assigned it to the seventh or eighth century, and, as it refers to the powerful Turuschas (or Turks) as foes overcome by the nameless hero whom it celebrates, it proves the fact of the extension of the Indian rule to this point of the Indus, and the early struggles of that race with the Tartar tribes beyond them. I subjoin the translation, and on the opposite page will be found a facsimile of the inscriptions and monograms.—

TRANSLATION.

1. . . blessings; whose kingly and priestly rule even among his enemies spreads.
2. Above his glory goes . . . for pleasure . . .
3. . . . the powerful flesh-eating *Turushcas*, causing alarm to . .
4. . . . lavishing bland speech on spiritual superiors and Brahmins without number.
5. Such a prince as attracts all things to him; persevering in the protection of his people.
   . . . what in the world is difficult (for him) to accomplish?
6. . . husband of Parbati . .went on a road . .
7. . . . elephant. .whose mothers (?) and fathers' virtue
8. . . . endure forages . . . glory and excellence.
9. Virtue . . . .
10. Of Deva the great riches, . . rule . . moon.
11. . . . great . . . sun . . living among
12. . . . the cheerful minded; . . . .
13. . . . then Seri Tillaka Brahmin . . (shall be made beautiful?)

On the 11th of August we set out for Acora. On our route the Sikh garrison of Jangeera, a fort that stands on the southern bank of the river of Cabool, sent a party to welcome us, and fired a salute. The next day we drove into Peshawur in

General Avitabile's carriage, who very kindly came out some miles to meet us, accompanied by a large suite. It afforded me great pleasure to renew my former acquaintance with the chevalier, and letters which I received from his compatriots at Lahore, Messieurs Allard and Court, carried me very agreeably back to former times. Peshawur was indeed changed since my former visit: a French officer now governed it, and certainly in a splendid style, whilst the former chiefs, Sooltan Mahommed and his brothers, came to see me in their fallen state. I found it somewhat difficult to steer through the maze of conflicting parties; but I endeavoured as much as possible to confine my communications to personal matters, and my remembrance of past kindnesses was so strong, that, if I could not meet the wishes of my old friends, I at least took care to point out the causes of my inability.

Our first visit after alighting at the Baghi Wazeer, which was assigned as our residence, was to the Prince Kurruck Sing. His imbecility is such that he can scarcely return an answer to the most simple question; he was, however, extremely obliging; invited us to visit the new fort of Sumungur, which is now building on the ruins of the Bala Hissar, and promises to be, when finished, a place of considerable strength. He also paraded his forces for our inspection, both infantry and cavalry: the first consisted of twelve battalions and twenty guns, and went through its brigade-exercise well. The sight, however, of 12,000 cavalry was much more imposing as they passed in review order before us in the fine plain of Peshawur. The only drawback to the enjoyment of these scenes was the weakness of the poor prince, which was really distressing: he could neither put a question, nor answer one, without being prompted. A Peshawuree told us an amusing anecdote of a half-witted king of Balkh, who was ruled by his minister. On one occasion, when a foreign ambassador was to be presented, the vizier, fearful that his master would commit himself, prevailed on him to allow a string to be tied to his foot, and passed under the carpet in such a manner that the minister might hold the other end; and it was arranged between them that, whenever the vizier pulled, the king was either to speak or to desist from any inappropriate speech. The audience took place: the ambassador spoke; and the king replied; but, alas, the reply was only " Kush mu koonud ! ! " (he pulls). Again the ambassador spoke, and even more deferentially than before; but again the poor king shouted out " Kush mu koonud ! kush mu koonud ! " to the unspeakable grief and dismay of his prime minister. " Now," added the Peshawuree, " our prince wants a guide-string as much as the king of Balkh."

I found that the Sikhs had changed everything: many of the fine gardens round the town had been converted into cantonments; trees had been cut down; and the whole neighbourhood was one vast camp, there being between 30,000 and 40,000 men stationed on the plain. Mahommedan usages had disappeared—the sounds of dancing and music were heard at all hours and all places—and the fair Grisis of the Punjab enchanted the soldiers with varied strains of Hindee, Cashmeree, Persian, and Afghanee. If, however, some things be changed for the worse, others are improved. The active mind of Monsieur Avitabile has done much to improve the town and tranquillize the neighbourhood: he was building fine bazaars and widening streets; nay, that most conclusive proof of civilization, the erection of a gallows, proved how much he had done towards bringing this wild neighbourhood under subjection. The general did not pretend to be guided by European ideas; and although at first his measures appeared to us somewhat oppressive, his proceedings were, I am sure, in the end, more merciful than if he had affected greater lenity. It is quite impossible for me to give an adequate idea of the princely hospitality and unvarying kindness of this gentleman to every one of our nation, and I hope he may soon return to Europe and enjoy his colossal fortune in his native city.

At Peshawur I was told of a signal service performed by an old favourite of mine, a fine iron-grey Toorkumun horse, which had been presented to me by Runjeet Sing. He was by far too splendid an animal to suit the appearance of poverty which I then deemed it prudent to assume, and, being constrained to part with him, I gave him to two Moollahs at this place, whose services I was glad thus to reward. They sent him down to their father, who was with Shah Shooja, at Loodiana, and in the defeat which that monarch sustained at Candahar, in 1833, he rode this very horse, and actually owed his life to the speed with which the gallant animal carried him away from the field. I had not anticipated that he was destined for such royal services, and was pleased to find that I had, indirectly, been enabled to render a good office to the king in his misfortunes.

During our residence in Peshawur Dr. Lord, accompanied by Dr. Falconer, proceeded to Cohat to examine its mineral formation; but the people there had metal in their human clay as well as in their earth, and the tone which they assumed, and also the disturbed state of the country, constrained the two geologists to return. Lieutenant Wood, however, passed up by Cohat; and as he had also descended the Indus, he had altogether examined three lines of route. The whole of our party now concentrated themselves at Peshawur, and prepared for an advance on Cabool; and as the thermometer was at 98°, we anticipated an agreeable change. The heat of Peshawur was less than I expected; still it was oppressive, and a constant haze hid the surrounding mountains. The fruits at this season were excellent and extremely grateful to the palate.

On the 30th we took our departure from Peshawur, and were driven by Monsieur Avitabile in his carriage to Jumrood, three miles from the mouth of the Khyber Pass, the scene of the late battle between the Sikhs and Afghans, and where the former were now actively engaged in building the new fort to which I have before alluded, and which has been named " Futtehghur," or the fort of victory, although in reality it was the scene of defeat. The village of Jumrood is in ruins, but is marked by a brick fountain: its little fort is also contemptible, and hence the necessity for erecting the new place of defence: they have chosen for its site an old mound, with which they, as usual, couple traditions of Man Sing; and it is certain that, whilst digging the foundations, coins similar to those obtained at the tope of Manikyala were found. The work was proceeding with great activity, and, as each Sikh commander had a portion assigned to him, it would soon be finished. The position is ill chosen, inasmuch as its supply of water is uncertain.

We found our situation at Jumrood by no means agreeable. The deputation sent to escort us through the Khyber Pass had not arrived; and although some months had elapsed since the battle, the effluvia from the dead bodies, both of men and horses, were quite revolting. Some camel-keepers who had left the place the day after our arrival, escorted by a few soldiers, were attacked by the Afreedee mountaineers, who came down upon them, drove off the camels, and beheaded two of the people, whose mangled trunks were brought into camp; and we were informed that this murderous outrage was one of very frequent occurrence. The garrison, in this instance, pursued the marauders and brought back the cattle.

At length, after a good deal of discussion, and very contrary to the advice of our worthy host, Monsieur Avitabile, we resolved to wait no longer for our escort, but at once to enter Khyber. Some half-dozen letters had already been exchanged between the chiefs of the pass and myself; and the individual commanding the small detachment of the

Cabool troops, a renegade of the name of Leslie, alias Rattray, who now figured as a Moslem, under the name of Fida Mahommed Khan, assured me they were to be relied upon. We set out on the morning of the 2nd of September. Monsieur Avitabile saw us a few hundred yards from his camp, where we parted from him, with many thanks for all the kind attentions which he had shown us. The Khuleels, a tribe of Afghans, escorted us for about two miles to Kudun, and then handed us over to the genuine Khyberees, who occupied the gorge of the valley. The first salutation which we received from them was a message directing us to get rid of our escort: we accordingly sent the Khuleels back, and at once abandoned ourselves to the tender mercies of Ullah Dad Khan, the chief of the Kokee Khyl, who, with his numerous followers, led us to Ali Musjid, a weak fort in the centre of the pass. Our march was not without a degree of anxious excitement: we were moving among a savage tribe, who set the Sikhs at defiance, and who paid but an unwilling allegiance to Cabool; we had no guard of our own, except about a dozen Arabs, and we had considerable property with us. We were also stopped at every by-road and defile as we came among the different subdivisions of the tribe. At Jubugee they, in conclave, requested us to halt for the night, and pointed out the rock near which Nadir Shah had slept on his advance to India: but not even the historical association attached to the sleeping-place of that "Persian robber," as Gibbon calls him, could convince me of the propriety of halting there; and, after a good deal of parleying, we were allowed to advance, and reached Ali Musjid about eleven o'clock, all our baggage preceding us—a very necessary precaution in journeying among Khyberees. By the road they showed to us many small mounds, built to mark the spots where they had planted the heads of the Sikhs whom they had decapitated after the late victory: on some of these mounds locks of hair were yet to be seen.

We had scarcely pitched our camp in the confined ground below Ali Musjid and in the dry bed of the river, when the rolling thunder gave notice of rain; and it soon came down in such torrents as must have washed us back to Jumrood, had it not been for the great activity of our own people and the assistance afforded us by the Khyberees. Tents, boxes, and everything were dragged by main force up the steep sides of the defile, on which we were constrained to remain, drenched to the skin and totally without shelter, and by no means in that placid state of mind which would enable us to have enjoyed the sublimity of the scene—for sublime it certainly was—the water rolling in a torrent down the bed of the pass, driving bushes and everything before it, whilst waterfalls in all directions and of all hues came rushing down around us, some of them in an unbroken leap of more than 300 feet— all of these bursting out, one after another, from unseen crevices in the towering rocks by which we were surrounded. In all this confusion, and indeed throughout our previous march, we had a good opportunity of studying the Khyber Pass, which must always be formidable, and more especially so in rainy and boisterous weather. We had found the road as good as it had been represented; and the people, lawless as their habits undoubtedly are, had been more friendly than we could have hoped for. Next morning we were joined by Agha Jan, the Governor of Julalabad; the Momund chief, Sadut Khan; and a Shahghassee, or officer of the court, who came with about 5000 men; and the hills rang with shouts and noise of men and arms, during all which din and tumult we remained looking on as patiently as we could, but heartily wishing ourselves fairly out of the defile. This we effected on the following morning by a march of twenty miles to Duka, and at length cleared the far-famed pass of Khyber without an accident. The last half of the pass is the most formidable; but even there it is pervious to heavy artillery. The formation is black slate and limestone rock, with deep beds of conglomerate, in which are rounded pebbles. At Ali Musjid the water jets beautifully out of the rock and flows towards Jumrood, but for some distance between these two places it has a subterraneous course. There is something in this water which renders Khyber extremely unhealthy in the hot weather; and we were told that after standing for a night it is covered with an oily substance.

In the last part of the road, at Lundee Khanu, a village composed of thirty or forty small forts, and built where the pass opens, we saw a "Tope" in good preservation and in a commanding position. Farther on, and before reaching a place named "Huft chah," or the seven wells, we passed to our left a hill crowned by a long fort, and called by the inhabitants the "Kaffir Killa," or infidel's fort, to which tradition assigns a very ancient date. There is a ruin of a similar kind north of the Cabool river, and my inquiries led me to the conviction that there are many such remains in Afghanistan: they are doubtless the relics of former kings, whether the word "infidel" has reference to a Bactrian, a Greek, or a Hindoo.

At Duka the whole of the chiefs of Khyber visited us: there are four principal and several petty ones.

They asserted that in the time of the kings of Cabool they received a lac and 32,000 rupees pay for guarding the pass, besides the transit-duties; and they offered, on a renewal of this, again to open the road to commerce. I found, however, that it was at this time actually open, and that Dost Mahommed had satisfied all their demands by the payment of some 15,000 or 20,000 rupees a year; but their religious animosity towards the Sikhs was the best safeguard against an advance of that nation on Cabool in this direction. There are, besides, more obstacles to commerce in the Punjab than in the mountains of Khyber. The easy terms on which we were enabled to satisfy the Khyberees for the friendly and really important services which they had rendered us did credit to their moderation. A few coarse gun-locks, some still coarser loongees and pelisses (choghas), with 375 rupees in cash, making the total value of the payment about 500 rupees, satisfied all parties. An Ornkzye Ruhmutoollah came with us all the way from Peshawur: he was an eccentric being, with a tongue much too large for his mouth. We gave into his charge a palanqueen, in which Dr. Lord, in consequence of indisposition, had been obliged to travel through the pass: no sooner was it intrusted to him than he very coolly seated himself in it, and ordered the astonished bearers to proceed. It was curious enough that we had been driven in a coach to Jumrood, and that one of our party had travelled in a palanqueen through Khyber. Too favourable ideas of Khyber society must not, however, be inferred from what I have stated: they live in miserable caves, and one tribe of them, the Momuzye Afreedees, I was positively assured, sometimes change their wives, paying the difference in value! When a man dies and leaves a widow without children, his brothers feel no hesitation in selling her. Altogether, the women are badly off, and do much of the laborious out-of-door work: their condition, however, is not such in all the tribes.

We passed through Bassoul and Butteecote to Mazeina, a village near the base of Sufued Koh, where we halted by a fine stream of running water and in a bracing climate, which we greatly enjoyed after having been so long roasted on the Indus. The mountains near us were thickly clad with pines and julgoozas, and the snow was on their summits; but it was that of last year, as none had yet fallen. We next passed up the fine valleys of Nungeenar, and the districts of Chupreeal, to Beea and Kuju, and encamped in the latter on the 11th. This is the place so famed for its pomegranates without seed, although the best fruit is brought from villages half way up the mountains. Kuju has a hot summer, the elevation not being great. We here received abundant presents of fruit from Cabool, chiefly peaches and pears; but we were admonished not to eat too freely of them until the autumnal equinox, when all food is considered to have become wholesome. We now found ourselves in a country altogether different from that which we had left: beggars and heat had ceased to annoy us, and, although the people crowded to see us, they were well-behaved and well-clad; many of them had books under their arms, and, more strange to say, on their heads, for such appears to be the fashionable way of carrying octavos in these parts. These *bookish* men were of course Moollahs and students. The Hindoos of Kuju were numerous: they were Sikhs, and had a temple; but, nevertheless, professed poverty, to save themselves from the exactions which were imposed on the people for the purpose of carrying on war with the Punjab—a war which, they truly said, required a greater treasury than Cabool could furnish.

In Kuju we found a park of artillery, which had been detached from Julalabad, that the men might not suffer from the excessive heat. The pomegranate-growers were now within twenty days of their harvest, and the traders who transport the fruit to

India were assembling in numbers. The tree differs altogether in appearance from the common pomegranate; and only grows at Kulghoo, Tootoo, Hissaruk, and one or two other villages, which are beautifully situated above Kuju: the fruit comes to greater perfection if sheltered from the sun. 1500 or 2000 camels laden with it leave the place yearly: it was selling for three rupees a hundred. The rind is also an article of considerable export, as it is used at Cabool in the preparation of leather, which, by means of it, they dress in a superior manner. The great carriers are the Lohanees and Sheenwarees: the former go to India, but it would appear that the latter only pass between Cabool and Peshawur. Very fine camels are to be had from the one region, and mules still finer from the other.

From Kuju we passed through the garden of Neemla to Gundamuk. This royal garden was in good order, and we halted to admire it: cypress-trees alternate with the chinar or plane; all of them reaching to the height of 100 feet, and, as the Persian verse has it, "holding each other by the hand and rivalling each other in beauty." The walks which they shade are lovely. We were here visited by the son of Shah Shooja's vizier, Akram Khan: he came with his two sons to express his devotion to the British, and his hopes that he would be remembered for his father's sake, who fell at the king's stirrup. He put the hand of one of his sons into mine and said, "He is your slave: I have brought him by his mother's desire, and she was the daughter of the great Futteh Khan." Both the grandfathers of this little fellow had, therefore, been viziers of the empire. Agha Jan, our conductor, speaking of Akram Khan, said "He had exalted ideas of kingly dignity, never relaxed into a smile, nor sat carelessly on the ground." I said that a great man should sometimes relax. He replied by relating an anecdote of Nadir Shah, to whom one of his courtiers once made a similar remark, adding "That he might safely so indulge himself, as there was no one present to observe him." "What," answered his master, "is not Nadir Shah *himself* present?" This said Agha Jan here took leave of us, being relieved by Nazir Ali Mahommed. Agha Jan was a sedate, good sort of man; tolerably well informed, and very fond of wine, which, however, he took care to drink in secret. The best wine he told me was to be procured from the Kaffir country, and in praise of the juice of the grape he quoted the Toorkee proverb: "Drink of it in moderation, that you may fight the lion; not in excess, that the crow may peck out your eyes."

On our way to Jugduluk we passed the bridge of

the Soorkhrood, the date of which is quaintly given in an inscription which is let into the rock, and of which the following is a translation:—

"In the reign of the impartial Shah Jehan, the founder of this bridge was Ali Murdan Khan: I asked Wisdom the date of its erection; it answered, 'The builder of the bridge is Ali Murdan Khan:'" which words give the year of the Hegira 1045; A. D. 1635.

On this bridge I was welcomed by my old friend Hyat, the Cafila-bashee, who, after convoying me safely over Hindoo Koosh, now saw me returning from the opposite direction again to represent my nation. He brought with him a dozen mule-loads of fruit from the Nawab, and our meeting was a very cordial one. The worthy fellow seemed to me to look younger than when we parted: I clothed him in a Cashmere shawl, and he could scarcely speak for astonishment and delight. We ran over together our adventures in Hindoo Koosh; and I did not fail to take care of him who had so long taken good care of me, and gave him a comfortable tent and a good pilao.

Here the chief, or, as he is called, Padshah of Kooner sent a messenger to tell me "his country was ours, and he hoped we would command his services: it extended," he said, "from Nijrow to Ba-

jour, and from Shew to Pushoot; and bordered on the Kaffirs, over whom he had influence." The bearer of this communication was a Mooftee of a facetious turn of mind, who had been in the Punjab, and amused us with his accounts of an interview with Runjeet Sing, who interrogated him closely regarding the habits of the people to the west, and the state of their affairs. At last one of the courtiers, who understood Persian, asked if it were true, according to the couplet, that every woman at Cabool had a sweetheart. The Mooftee replied that he had seen nothing but courtesans since he had left his country, and gave in return a wittier verse than the one alluded to.* The Maharaja at length gave him a dress of honour, and the Afghan was no sooner clad in it than some thirty cormorants demanded each his perquisite. This was too much—he returned into the presence of the Raja, placed his dress at his feet, and upon it the 200 rupees which he had received with it; and began as follows: "A person gave some cloth to a tailor to make into clothes, who, when it was brought home, demanded more for it than the value of the cloth. 'Take the garment,' said the man, 'and wait till I can return with some

---

* Adam wu Huwa humih ek-abee und
Wahee! bur an quoum ki Punj-abee und!

borrowed money to discharge the demand.' So is it with me, Raja! Pray receive back the dress and money, till I can sell one of my horses and pay the balance of the fees which your courtiers demand." The merriment occasioned by this illustration saved the Mooftee from the usual exactions, and he left the court with his dress of honour, and his 200 rupees to boot.

Near Jugduluk we saw holly-trees (beloot) to our left; and crossing a lofty pass of about 8500 feet, clad with pine-trees, descended direct upon Tezeen by a short route. From the summit of this, Lughman and Togour lay in sight beneath us: the distant hills over Cabool were pointed out to us; and behind us were the forests of Kurkuju. As we descended we observed the bitter almond and the mulberry, and a pleasing fragrance exhaled from the aromatic grass: there were also the wild lavender, the wild rose, and the thistle. Half way up this mountainpass our road led through the bed of a water course, which was strewed with rounded pebbles; and, as we got higher up, the rock cropped out in vertical dykes. From Tezeen we passed the "huft kootul," or seven passes, to Khoord Cabool and Bootkhak, where we were joined by Mr. Masson, the well-known illustrator of Bactrian reliques. It was a source of great satisfaction to all of us to make the acquaintance of this gentleman, and we were highly gratified by our intercourse with him. On the 20th of September we entered Cabool, and were received with great pomp and splendour by a fine body of Afghan cavalry, led by the Ameer's son, Akbar Khan. He did me the honour to place me on the same elephant upon which he himself rode, and conducted us to his father's court, whose reception of us was most cordial. A spacious garden, close by the palace and inside the Bala-Hissar of Cabool, was allotted to the mission as their place of residence.

CHAPTER VII.

Interview with Dost Mahommed Khan—Gracious reception by the Ameer—Nawab Jubar Khan—State of affairs at Cabool—Siege of Herat—A Russian agent—Fears and hopes of the Ameer—Alchymy—Famous swords—Visit Koh-damun and Kohistan—Istalif—Its fine scenery—Wild inhabitants—Blood feuds and customs—Chareekar—Pass of Hindoo Koosh—Mines of Fureenjal—Ghorbund and Purwan rivers—Value of irrigation—Expenses of farming—Reg Ruwan—Frequency of earthquakes—Objects of our tour—Begram—Topes—Water-fowl and animals—Return to Cabool.

On the 21st of September we were admitted to a formal audience by Ameer Dost Mahommed Khan, and I then delivered to him my credentials from the Governor-General of India. His reception of them was all that could be desired. I informed him that I had brought with me, as presents to his highness, some of the rarities of Europe: he promptly replied that we ourselves were the rarities, the sight of which best pleased him.* Seeing our draftsman, Mr. Gonsalvez, he asked of what country he was, and, upon being told that he was a Portuguese, made many inquiries as to the present power and prospects of that nation. When he

* I am indebted to my friend Lieut. Jas. Rattray, of the 2nd Bengal N. I., for the portrait of Dost Mahommed, which is a striking likeness.

DOST MAHOMED KHAN,

EX CHIEF OF CABOOL, IN MARCH, 1841

heard that the Portuguese had intermarried with Indians, he observed that their spell as Europeans was broken, and their fall certain. From the Ameer's audience-chamber we proceeded to the Nawab Jubar Khan, who received us in his bath, and invited us to breakfast. As we passed through the city some of the people cried out, "Take care of Cabool!" "Do not destroy Cabool!" and wherever we went in this fine bustling place, we were saluted with a cordial welcome. Our visits were soon returned, both by the Ameer and his brother the Nawab. Power frequently spoils men, but with Dost Mahommed neither the increase of it, nor his new title of Ameer, seems to have done him any harm. He seemed even more alert and full of intelligence than when I last saw him. In reply to my inquiries regarding the descent of the Afghans from the Jews he said, "Why, we marry a brother's wife, and give a daughter no inheritance;—are we not, therefore, of the children of Israel?"* Speaking afterwards on our English law of inheritance, and of a daughter sharing with a son, the Ameer observed that it must have originated from the respect paid by Christians to the Virgin Mary. I did not

* I since find that the book from which the Jewish lineage of the Afghans is derived is the "Mujmoo i ausab;" and it is said that the Urz Bege of Hajee Feroz at Herat possess elaborate genealogical trees on the same subject.

deem it court etiquette to inform him that it was unnecessary to go so far to find a reason for an act of common justice.

It is difficult to proceed without saying a few words on the state of parties at Cabool: were I to omit doing so, I must fail to make my narrative intelligible. After the action at Jumrood with the Sikhs, both parties withdrew from the contest, and the presence of the British had therefore the good effect of putting an end to the horrors of war. Scarcely however had tranquillity dawned on the east, when the Persians invaded Afghanistan on the west, and besieged Herat, from which, as is well known, they only withdrew under an actual demonstration of our force in the Gulf of Persia, and in consequence of the threatening admonitions of the British Government. These circumstances had a prejudicial effect at Cabool, which was further heightened by the presence of an agent from Russia, who reached the place some time after my arrival. To the east, the fears of Dost Mahommed Khan were allayed—to the west they were increased; and in this state of things his hopes were so worked upon, that the ultimate result was his estrangement from the British Government. For the information of those who are interested in the exact condition and relations of Cabool, as it stood while these events were passing, I have, in an Appendix, given a sketch (see Appendix No. III.) extracted from the printed records of Government.

One of the first applications which we received was from the Nawab, who requested us to supply him with some platina wire, to aid his studies in alchymy. I took the occasion to inquire into the state of the science, which has always been in such high favour among the Afghans, and was forthwith made acquainted with several ways of *making gold*, by which the adepts trick their credulous employers. One of these is by secretly introducing some gold inside the charcoal, and, after the quicksilver has been evaporated, the more precious metal is left to delight the wiseacre, and to tempt him on to further expenses. Another method is to put the filings of gold into a stick or pipe, and fasten the end with wax; with this rod the materials in the crucible are stirred, and the desired result obtained.

We found greater cause to admire the Afghans in their taste in swords than for their chemical studies. Some very fine blades were sent to us for our inspection by a decayed widow lady, whose husband had been one of the former Dooranee lords. One of these scimitars was valued at 5000 rupees, and the other two at 1500 each. The first of these was an Ispahan sword, made by one Zaman, the pupil of Asad, and a slave of Abbas the Great. It was formed of what is called "Akbaree steel," and had belonged to Ghoolam Shah Calora of Sinde, whose name was upon it, and was brought from that country during the wars of Mudad Khan. The especial cause of its great value was that the *water* could be traced upon it, like a skein of silk, down the entire length of the blade. Had this watering *been interrupted* by a curve or cross, the sword would have been comparatively valueless. The second was also a Persian sword of the water called "Begumee." The lines did not run down straight, but waved like a watered silk fabric. It had the name of Nadir Shah on it. The third was what is termed a "Kara" (black) Khorasan blade, of the water named "Bidr," and came from Casveen. There were neither straight nor waving lines in it, but it was mottled with dark spots. All these swords were light and well-balanced, the most valuable one was the most curved: the steel in all the three tinkled like a bell, and is said to improve by age. One test of the genuineness of a sword is that it can be written upon with gold; others, more certain, are its cutting through a large bone, and severing a silk handkerchief when thrown into the air.

After the turmoil of eating dinners and receiving visitors had been got over, and our business put in train, we all of us determined to visit the far-famed mountain-skirts of Kho-damun and Kohistan, which are situated north of Cabool. The Ameer very readily granted us permission to do so, and appointed an individual of influence to conduct and protect us, several parts of the neighbourhood, particularly north of the Ghoorbund river, or what is called Kohistan Proper, having only of late been brought under subjection. We set out from Cabool on the morning of the 13th of October, and halted at Kareez-i-Meer, about fifteen miles from which we could see, in the hazy distance, a vast vista of gardens extending for some thirty or forty miles in length, and half as broad, terminated by Hindoo Koosh itself, white with snow. Next day we reached Shukurdura, where there is a royal garden, but which is now in a state of decay. Our next march was to Kahdura, and thence to Istalif, the great point of attraction. No written description can do justice to this lovely and delightful country. Throughout the whole of our route we had been lingering amidst beautiful orchards, the banks of which were clustered over with wild flowers and plants, many of them common to Europe, and which were also in profuse abundance along the margins of the innumerable brooks which intersect the valleys.

The roads were shaded by noble and lofty walnut-trees, which excluded the sun's rays, never powerless in this climate. Every hill with a southern aspect had a vineyard on it, and the raisins were spread out on the ground, and imparted a purple tinge to the hills. There were very few songsters however to enliven the scene, most of the feathered tribe having flown to a warmer climate. The coldness of the air, which had driven them away, was to us bracing and delightful, and only served to increase our enjoyment. I must not, however, speak in detail of this charming country, nor do the far-famed gardens of Istalif require any aid from me to establish their supremacy. We pitched our camp on one side of the valley, and directly opposite to us, at a distance of about a thousand yards, rose the town of Istalif in the form of a pyramid, terrace on terrace, the whole crowned with a shrine embosomed among wide-spreading plane-trees. Between us lay a deep and narrow valley, at the bottom of which was a clear, rapid, and musically-sounding brook, on both sides of which the valley was covered with the richest orchards and vineyards. Looking down this stream, the dell gradually opens out, and presents to the eye a vast plain, rich in trees and verdure, and dotted over with innumerable turreted forts: beyond all this, rocky mountains are seen with the fresh snow of yesterday upon them; and over these again tower the eternal snow-clad summits of Hindoo Koosh. The scene was as sublimely grand as it was beautiful and enchanting. The yellow autumnal leaves rustled in the breeze, and the crystal waters rushed in their rapid course over craggy rocks with a noise which reached the summit of the valley. Thessalian Tempé could never have more delighted the eyes of an Ionian, than did Istalif please Bœotian Britons. The people illuminated their town in the evening, in honour of their visitors. It had a pretty effect, but the beauties of art could not in our opinion compete with those of nature. Not so with our escort: they declared that Istalif had at all times been the abode of pleasure, and that, without wine, not only would the illumination lose its value, but Nature herself would be worth nothing. We accordingly sent a few bottles of wine, to which they did the amplest justice, although the "Moohtussib," a chief constable of Cabool, was of the party. On the following day I taxed him with this departure from the rules of his sect. He bore my bantering with great equanimity, and replied, with mock heroic dignity, "Who, my lord, suspects me,—me, the 'Moohtussib,'—of indulging in wine? My duty is to reform the morals of others."

It is a source of deep regret that this beautiful country should be inhabited by a race of men so turbulent and vindictive as the Tajiks have here proved themselves to be; and yet, throughout Afghanistan generally, these same Tajiks form the most peaceable classes of the population. Here, however, their blood-feuds are endless: a week never passes without strife or assassination, and I have been assured, on the best authority, that a man frequently remains immured in his own tower for two and three years from a fear of his enemies, leaving his wife to take care of his property, and discharge his duties; nay, that in some instances this durance has lasted for eight and ten years. It is rare to see a man go to bathe, hunt, or even ride out, without a part of his clan attending him as a guard. Lately a strong government has in some respects softened down these asperities; but the retribution of blood, which the Mahommedan law allows, fatally perpetuates these sanguinary habits. "Blood for blood" is their motto and their rule; and as they still rigidly follow it up, every fresh act of violence increases the number of feuds, and extends the misery resulting from them still more widely.

Children born of different mothers and the same father are seldom cordial friends; and, singular enough, the word "turboor" among them has the double signification of cousin and rival. When any rebellion is excited, it is customary for the government to expel the traitor, and raise up his "turboor," or cousin, to govern in his stead. If you ask the natives of Kohistan why such desperate habits have become familiar to them, they will gravely tell you that they result from their heating diet of mulberries—that fruit, dried and pounded into flour, being the general food of the population. These people have the reputation of being the best foot-soldiers in Afghanistan, and from all I could learn they merit the distinction. They are a healthy and handsome race, and are alike fond of sport and of war. In time of need as many as twenty thousand of them have taken the field, well armed with flint-lock muskets. Dost Mahommed rules them with a rod of iron, and has executed many of the principal men. Many others, to whom independence and lawless liberty were dearer than their possessions, have fled the country, and now cultivate fields among the fens of Koondooz and Balkh, voluntarily exposing themselves to poverty and hardship, rather than submit to any regularity of government in their native glens. In bygone times Nadir Shah himself is said to have been satisfied with a tribute of three hundred tent-pins from Doornanu, one of their districts; and the kings of Cabool apportioned this country under an easy tenure to their nobles, contenting themselves with the military services of the people. The present chief of Cabool has, on the contrary, been constrained, in order to maintain his power, to destroy many of their forts, which were scattered in clusters all over the valley, and is anxious to reduce the inhabitants to the state of citizens. On our return route from Istalif we passed through Isterghich, Sinjet-dura, Tope-dura, Si-yaran, and Chareekar, the last a large bazar-town of about ten thousand inhabitants. All these places are faithfully described by the Emperor Baber. They are a succession of separate valleys at the base of lofty mountains, glowing and rich in foliage, which forms a striking contrast to the bleak ground by which they are divided, and the still bleaker hills that rise above them. Wherever nature or the hand of man has conducted water, there are to be seen gardens and orchards; and the surplus water, which runs down lower into the valley, nourishes rich crops of grain.

Chareekar lies on the high road between Cabool and Toorkistan, and we saw many travellers hastening to and from both places, as the approaching winter would soon put a stop to all journeyings. Conversation with these people so much excited the curiosity of Lieutenant Leech and Dr. Lord, that they resolved to attempt to climb the mountains, and examine the celebrated pass of Hindoo Koosh. This they effected in a satisfactory manner by a route through the valleys of Ghoorbund and Konshan, dressed as Asiatics, and under the guidance of honest Hyat, the Cafila Bashee. They found the actual pass to be about 15,000 feet high, consequently in elevation little inferior to that of Mont Blanc. They attained it on the 19th of October, and learned that it would be finally closed by the snow in about ten days; after which, until the spring, no caravan could pass. The ascent had been very gradual to within twelve or fifteen miles of its summit, nor was any considerable difficulty experienced till within a mile of the pass. The track then became very steep, and in consequence of a partial thaw, very slippery and dangerous. The horses fell and appeared much distressed, and the party was obliged to dismount and proceed on foot. They did not experience any personal inconvenience, but the natives informed them that they, themselves, were frequently seized with giddiness, faintness, and vomiting. The summit of Hindoo Koosh was of pure granite. On the southern side the snow only extended for four or five miles, while on the northern it reached eighteen or twenty. This difference of climate appears to be characteristic of these regions, for Dr. Lord afterwards found at the pass of Sir-alung, which is next to that of Hindoo Koosh, that on the southern side the ground was clear of snow within ten miles of the summit, although on the northern face it extended for sixty miles. On their return they visited the rich lead-mines of Fureenjal, the underground workings of which are so extensive, that they were occupied nearly three hours in examining them. Farther down the valley of Ghoorbund, they came to the magnificent cavern of Fulgird, which they explored for three or four hundred yards, but found nothing to reward them, except some very large and transparent stalactites. The whole country appears to be rich in minerals.

While our two fellow-travellers were employed in their exciting journey, Lieutenant Wood and myself continued our wanderings in Kohistan. About four miles north of Chareekar, we found the country abruptly sink nearly an hundred feet, and presenting a scene of unrivalled cultivation. Through this basin or valley ran the rivulets of Ghoorbund, Purwan, and Punjsheer, all of which we crossed. At this season they were clear, rapid brooks, with stony beds, and easily forded: in spring and summer they are much swollen. They all unite at the celebrated ruins of Begran, and, passing Joolga and Tugow, reach Tungi Gharoi twenty miles from Cabool, where there is a waterfall which interrupts the navigation. It is one of the great amusements of the people to ensnare the fish as they leap up this cascade. Immediately on crossing the river of Ghoorbund, we entered Kohistan Proper, a country rich without parallel. It is of no great extent, its form being that of the segment of a circle, the length of which is about sixteen or eighteen miles, and five or six its greatest depth. The fertility and productiveness of the soil is equalled by the industry of the people, who, forming bank above bank, acquire, as it were, land from their stony hills, all of which they irrigate with a care and zeal greatly to be admired. Aqueducts may be often seen fifty and sixty feet up the hill, conducted round every swell and valley, till at last they pour out their contents on the embanked fields. Irrigation from natural rivulets is, of course, more economical than by canals or subterraneous watercourses. Near Chareekar there are some magnificent artificial canals, which, according to the people, are as old as the days of Timour. The canals are either dug by the government, or the villagers make common cause. If the former, the revenue derived is considerable, one hundred rupees per annum being charged for every place through which the supply passes. In some parts of the country the water, after being conducted, is made free property: in others it is carefully distributed and sold. A cut from a canal ten fingers broad and five deep is sufficient to irrigate eight khurwars of grain. Much abuse, however, attends the subdivision of the water, and the owners of lands at the lower extremity of a canal are often obliged to watch over the proceedings of those who live higher up, and even to bribe them not to damage their fields by stopping the supply; nay, battles are sometimes fought for the water. For one night's supply to a crop of twenty khurwars, from fifty to one hundred rupees are sometimes given.

On the prices of farming and labour in this country I gathered the following particulars. A landlord who farms his estate is understood to pay one-third of the total produce for sowing, rearing, and reaping. The state takes a third, and the remaining third falls to the proprietor. In this case, however, he furnishes the seed, and water for irrigation. If the proprietor also furnish cattle, and all the materials, &c., which are required, the labourers then receive only one-sixth for their trouble. It is not usual to hire daily labourers; but when a plough, two men, and a pair of oxen are so employed, the wages are half a Khan rupee, or three-eighths of a Company's rupee, per diem. Afghanistan is a cheaper country than Persia, for grain is more abundant. The returns of seed sown vary, of course, with the nature of the grain and the quality of the soil. Wheat yields from ten to sixteen-fold, seldom more than fifteen; rice gives sixteen or eighteen; juwaree as much as fifty-fold. The best soil in the district of Cabool is at Deh Afghanee, a village in the suburbs, where a jureeb of land, or half an English acre, produces a rent of ten tomauns or 200 rupees, and yields, besides the profits of the proprietor, a revenue as high as forty rupees to Government; but this is ground on which vegetables are reared, the sale of which is highly advantageous, for the Afghans preserve cabbages, carrots, and turnips, as we do potatoes, placing them on the ground, with a little earth over them and leaves, so that they are thus kept fresh till April.

Some of the natives of Kohistan bore a strong resemblance to the people beyond the mountains, and they repeated to us traditions which went to prove that they had crossed them in the days of Timour. In several places they spoke corrupted Toorkee, and among the villages two were named Togh Verdee and Togh Bogha. There was, however, a more remarkable race inhabiting the valley of Punjsheer, who spoke the Pushye dialect, and whom I shall shortly mention. A few of the people were Safee Afghans, or of the tribe which inhabits Nijrow, an extensive valley eastward of Kohistan, and deeply indenting the range of Hindoo Koosh.

As we were now in the vicinity of "Reg-Ruwan," or the moving sand, we made an excursion to it. It is a phenomenon similar to what is seen at Jubul Nakoos, or the sounding mountain, near Too in the Red Sea. The Emperor Baber thus describes it:—"Between the plains there is a small hill, in which there is a line of sandy ground, reaching from the top to the bottom. They call it Khwaju Reg-Ruwan: they say that in the summer season the sound of drums and nugarets issues from the sand."

The description of Baber, however marvellous it appears, is pretty accurate. Reg-Ruwan is situated about forty miles north of Cabool, towards Hindoo Koosh, and near the base of the mountains. Two ridges of hills, detached from the rest, run in and meet each other. At the point of junction, and where the slope of the hills is at an angle of about forty-five degrees, and the height nearly 400 feet, a sheet of sand, as pure as that on the seashore, is spread from the top to the bottom, to a breadth of about 100 yards. When this sand is set in motion by a body of people sliding down it a sound is emitted. On the first trial we distinctly heard two loud, hollow sounds, such as would be produced by a large drum. On two subsequent trials we heard nothing: so that perhaps the sand requires to be settled and at rest for some space of time before the effect can be produced. The inhabitants have a belief that the sounds are only heard on Friday; nor then, unless by the special permission of the saint of Reg-Ruwan, who is interred close to the spot. The locality of the sand is remarkable, as there is no other in the neighbourhood. Reg-Ruwan faces the south, but the wind of Purwan (bád i Purwan), which blows strongly from the north for the greater part of the year, probably deposits it by an eddy. Such is the violence of this wind, that all the trees in the neighbourhood bend to the south, and the fields, after a few years, require to be re-cleared of the pebbles and stones, which the loss of soil lays bare. The mountains around are, for the most part, composed of granite or mica, but at Reg-Ruwan we found sandstone, lime, slate, and quartz. Near the strip of sand there is a strong echo, and the same conformation of surface which occasions this is doubtless connected with the sound of the moving sand.

In a late number of the 'Journal of the Asiatic Society of Calcutta' there is an extract of a letter from Lieutenant Wellsted of the Indian Navy, in which he describes the sounding mountain in the Red Sea, which has also been mentioned by Gray and Seetzen. There would appear, however, to be some variation in the kind of sound produced in the two places; but both are, I suppose, explained by the theory laid down by Mr. James Prinsep regarding Jubl Nakoos, who says that the effect is there produced merely by "a reduplication of impulse, setting air in vibration in a focus of echo." At all events we have at Reg-Ruwan another example of the phenomenon, to excite the curiosity of those interested in acoustics. Reg-Ruwan is seen from a great distance; and the situation of the sand is so peculiar, that it might almost be imagined the hill had been cut in two, and that it had gushed forth from the opening as from a sand-bag: the probability, however, is, that it has been brought together by the wind.

Convulsions of nature are exceedingly common in this part of the world. Baber mentions one to have occurred in his time, and in this very plain: " so that in some places the ground was elevated to the height of an elephant above its old level, and in others as much depressed." A severe earthquake took place in Cabool six years ago, and shocks happen as frequently as twice or thrice in a month. We had no less than three of these on the 14th of December, and many before and after that day: but they were all slight. A passing shake, with a rumbling noise, is called "goozur," to distinguish it from "zilzilla," or earthquake, the term used by the inhabitants when a tremulous motion takes place.

Our geological and other similar researches in Kohistan naturally led to our being questioned as to the particular object of our pursuit. "We are seeking," said I to a Mahommedan, "for the organic remains of a former world." After ascertaining from me that Christians and Mahommedans agreed on the subject of the deluge, he observed that, "when Mahomed was asked what existed before the world, he answered, the world; and he repeated the same answer seven times. I can therefore," continue the Moslem, "well understand the motives of your search." Another individual with whom I fell into the same conversation observed, "We do not even know ourselves; what can we know, therefore, of the past and present world?" The remark, however, of my first acquaintance will serve to show that it probably will not be a difficult task to explain to the Moslem the mysteries which geologists have of late years so successfully unravelled.

After a delightful tour we turned our steps towards Cabool, taking the ancient city of Begram by the way. It is supposed to be the " Alexandria ad calcem Caucausi;" and the merit of its discovery is due to Mr. Masson, who, during many successive years, disinterred thousands of coins on its site, which is in a vast plain, extending for miles and covered with tumuli. A citadel of natural strength and in a commanding position overlooks the low land of Kohistan, and the three rivers in one wash its base. It is called by some " Kaffir Killa," the infidel fort; and by others Abdollas tower (boorj). No part of it is now inhabited, but its extensive aqueducts may yet be traced, and if repaired would greatly increase the fertility of the country. The position is one well suited for a capital; dry, flat, and elevated, in a rich country, and near the foot of the passes which lead to and from Tartary. Within a few miles of it, at Tope-dura and Joolga, are two of those curious remnants of former ages called " Topes." They have been opened, and their contents of boxes and coins prove their age. Another of them, called Sir Baolee, in Nijrow, near a cave, and covered with a glazed blue coating, yet remains intact to stimulate future inquiry. I will not enter upon the *questio vexata* of these works. Their antiquity is undoubted, and merely in crossing them we picked up coins. I contented myself with having a careful topographical drawing of the whole prepared, which I transmitted to my friend, General Court, at Lahore, who had expressed great anxiety for it. I believe he has since transmitted it to Paris, and that it now lies in the archives of the Asiatic Society of that capital.

The rivers in this vicinity were well stored with fish, and, as it appeared to me, with ducks also, at which I fired; when, to my great surprise, I found they were but decoy-ducks, admirably executed, and which deceived their natural representative as they did me, for thousands are at this season enticed by them, and ensnared during night by the villagers. Water-fowl abound in these parts: I made a collection of no less than forty-five different species of ducks, and it was quite evident that many additions might have been made. The finest are the large red duck, and the mallard, which looks like the tame duck in its wild state. Besides the water-fowl, they brought to us the skin of another bird of passage, called "kujeer," which, when stripped of its feathers, has a rich down left on it, which is much used in pelisses.

But the *rara avis* of Kohistan was the " kubk i duree," a bird somewhat less than a turkey, and of the partridge or chiccore species. It was first procured for us in Ghoorbund, but as the snow falls it may be had nearer Cabool. For the table, it is not surpassed by any bird; but it must be killed when caught, since it loses its flavour in a tame state. The "dughdour," a kind of bustard, was also seen here. In Kohistan the most active search is made for all animals which yield fur, that being an article in high demand in Cabool. There are eight or ten different species to be found here, amongst which are the lynx, the gor-kun, and the moosh-khoorma; but the one most sought after is the "dila khufuk," a large weasel, of greyish colour, and white in the neck. The Galago crassicaudatus of Cuvier was also brought to us; and the Huzara rat, which is a creature without a tail. Porcupines and hedgehogs abound. Marmots were likewise caught, but the hares in this country are few, and small in size; and, with the exception of water-fowl, there is little which a sportsman calls game, although the Afghans hunt everything that yields a fur. Bears of a reddish-brown colour and wolves make their appearance in winter; as also the red fox, and the common reynard, which is larger than in India, and would not disgrace an English field. The people spoke much of the "sug i kohee," or dog of the hills, brought from the Huzara country, but I doubt if it be really the wild dog, as the region has no wood or jungle. Its young are most sought after. There is also in the same region an animal of a like nature to our badger, and called "tibbergam," which takes to the ground in winter. From Nijrow they brought to us a large bird called "unkash:" it was either the condor or a vulture. Some fine specimens of wild sheep and goats were seen here. They are natives of Hindoo Koosh; and for full particulars regarding them I refer the naturalist to Dr. Lord's very accurate account, which will be found in Appendix V.

On our route we alighted at Ak-Surai, a flourishing village about twenty miles from Cabool. In one of its gardens many families were residing under the trees, as is common during summer in this country. Several of them were preparing grape-jelly, called "sheeru." They first squeeze the ripe Kismiss grape in a wicker basket, from which the juice escapes into a jar, after which it is put on the fire and boiled: it is used in making sherbet. The squeezed husks of the grapes they give to cows and horses. While resting under a tree at a little distance and watching this process, a damsel sent me some kabobs, spitted on a twig of willow and well roasted, which I enjoyed vastly after a march of nearly thirty miles. I suppose I was indebted to the intervention of the officer with me for the fair lady's civility; but as my baggage was in the rear I was doubly thankful. I afterwards retired to the house of a Hindoo in the town, where I rested for the remainder of the day, evidently affording great amusement to all the neighbours of my host; the situation in which I sat enabling them to peep down upon me from every direction, as if I had been shut up in one of the central cells of Bentham's Panopticon. Next morning we rose early, and, crossing the pass of Paeen Moonara and the lake, soon found ourselves in Cabool. On the way we met many travellers, most of them women, still hurrying across the mountains, chiefly to Inderab. They were all on horseback; one horse sometimes carrying a woman, her child, and a slave-girl. They were well clad to keep out cold, and the men had mottled stockings, or overalls, of worsted, that came up the thigh and looked extremely comfortable. Entering Cabool from this side, we were shown two mounds close to the Bala Hissar, called the "Khak i Balkh," from a tradition that when the Afghans took that city they half-filled their grain-bags with earth taken from it, and which they threw down where it now lies as a trophy of conquest. I fear the mounds are too large, and too closely resemble the neighbouring soil, to admit of the reception of this proud legend.

CHAPTER VIII.

Cabool—Agent from Moorad Beg of Koondooz—Letter from the Chief—His change of policy—Answer given to it—The Envoy's character of his Chief—Dr. Lord's journey to Koondooz—Extracts from his letters—Arrival and reception—Conversations with Moorad Beg—The invalid's a hopeless case—The Chief's friendship—Lieutenant Wood's journey—Syud of Talikhan, the friend of Moorcroft—Atalik Beg—Moorcroft's books, &c.—Date of his death—Mr. Trebeck's character—Customs of Uzbeks—Marriages—Man-selling—Traffic in wives—Mode of salaam—Circumcision—Enormous eating—Horse-racing and prizes—Amusements.

On our return to Cabool I had the unexpected pleasure of finding there an Elchee, or agent, from Moorad Beg, the chief of Koondooz. Ever since my arrival in the country I had been endeavouring to conciliate this hostile personage: I had addressed not only his minister, but the ruler himself, by the intervention of certain merchants. I had not forgotten the dangerous situation in which I had once found myself in his country; and, as subsequent conduct on his part towards Dr. Gerard and Mr. Vigne showed that his asperity towards Europeans was little abated, I was not prepared for the gratifying prospect that now developed itself. The Elchee waited upon me, and presented to me the following letter from his master. It was addressed to "Sikunder Burnes, Firingee Angrez," and after sundry compliments ran thus: " I have heard much of you and the great wisdom you possess: I have learned from many quarters that you are as the renowned Hippocrates among wise men. My younger brother has become dim-sighted: if you can cure him I will be very thankful to you, and send him to Cabool. If it please God that the eyes of my brother be cured, you will have a great name throughout Toorkistan (Tartary). The bearer of this, Mirza Budeea, will tell you all, and rely upon what he says. Accept also the horse, which I send to you as a rarity from this country and a remembrance of me."

Here indeed was a change of fortune, when contrasted with that day on which I had been dragged as a suspected culprit to Koondooz. An opportunity was now afforded us not only of terminating Moorad Beg's hostility, but also of making him our friend, and, by his means, of pushing our inquiries even to Pamere and the sources of the Oxus. The time was not one for hesitation, and the plans determined upon will be fully shewn by my reply to his epistle, which was as follows: "I have received your letter with the greatest satisfaction, and I feel sensibly the confidence which you place in me, and still more so the high opinions which you entertain of European knowledge. It is a source of much regret to me that one so dear to you as a brother should labour under a disease so afflicting as a threatened loss of sight; but where would be the proof of the friendly feelings which I entertain towards you, if I allowed such a one to cross the snows of Hindoo Koosh and seek for medical aid in Cabool? In company with me is a physician renowned and skilled in the sciences of Europe: the cure of disease is in the hands of God, but Dr. Lord and Mr. Wood will omit nothing which can render their services valuable to you. These gentlemen are servants of the Government of India, and my fellow-travellers: they are very dear to me, and I commend them to your care. That which has passed between your confidential agent, Mirza Budeea, and myself will be made known to you: the promise which he has made to me, as to the restoration of the papers and books of the lamented Moorcroft, is worthy of yourself. As the sight of your own brother is dear to you, so are the relics of a countryman who died in a distant country dear to all his friends and relations." Dr. Lord and Lieutenant Wood forthwith made every arrangement for commencing this highly interesting journey, as it was resolved that they themselves should be the bearers of this letter, and also of sundry curiosities as presents to the chief. All this was arranged not without reluctance on the part of Dost Mahommed Khan, who wished to summon the Uzbek to Cabool: his objections, however, were at last overcome, and the prediction of the 'Edinburgh Review,' when speaking of my last work, was thus fully verified: "The turbulence of Moorad Beg *has* been subdued by a mission."

Before, however, I relate the departure of my fellow-travellers, I must give a few particulars of the information which I received from Mirza Budeea, a loquacious, simple-minded, but honest Uzbek, who stood high in the confidence of the chief of Koondooz; nor am I deterred from doing so by the subsequent and more accurate information acquired during the journey of the two travellers.

The Mirza faithfully promised me to attend with zeal and fidelity to the wants of my companions, and enlarged on the bounty of his master to every one, even to those he subdued. He dwelt at great length on the activity which he evinced in his "chupaos," or forays; on the liberality which led him to kill fifteen sheep a-day in his own house, and sometimes to entertain 1000 persons; and seemed, in fact, lost in admiration of the "tyrant of Koondooz," on whose fame and power he discoursed *con amore*. "My master," said he, "can bring 20,000 good cut-horses to proceed on 'allamanee' (plunder) for forty days; and man and beast will exist, each day, on three handsful of grain and a bit of bread as large as the hand." He stated that the Mir was accustomed to assemble these men at a certain place, and that none knew what would be the direction of the foray, whether to the Huzara country, to near Candahar, Balkh, Durwaz, Shughnan, Shah Kutore's country, or to that of the Kaffirs. He added that the only people who were harshly treated in the Koondooz dominions were those whose countries had been captured, and that this was necessary for the preservation of peace; but Shah Mahmood of Doornaz, whom without interrogation he called the descendant of Alexander the Great, had, he said, been much favoured. "We Uzbeks," said Mirza Budcea, "live on horseback: we have none of your trading as in Cabool. Dost Mahommed bids me inform my master that man-selling is discreditable; but I tell him to negotiate with his new ally, the king of Bokhara, and make him prohibit man-purchasing, and that then the enormity of man-selling would soon cease. We have the power to shut up the caravan-roads from Cabool to Bokhara," continued he, "which would injure both places and not in the least affect us—we scorn to do it: we dress in mottled garments, the produce of our own country and Toorkistan, while every one here wears European chintzes, &c., and their ruler's subsistence is largely derived from the duties levied on those articles: from such a source Moorad Beg has never sought profit. He lives contentedly at Koondooz: the eastern part of his country he gives to his son, Shah Moorad Khan, who has the title of Atalik Khan, and also rules over Budukshan, Shughnan, and Talighan: to his brother, Mahmood Beg, he intrusts his northern limits, Buljeewan, &c.; while he himself at Koondooz manages the country south and west of it. The whole stretch of his power is about fifty days' journey, from Sir-i-kool to near Balkh, although he interferes but little with some of the intervening tracts. From Shughnan he takes but 500 'yamoos,' or ingots of silver: from Chitral he receives slaves more beautiful than the Kaffirs, and these he distributes to his Begs, or sends to Bokhara: he mulcts no strangers who come to his country, and even Chinese may pass through it." I have thus left the Elchee to speak for himsel, and my own leading questions to be inferred. He said he had *partly* satisfied himself that we were not infidels, but had a good book of our own and much knowledge; adding that he had five sons, and begging me to write their names down in the book of Firingees. After this long conversation we strolled about the garden in which was our residence, and which was beautifully adorned with variegated stock and other flowers; and I asked him if Toorkistan had such a display? His reply did not do much honour to his taste: "Fools and fakeers (devotees)," he said, "only attend to such things." Mirza Budeea, however, proved himself an amiable, worthy man. I regret to add that he was barbarously assassinated a few months after this interview.

On the 3rd of November Dr. Lord and Lieutenant Wood set out on their journey by Purwan* and the Sir-aulung Pass, in ascending which they experienced a terrific snow-storm: some of their followers became incoherent in their speech, others went raving mad; and the party were compelled to return to Cabool, and finally took the road by Bamian. I shall leave them hereafter to describe their own adventures, and will at present only give the following extracts from Dr. Lord's letters to myself:

* It was at this very place that Dr. Lord afterwards fell, in the last action with Dost Mahommed Khan, on the 2nd of November, 1840, when two squadrons of the 2nd Bengal Cavalry basely fled before our eyes and sacrificed their officers. I had to deplore the loss of two dear friends, Dr. Lord, and Lieutenant J. S. Broadfoot, of the Bengal Engineers, an officer of the highest promise.

they will be read with deep interest, and with a melancholy regret at the death of their energetic and accomplished writer:—

"*Koondooz, 7th Dec.*, 1837.

"We left Cabool on the 15th of November, and arrived here in perfect health and safety on the 4th of the present month, having experienced no difficulty worth mentioning on the way. On the 21st we had reached Bamian, and next day entered Mir Moorad Beg's territories, from which moment the Mirza Budeea took on himself the duties of Mihmandar, and continued to perform them with the utmost regularity and attention. We held the direct road as far as Koorum, which being his jaghire, we halted there one day to oblige him, and had the satisfaction to receive a letter from the Mir expressing his regret at the difficulties he heard we had experienced in our first attempt at crossing Hindoo Koosh, and his satisfaction at hearing that we had now safely reached his country. There was a letter from Atma Dewan Begee, requesting we would send him full information of our movements, and when we might be expected. To this I despatched an answer; but our messenger had delayed so much on the road, that we reached Aleeabad, within one stage of Koondooz, before he had delivered his letter. In consequence, on our arrival at Aleeabad there was no one to meet us as had been intended. The Mirza expressed much disappointment at this, and requested leave to precede us next morning, saying he was certain the cassid could not have arrived. He did so, and about four miles from Koondooz we were met by the Dewan Begee himself, who, on receiving from the Mirza news of our approach, had hurried out to receive us with whatever horsemen were at hand. We afterwards learned it was intended the Mir's brother (my patient) should have come, but he happened to be asleep when the Mirza arrived: he came, however, to visit us on the very evening of our arrival, at a most comfortable house of Atma's, where we dismounted, and which has been placed entirely at our disposal. We received also a congratulatory message from the Mir, desiring us to consider the country as our own: this was followed by a present of tea and sweetmeats; and next morning, having heard that we had used native costume on our journey, he sent each of us a full suit of Uzbek clothing and a present in money of 200 rupees. He also intimated that we might name our own time for paying him a visit, which, as we required a day to prepare, we arranged for the following morning. In the evening I had a long visit from Atma, who came after dinner and sat with me more than three hours; during which I took occasion to explain to him the objects of your mission as far as they could be interesting to him; mentioned the views of our Government in opening the navigation of the Indus, and their intention of establishing a fair somewhere on its banks. He appeared much pleased and struck with the intelligence, and made many inquiries respecting the rate of tolls, duties, &c. I mentioned Runjeet Sing's fleet of twenty boats going to Bombay, and said our Government as an encouragement had promised they should enter free of all duties.

"Just as I had written this, Atma called and brought with him a letter of yours, which had been round by the way of Khooloom, and had only just been forwarded by his agent, Chumundass. It was opened and read in my presence, and he was evidently most highly gratified by the expressions of friendship it contained, and which I assured him were no more than what you really felt: he has desired me in return to give his best salaam, and assure you that himself and everything he has shall be at our service as long as we remain here.

"But to continue my journal.

"Next day, December 6th, we went to wait on the Mir. He appeared to us quite a plain, good old man; came outside his door and down his steps to receive us; gave us his hand, invited us in, and placed us at the top of the hall, while he himself sat down at one side, and those few courtiers who were allowed to sit occupied the other: the greater number stood below a couple of pillars which divided the upper from the lower end of the hall. The Mir then inquired after your health, and said it was an honour that Firingees had come to visit him. After a little conversation I produced your letter, which was read, and which he pronounced at its termination to be full of kindness. I then said you had sent some presents, of which, though not worthy of him, you begged his acceptance. This, he said, was quite unexpected—our coming he looked on as a great thing, and never looked for anything more: on the presents being produced he examined each of them with much attention, appeared pleased, and, I heard afterwards from the Mirza, was highly satisfied. He then resumed the conversation, inquired about the relative size of Firingistan (Europe) and Hindostan, the nature of our power in the latter, and whether it had any other king than ours: this enabled me to mention the kings whom we had pensioned, with which he seemed much struck; and one of his Mirzas explained to him that it was the policy of the English, when they conquered a country, to keep in place those whom they found in it, by which means they avoided driving people to despair, and more easily attached them to their government. He then inquired whether the Russians or English were the cleverest: to which the same Mirza, a Peshawuree as I have since learned, at once replied that the English were far the cleverest people in all Firingistan; an assertion which I did not feel myself called on to contradict. After a little further conversation we took our leave, and I next went to visit my patient, and regret to say his case is almost hopeless, being amaurosis (gutta serena), complete and of eight years' standing in one eye, incomplete and of eighteen months' duration in the other. I have fairly informed him that I consider the former quite gone, and that I have but slender hopes of benefiting the latter; but that, as his general health, and particularly his digestive powers, seem much impaired, I shall require some time to improve these before I give him a definite answer regarding the chances of recovering his eyesight. On this understanding I have commenced his treatment.

"I had almost forgotten to say that during our interview with the Mir, though he spoke freely of Moorcroft, and mentioned his knowledge of Persian and Toorkie, yet he avoided saying anything of his books and papers, which were expressly mentioned in your letter. I have since heard that there has been some difficulty about procuring them, and that they are not yet arrived, which probably may account for his silence."

"*Khamu-abad*, 13*th January*, 1838.

"You will perceive by the date that I am at the place where your anxieties reached their acmé, and received their happy termination. I came here four days since to give my patient the last chance in the benefit of a purer air than Koondooz: I am now perfectly convinced that the case is utterly hopeless, and should have announced this before but for my fear of compromising Wood, and my anxiety to have him back and ready to start with me, should it be necessary, as soon as I have made the communication. I have, however, told my patient that I am now trying the last and most powerful remedies, and that, if within forty days no effect is produced, it will be in vain to continue them any longer, and he must submit to what is written in his destiny.

"The way is thus paved; and meantime I am looking round for some other way of maintaining my footing here, as the road back will not be open for nearly four months.

"And your letter has given me, I think, no bad

commencement. On receipt of it I rode into Koondooz, and, waiting on the Mir, said I had come, by your orders, to offer your best thanks for all his kindness to Wood and myself since we arrived in his country, more particularly his having allowed Wood to go to the source of the Oxus, a favour which Firingees highly appreciated. This was received most graciously; and I then went on to inform him that Candahar had seceded from the Persian interest and was now anxious for the friendship of our Government, in consequence of which a Firingee had been despatched there. In telling him this I only told him what common report would have brought to him in half an hour afterwards, as the cassid had begun to spread it everywhere. This intelligence proved as highly satisfactory as I had anticipated, for the Persians are equally hated and feared here: it also produced divers exclamations of astonishment—'What wonderful men these Firingees are! Three months ago four of them came into the country; now one is at Cabool, one at Candahar, one here, and one at the source of the Oxus. Wullah! billah! they neither eat, drink, nor sleep: all day they make syl [enjoy themselves], and all night they write books!' When these exclamations were over I inquired what news he might have from the seat of war: 'Hech,' (nothing,) he said; 'people will talk' (gup me zunund), 'but the news of one day is the lie of the next: however,' said he, 'I wish very much I had some sure information what these Kuzzilbash dogs are about, as some people say they are coming this way.' This was the very point I wanted to bring him to, as I was myself just at the same loss for information to send you: so I said at once, 'What difficulty can there be about this? If it is your pleasure, I will send off a man who will go to Mei-muna, and, please God, even to the Persian camp, and will tell us all that is going on.' 'By all means,' said his Highness, who, much as he wanted information, seems never to have thought of this simple way of getting it—'by all means, send three, four, six men: let us have good pookhtee (information) every day, and when it comes let me know of it.' 'Bu chusm,' (on my eyes,) said I; and, fortified with this permission, I have started off Rujab Khan this morning, who is to go first to Balkh, where he is acquainted with some few families who have connexions in Herat, and will probably have good information. He is then to go on through Akchu, Siripul, and Shibberghán, to Mei-muna, getting the statistics of these little independent states on his way. From Mei-muna he is to send me another cassid, and also either to go himself or procure some one to go and reconnoitre the Persian camp. He is also, on leaving it, to engage some of his friends there to write him occasionally, should there be anything new: so that I hope by this arrangement to get you not only present information, but a continuance of it while the war is in that quarter, and that without committing either you or myself.

"During the whole interview Moorad Beg was, I think, in better humour than I have seen him before, though he has always been gracious; and I afterwards heard from Atma that he was much pleased at the idea of my coming in from Khánúábád to make 'salaam,' as attending his durbár is called here.

"Before taking my leave I represented that, as Talikán was but a short distance from Khánúábád, I meant, with his permission, to go down there for one night, in order to make my salaam to the holy man there. 'Why not?' said he: 'Go everywhere, and see what you like.' I here terminated our interview, with which I am the more satisfied as some unpleasant rumours had reached me respecting his dissatisfaction at my not having done his brother any benefit; and it was in some measure to test their accuracy that I made the visit, and to his inquiries after his brother's eyes answered distinctly that I saw no improvement. I therefore entertain hopes that, even after I have announced the melancholy truth, I may not find my situation here wholly untenable; and may even get permission to ramble along the banks of the Oxus, the fords of which I wish to examine, as Wood seems to have turned his back upon them.

"Yesterday was altogether, as Dominie Sampson would say, 'a white day;' for, on returning here in the evening after this successful interview, I was saluted by a man who turned out to be a messenger bearing a letter from the 'holy man of Talikán,' every word of which was a full-blown rose in the garden of friendship. Of course I 'khoosh amudeid' the worthy gentleman; told him of the leave I had that day received to pay my respects to his master, who, I said, was well known through all Firingistan as the friend of our nation; tied a turban round his head; and sent him back with a letter containing as many peonies as his master's had roses, and announcing my intention of making my salaam within a few days at furthest. I look on this man as no bad peg to hold by in case of accidents, and have prepared a grand posteen (fur pelisse) to invest him with on occasion of my visit."

"*Koondooz*, 30*th January*, 1838.

"You will be prepared to hear that I have given up my patient's case as hopeless; but the resignation with which this destruction of all his hopes of regaining his sight has been borne, both by himself and Mir Moorad Beg, is far greater than either you or I could have anticipated, and in fact is such as to do high honour to the Uzbek character. I had from the first declared the case to be one of extreme difficulty; and, latterly, told him that one after another of my remedies had proved ineffectual, and that the slight hope I originally might have had was daily becoming less. My final announcement he anticipated by sending me a message on the evening of the 17th to this effect :—'He felt it was written in his destiny that he was not to recover his sight: he was satisfied I had done everything possible, but that he was now resigned to the will of God, and content to go back to his own house convinced that a cure was not to be expected.' These were so nearly my own sentiments on the matter that I did not offer much opposition. I said, 'If he wished for my advice it was this—that he should persist in the use of the remedies twenty days longer, within which time, if there was no amendment, I was hopeless; but that if he determined on going now I had little to say against it, as my hopes of ultimate improvement were now very slight.' I added, 'It would be well he should think it over for the night, and that in the morning I would call and hear his decision.' With these words I dismissed the mission, which consisted of Mousa Yessawul, the governor of Khánúábád, at which place we then were, Zohrab Khan, the governor of Inderab, and a Mirza.

"About 8 P.M., having heard that the Mir had finally determined no longer to struggle against his fate, I went over to take leave of him and offer such consolations as might occur to me. He expressed himself in every way satisfied with the exertions I had made, said he was under obligations which he never should forget, and begged I would continue his guest as long as it suited me to remain in the country, every part of which I was at liberty to visit. He added numerous other expressions of kindly feeling, and explained that he had given orders to Mousa Yessawul that all my wishes were to be attended to. He then reverted to his own melancholy condition, and, losing all composure, burst into tears, accusing himself loudly of the many crimes he had committed, and acknowledging the hand of God in the judgment which had now overtaken him. The scene was a strange mixture of the pathetic and the ludicrous. I could not help sympathising sincerely with the poor old man and his son, a fine lad of fifteen, who shared deeply in his father's grief; but then every broad-faced Uzbek about the room, seeing his chief in tears, thought it incumbent on him to blubber a little also, and the wry faces some of them made in attempting to look melancholy were perfectly irresistible.

"I was obliged to bury my face in my sleeves, and hope I too got credit for crying a little. After the first burst of grief was over, I took on me the office of comforter. I said 'He had undoubtedly committed crimes, as all men had, but then he had also done much that was good: he had cherished the ryot, distributed justice, and I had with my own eyes seen that the people who lived under him were contented and happy.' I added that God had taken away one blessing, but had given him many—lands, houses, children, wealth, and power; that it became him to look on these, not on what was taken away, and to be thankful. I further advised him to have the Koran constantly read to him, and to reflect on the instability of this world; and having so said I got up and went away.

"Next morning the old man returned to Koondooz, and I, wishing to commence my new game by leading off a trump card, started to pay my long-promised visit to Moorcroft's Syud.

"The village of the Holy Man is about six miles on the other side of Talikán, in all thirty miles from Khánúábád. I reached it about four in the afternoon, and on dismounting was conducted to a small, neatly-carpeted apartment, where I was told to expect a visit from the Syud as soon as he should have finished his afternoon devotions. In about half an hour he came. I stooped to kiss his hand in acknowledgment of his sanctity, when he gently raised and embraced me: I then endeavoured to express to him the obligation which I, in common with all Firingees, felt to him for the service he had rendered our ill-fated countryman, Moorcroft, and added that it was a favour which none of us should forget. I explained to him that this was the very first day I had been disengaged since my arrival in Moorad Beg's territories, and that I had impatiently awaited the opportunity it afforded me of expressing to him these the common sentiments of my nation. He appeared gratified, but modestly disclaimed any merit, saying it was not in his power to do much for Moorcroft. He added that it astonished him not a little to find that so trifling an action as it had appeared to him at the time should have reached a country so remote and so great as ours. After a little further conversation, in which I said I had been charged to add your acknowledgments to my own, he retired, and soon after slaves made their appearance, leaving trays of pilaos and sweetmeats, to which my long ride induced me to do ample justice.

"After dinner he again came, and sat with me nearly an hour. The conversation ran chiefly on European politics, and commerce, as connected with India and Persia. Knowing his influence over the mind of Moorad Beg, I took occasion to explain to him the objects of your mission, and more particularly the intention of our Government to establish a great annual fair on the banks of the Indus, and showed the benefits which must arise from this to the Mir, whose country would necessarily be the grand line of communication between Hindostan and Toorkistan. He seemed perfectly to comprehend all my sentiments, and made several inquiries that evinced his intelligence. He then inquired what I meant to do with myself until the road back should be open. (I had informed him that I had relinquished Mahomed Beg's case as hopeless.) I replied, that, if the Mir would permit me, I wished to travel a little about his country, as it was the custom of Firingees to observe everything that came in their way. He said he had heard this from Moorcroft, and thought I should find no difficulty here. Before I went away he again expressed his astonishment at our being acquainted with what he had done for Moorcroft. 'Is it really a fact,' said he, 'that this is known in Firingistan?' 'Wullah, billah,' said I; 'the very children repeat the name of Syud Mahomed Kasim, the friend of the Firingees.' He did not attempt to conceal his satisfaction. 'God is great!' said he; 'feel my pulse.' 'Praise be to God,' said I, 'what strength and firmness! If it please God, one half your life is not yet passed.' We stroked our beards, said a 'fatha,' or blessing, and the old man departed. I saw him again in the morning, when I was about to return: he had been praying from cock-crow until past nine o'clock. He stopped for a few moments as he passed my door, said a few words of inquiry, asked for some medicine for his eyes, and, having ordered breakfast to be brought me, took his leave.

"On proceeding to mount I found a handsome young horse, which he had ordered to be presented to me in return for some articles I had given him. A man also was in readiness to show me the salt-mines, which I had expressed a wish to see.

"Having visited them, I thought it well to make my salaam to the heir-apparent, Atalik Beg, as I was in his vicinity. He received me in the same distinguished manner his father had done—standing outside his own door, with all his court drawn up around him—placed me in the highest seat, and at my departure presented me with a horse and a dress of honour. The two first tricks being thus clearly won, I thought it proper to lose no time in going to Koondooz, to ascertain my fate there.

"The day after my arrival (22nd January) I had visits from Atma and Mirza Buddeea, who both assured me that the Mir's friendly disposition towards me was not in the least altered by the result of his brother's case, which, he said, was his destiny. Atma further added that Mahomed Beg, my patient, in passing through, had spoken of me in the highest terms, as not only possessing professional skill, but as 'being perfectly acquainted with good manners,' and as having paid him every possible attention. This is all as it should be."

* * * * *

In the middle of April Dr. Lord and Lieutenant Wood set out from Koondooz, on their return to Cabool; and previous to their departure the books of Moorcroft, with a few of his papers, were made over to them: with these poor Lord sent to me the following interesting memorandum:—

"I have to present to you a list of books and

papers belonging to the late Mr. Moorcroft, which I have been so fortunate as to recover during my recent journey to Toorkistan.

"For the greater part of them I am indebted to Mir Mahommed Moorad Beg, who, immediately on my arrival at Koondooz, wrote to the Khan of Muzar, desiring that all such relics of the European traveller should forthwith be sent. In reply to this, fifty volumes, all of printed works, were immediately forwarded; the remainder, including the map, Mr. Moorcroft's passport in English and Persian from the Marquis of Hastings, and a MS. volume, with several loose MS. sheets, chiefly of accounts, I was enabled to recover when, by the Mir's permission, I myself made a visit to Khooloom and Muzar.

"I think the evidence I have received proves, as strongly as the nature of negative evidence will admit, that no MS. papers of any value belonging to that ill-fated expedition remain to be recovered.

"I paid every person who brought books; and always explained that I would give double reward for anything that was written; and though in consequence of this several sheets of MS. were brought me, they never appeared, on examination, to contain anything beyond accounts and such routine matters. Now, as the natives must be unable to make the distinction, the chances evidently are, that, if any papers of importance existed, one or two of them at least would have found their way to me amongst the number presented.

"I append a letter from Mirza Humeedoodeen, the principal secretary to the Khan of Muzar, and a man who attended Mr. Trebeck in his last moments, saying that two printed and one MS. volumes are in existence at Shehr Subz, and that he had sent a man to recover them for me. As I have since been obliged to leave the country, and as all communication is, by the present state of affairs at Cabool, rendered impossible, I mention this fact as well worthy the attention of some future traveller.

"The map is in itself a document of much interest, as containing Mr. Moorcroft's route, traced evidently with his own hand, and continued as far as Akcha, within one stage of Andkhoee, where he is known to have fallen a victim, not more I believe to the baneful effects of the climate than to the web of treachery and intrigue by which he found himself surrounded and his return cut off. On the back of the map is a MS. sketch of the route through Andkhoee to Mei-muna, and back through Sireepool to Balkh, as though he had planned a tour through these little independent states, partly perhaps to see the horses for which they are famed, and partly to while away the uneasiness of expectation till a safe-conduct should be granted him through the territories of the ruler of Koondooz. We can thus almost trace the last object that engaged his mind, and in the prosecution of which he laid down his life.

Connected with this I beg to subjoin a slip of paper which I found amongst a pile of loose accounts, and which bears, in Mr. Trebeck's writing, the following entry, date September 6th, 1825:—

"'Arrived at Balkh, August 25th. Mr. M. died August 27th.'

"This places the date of Mr. Moorcroft's death beyond a doubt; and also, I think, affords negative evidence against the supposition of its having been caused by any unfair means.

"But the same paper is further interesting from an accidental coincidence. The Mirza, I have before mentioned, accompanied me from Tash Koorghan to Muzar, and in the course of conversation, which naturally turned in a great measure on the melancholy fate of Moorcroft's party, he said that, about a month before the death of Trebeck, he had one day gone to him, by desire of the Khan, to purchase some pearls which he heard he had. Trebeck produced the pearls; but, when questioned about the price, said, in a desponding tone, 'Take them for what you please;—my heart is broken: what care I for price now ?' The entry is this:—

Total on the strings	. .	280 grs.
Oct 15th. Taken by Mirza	.	131 grs. or 4 miskals.
„ 16th. Taken by Dewan Beghee		33 grs. or 1 miskal.

"It will be observed no price is affixed: probably none was received. A stranger in a foreign land, far from the soothing voice of his countrymen or kinsfolk, surrounded by rude hordes, who looked on him as the only obstacle to possessing themselves of the countless treasures which they believed to be in his charge, his youthful spirit pined and sunk. The bright visions with which he had commenced his career had long since vanished; where he had looked for pleasures he had found toils; where for rest he had to guard against dangers; sickness had carried off many of the companions with whom he had set out; and when at last it struck his guide, his own familiar friend, to whom he looked for support under every adversity, and for rescue from every difficulty, and when in addition he found that all hopes of return to his native land seemed, if not cut off, at least indefinitely deferred,—his heart, as he too truly says, was broken, and in a few short weeks he sunk into an untimely grave. I should apologise for a digression unsuited, I confess, to the character of an official paper, but it is impossible to hear the warm terms in which poor Trebeck is still mentioned by the rude natives among whom he died, without feeling the deepest sympathy in the fate of one who fell

'So young, and yet so full of promise.'

"It is only necessary I should add one or two more observations. The account-book, which I now forward, is a valuable document in more respects than one. It contains an accurate list of the stock originally purchased by Mr. Moorcroft when starting for his journey, and will serve to modify considerably the extravagant ideas that have been entertained of the quantities of goods which he carried. Taken in connexion with the loose MS. accounts, it will serve also to evince that the greater part of this stock was sold off previous to his leaving Bokhara, and, as far as my information goes, I am inclined to believe the proceeds were chiefly expended in the purchase of horses, of which I understand he had when he died somewhat under a hundred, including specimens of all the best Uzbek and Toorkooman breeds.

"The account-book is further interesting, as containing, in Mr. Moorcroft's own handwriting, a list of the articles which he offered on his presentation to the King of Bokhara; and a note at the end, to the effect that the King had in return ordered him a remission of the duties on his merchandize, rather more than equalling the estimated value of the goods. It is further satisfactory to be able to add, on the authority of several Bokhara merchants who were on terms of intimacy with him during his stay in that city, that his character was highly appreciated by the King, who frequently sent for him to enjoy the pleasure of his conversation, and conferred on him the high privilege, never before granted to a Christian, of riding through the city, and even to the gate of the King's palace, on horseback.

"In addition to the list of his merchandize, this account-book contains also a list of his private property, which, it appears, Mr. Moorcroft was obliged by order of the Koosh Begee to make out on entering Bokhara. From this list we learn he possessed ninety volumes of books. The number I have recovered, and which I have now the honour to place at your disposal, is fifty-seven. Amongst them are several odd volumes, of which the sets, if complete, would give an addition of about thirty—total eighty-seven; so that there are probably not more than two or three volumes of which we may not consider ourselves to have ascertained the fate. As to MSS., I have already shown the high improbability that any of consequence have eluded our researches.

"Scattered through the printed volumes, numerous notes and corrections in Mr. Moorcroft's own handwriting will be found. Of these some, referring incidentally to the dangers of his journey, or laying down plans as to the route by which he meant to return, cannot be read without emotion.

"In conclusion, it is but justice to add that the impression everywhere left by this enterprising but ill-fated party has been in a high degree favourable to our national character.

"Translation of a letter from Mirza Humeeoodeen to P. B. Lord, Esq.:—

"'A. C. Two books and one MS. are in the city of Shuhr Subz. I have sent a person to bring them, and when they reach me I shall send them to you. In all things I will never forget your kind offices. Let me always hear of your welfare. Believe what this man says, and that I am your well-wisher. Dated Mohurrum, 1254, A. H.'"

While at Koondooz, Dr. Lord wrote a single sheet on the customs of the Uzbeks, which I give entire, as illustrative of their manners:—

"At weddings, a party of the friends of the bride and bridegroom, provided with large quantities of flour mixed with ashes, meet in the open plain, and have a grand engagement until one party is obliged to turn and fly. After that, peace is made; and they both join at a great entertainment. Sometimes serious consequences arise if the beaten party get enraged. It is only a few years since the Mir's son, Malik Khan, married the daughter of Nuzry Min Bashee, a Kutaghan of his own tribe of Kaysumúr. On this occasion each party came provided with twenty-one jowals of wheat and an equal quantity of ashes, the Mir himself heading his own party: he was beaten, and pursued about two kos from the field; when, suddenly losing his temper, he turned about, and ordered his party to draw swords and charge, to the no little dismay, it may be supposed, of the victor. Some white-beards, however, interfered, and prevented the effusion of blood.

"Men here sell their wives, if they get tired of them. This is by no means uncommon: but the man is obliged to make the first offer of her to her family, naming the price, which if they do not give, he is at liberty to sell her to any one else. On the death of a man his wives all become the property of his next brother; who may marry them or sell them, giving the pre-option, as before, to their own families.

"Jándad, a Kaboolee Attari, to whom I spoke of the custom of selling wives, which I did not entirely credit, said, 'I'll tell you what happened to myself. I was one day returning from Khanuabád; and, being overtaken by darkness, halted for the night at Turnáb, three kos short of this. After feeding my horse and going to the house for shelter, I found three men busily engaged; and, inquiring the subject of their conversation, was told that one of them was selling his wife to the other, but that they had not agreed about terms. Meantime, Khúda Bérdí Ming, Bashí and chief of the village, came in, and whispered to me that, if I could go halves with him, he would purchase the woman, as he had seen her and found her very beautiful. I agreed; upon which we purchased her for seventy rupees, thirty-five each, and she went home with me for that night. Next morning Khúda Bérdí came, and said that partnership in a woman was a bad thing, and asked me how I intended to manage. I said she should stay with me one month, and then go to him next. To that he would by no means agree; because, if sons or daughters were born, there would be disputes to know to whom they belonged. "In short," said he, "either do you give me five rupees profit on my share, and take her altogether, or I will give you the same profit on your share, and she shall be altogether mine." To this latter alternative I consented;

and she is now living with him, as every one well knows.'

"A man who has a daughter marriageable must give intimation of it to the Mir, who sends his chief eunuch to inspect her: if handsome, he takes her; if not, he gives permission that she should marry another.

"Every man who meets the Mir out riding dismounts as he passes, and gives him the 'salâm alaikúm.' The rulers of districts, and other employés, are expected to come at least four or five times a-year to make their salâm. The mode is,—on entering the door each shouts out 'Salâm alaikúm' as loud as he can; then runs forward, falls on his knees, and, taking the Mir's hand between both of his, places it to his forehead, or kisses it, I could not clearly see which, and exclaiming 'Tukseer' (pardon me), retires to the wall, where he stands, and answers any questions the Mir may ask about his government; after which he mixes with the crowd, or walks out as soon as he pleases. On these occasions an offering is brought,—horses, slaves, &c.,—which are paraded for the Mir's approval.

"A child is circumcised at the age of seven or ten years. This is a time of the greatest festivity among the Usbeks; and on such occasions considerable expense is incurred, and feasts given which last fifteen or twenty days. The eating is truly enormous; but, indeed, to our ideas, it is always so: two Uzbeks not unfrequently devouring an entire sheep, with a proportional quantity of rice, bread, ghee, &c., between them; and afterwards cramming in water-melons, musk-melons, or other fruit: but these they say go for nothing, being only water. On the occasions to which I have referred horse-racing is a favourite amusement, and the horses for the purpose are generally trained for a fortnight or three weeks preceding; and they require this, for a race here is not a matter of one or two mile heats, but a regular continued run for twenty or twenty-five kos (forty or fifty miles) across the country, sometimes wading through morasses and swimming rivers, but more frequently crossing their magnificent extended plains; one of which, as level as our best race-courses and with a beautiful green turf covering, not unfrequently extends the entire distance to be run. The scene on these occasions is highly animated, as not only the racers, generally about twenty in number, set off, but the whole of the sporting assembly, perhaps 100, or even 500 in number, accompany them, at least for the first three or four miles. A judge has been sent on in advance; and the competitors seldom return till the next day. The prizes are certainly worth some exertion; and in one case, when the donor was a man of good substance, they were as follows: the first, and most classical, was a young maiden, generally a Huzarah or Chitráli, both prized for their personal attractions; the second, fifty sheep; the third, a boy; the fourth, a horse; the fifth, a camel; the sixth a cow; and the seventh, a *water-melon*, the winner of which becomes an object of ridicule and banter for the rest of the meeting.

"Another and more amusing kind of race is the following:—One man places a goat on the horse before him, and sets off at full gallop; fifteen or twenty others immediately start off after him, and whichever of these can seize the goat, and get safe off with it beyond the reach of the rest, retains it for his prize. The rapidity with which the goat sometimes changes masters is very laughable; but the poor animal is occasionally torn to pieces in the scuffle.

"A third game, called Kubach, requires no little dexterity in the use of fire-arms, and, indeed, looking at the wretched matchlocks which they usually carry, I doubt whether success in it can ever be more than a matter of chance. A kuddoo (a small kind of gourd), hollowed out and filled with flour, is erected on the top of a pole two spears high.

Those who are to make trial of their skill stand in a row, about four hundred yards distant, and each in succession, putting his horse to full speed, discharges his matchlock at the object whenever he pleases. Most fire when just under it, others on the advance; but the acmé of perfection is to turn round on your horse and strike it after you have passed. The flour flying out at once proclaims success, and the victor at this sport is rewarded with one hundred rupees, and a khillât, or dress of honour. The prize is generally given by the Mir himself, when he happens to be present on those occasions.

"On an attentive examination, I fully satisfied myself that anything like deliberate aim was totally out of the question; even the Uzbeks themselves, when questioned, admitted that it was all by chance."

These interesting details were not, however, the full fruit of Dr. Lord's labours at Koondooz. He accidentally heard from my old friend Atmá Dewán Begee, the minister of the chief of Koondooz, that he had in his possession two silver plates, or, rather, paterӕ, which he had procured from the family of the dethroned chiefs of Budukhshán, who claim descent from Alexander. My poor friend soon made these two treasures his own, and was justly proud of possessing them. One of these pateræ represents the triumphal procession of the Grecian Bacchus, and is of exquisite workmanship: the subject of the other is Sapor slaying the Lion. It is in the style of the monuments at Persepolis, and is less chaste than its companion. I have no hesitation in assigning them to the age of Bactria, from their appearance and the site in which they were found. The annexed engraving, taken from a drawing by my friend Captain H. Wade, of H. M. 13th Regiment, gives very accurate representations of both of them.

I received Dr. Lord's permission, very shortly before his death, to present the first of these pateræ, and some valuable coins, to the Museum at the India House, where they now are. The other relic is at present in my own possession. In coins also Lord's fortune was singularly great, as he procured, from the same quarter, one which is as yet quite unique. It is figured on the plate; and with the gay words in which the lamented discoverer described his treasure I will conclude this long chapter:—" Pends-toi, brave Crillon; nous avons combattu, et tu n'étais pas. I have got such an Eucratides! The great king, Eucratides, with a helmeted head on the obverse (God knows, it may be reverse for all I know), and on the other side the same king with a more melancholy expression of countenance,—no doubt of the cause, for this time he is accompanied by his wife,—two busts on one side, inscription of Eucratides, the son of Heliocles and Laodice. There's something for an article in Prinsep for you." And to the Journal of that ever-to-be-lamented individual I must refer for the article which he did send forth regarding this rarest of all Bactrian reliques.

Pl 18

BACTRIAN COIN FOUND AT KOONDOOZ.

ANCIENT PATERÆ FOUND IN BUDUKHSHAN.

CHAPTER IX.

The Siah-poosh Kaffirs—Character and customs—Mode of life—Language—Inscriptions at Bajour—Idols—Cashgar—Commerce—Climate—Clouds of red dust—The hot sand of Aksoo—Khoten—Kokan—Maimanu—Andkho—Shibbergam—Siripool—Akehu—Huzara Country—Population and descent—Customs—Curious tradition.

I will now digress for a while, and revert to the information which I gathered at Cabool relating to some of the countries north of Hindoo Koosh: it is not, however, my intention to carry the reader over any of the ground of which Lieutenant Wood has treated. I shall endeavour to bear in mind the true spirit of general geography, as defined by the illustrious Rennell, and contemplate not only the objects immediately in view, but direct inquiry to all around. To none did I more anxiously turn my attention than to the Siah-poosh Kaffirs, who occupy the mountainous regions of Northern Afghanistan, and whose history and condition have excited so much interest. In Cabool I met several Kaffirs who had been captured at an advanced age, and were still familiar with the language and manners of their countrymen. I also saw people, both

Hindoo and Mahomedan, who had visited the habitations of the Kaffirs, and I had thus an opportunity of hearing what these people thought of themselves, and also how they were viewed by foreigners. The account of the Kaffirs given by Mr. Elphinstone renders it unnecessary for me to repeat many of the details which I received, and which corroborated his statements: on these therefore I shall not touch, my object being to improve our present knowledge, and clear up, if possible, some of the obscurity which still exists.

In speaking of their nation the Kaffirs designate themselves, as the Mahomedans do, Kaffirs, with which name they, of course, do not couple any opprobrious meaning, though it implies infidel. They consider themselves descended of one Korushye, and their Mahomedan neighbours either corrupt the word, or assign them a lineage from Koreish, one of the noblest of the tribes of Arabia, to the language of which country they further state that of the Kaffirs to be allied. A Kaffir assured me that his tribe looked upon all men as brothers who wore ringlets and drank wine.* They have no

---

* Since the British entered Afghanistan one of the Kaffirs, near Jullalabad, sent a congratulatory message at the arrival of so many Kaffir brethren as ourselves!

definite idea of the surrounding countries, Bajour and Kooner, to the south, being the limits of their geographical knowledge. They have no books, nor is reading or writing known in the nation, so that they have no written traditions. Their country has many table-lands, some of which extend for fifteen or twenty miles, and on these there are always villages: Wygul and Camdeesh are on one of those plateaux, and eastward of the latter lies the country of the Mahomedans. The winter is severe, but in summer grapes ripen in great abundance.

The words of a young Kaffir, about eighteen years of age, now in Cabool, will afford the best explanation of many of their customs. His name, as a Kaffir, was Deenbur, as a Mahomedan it has been changed to Fureedoon. He fell into the hands of the Mahomedans eighteen months since, by losing his road when passing from his native village of Wygul to Gimeer, to visit a relative. He is a remarkably handsome young man, tall, with regular Grecian features, blue eyes, and fair complexion, and is now a slave of Dost Mahomed Khan. I give an accurate portrait of him, and the costume of his country as he described it. Two other Kaffir boys, eight and nine years old, who came with him, had ruddy complexions, hazel eyes, and auburn hair. They had high cheek-bones and less regular features, but still they were handsome and extremely intelligent. Their Kaffir names were Teeuzeer and Choudur, and that of their mothers Rajmal and Biaspagly. None of these three Kaffirs, or two others whom I saw, had any resemblance to the Afghans or even Cashmerians. They looked a distinct race, as the most superficial observer must have remarked on seeing them.

Deenbur said that there was no chief of the Kaffirs, but that great men were called Sabuninash. They do not appear to carry on any combined operations against their neighbours, but retaliate upon them when an invasion of their frontier takes place: they are very inveterate against the Mahomedans, and give no quarter to captives. They possess great ability and activity, qualities which their enemies accord to them. Mahomedans seldom venture to enter their country as travellers, but Hindoos go as merchants and beggars (fakeers), and are not ill-used. I met a Mahomedan who had passed into Budukhshan and was not molested. In killing animals for food, the Kaffirs use no ceremonies: they sacrifice cows and goats to Doghán, the Supreme Being, particularly at a great festival which occurs in the beginning of April, and lasts for ten days. They have idols, and know the Hindoo god, Mahdeo, by name; but they all eat

DEENBUR A SIAH-POSH KAFFIR

beef, and have either lost their Hindoo belief, or never had anything in common with it. They neither burn nor bury their dead, but place the body in a box, arrayed in a fine dress, which consists of goat-skins or Cashgar woollens: they then remove it to the summit of a hill near the village, where it is placed on the ground, but never interred. Kaffir females till the land: in eating, the men sit apart from the women. They have no tables: the dish containing the meal is placed on a tripod, made of iron rods, of which Deenbur and his companions made a model for me with twigs. They assemble round this and eat, sitting on stools or chairs without backs. They are very fond of honey, wine, and vinegar, all of which they have in abundance. They have no domestic fowls; nor is there a horse in their country: wheat and barley are their grains: there is no juwaree. They are very fond of music and dancing; but in dancing, as in eating, the men separate themselves from the women, and the dance of the one sex differs from that of the other. Both were exhibited to me: that of the men consists of three hops on one foot and then a stamp: the women place their hands on their shoulders and leap with both feet, going round in a circle. Their musical instruments are one of two strings, and a kind of drum.

By Deenbur's account, the mode of life among the Kaffirs would appear to be social, since they frequently assemble at each other's houses, or under the trees which embosom them, and have drinking parties. They drink from silver cups—trophies of their spoils in war. The wine, which is both light and dark, will keep for years, and is made by expressing the juice of the grape under the feet into a large earthen jar, which is described to be of delicate workmanship. Old and young of both sexes drink wine, and grape-juice is given to children at the breast. A Kaffir slave-girl, who became a mother shortly after her arrival in Cabool, demanded wine or vinegar on the birth of her child; the latter was given to her: she caused five or six walnuts to be burned and put into it, drank it off, and refused every other luxury.

The costume of the nation is better explained by the sketch than it can be by description. A successful warrior adds to it a waistband, ornamented with a small bell for every Mahomedan he has killed. His daughter has the privilege of wearing certain ornaments entwined in her hair, made of sea-shells or cowries, which no one else can put on without signal punishment. A Hindoo, who was present at a Kaffir marriage, informed me that the bridegroom had his food given to him behind his back, because he had not killed a Mahomedan. Enmities frequently arise among them; but the most deadly feud may be extinguished by one of the parties kissing the nipple of his antagonist's left breast, as being typical of drinking the milk of friendship. The other party then returns the compliment by kissing the suitor on the head, when they become friends till death. The Kaffirs do not sell their children to Mahomedans, though a man in distress may sometimes dispose of his servant, or steal a neighbour's child and sell it.

I asked my eldest Kaffir informant if he regretted the loss of his country? and he at once replied that *there* Kaffir customs were best, but *here* he preferred those of Mahomed. He had, however, imbibed a taste for Islam; and observed, that here there was religion, and in his country none. He told me a singular fact of a Kaffir relative of his own, named Shubood, who had been captured, and, becoming a Moollah, travelled, under the name of Korosh, into India, returned about three years ago into Kaffiristan, when he made known many things to the Kaffirs which they had never before heard. After a short stay he wished to quit the country, but he was not permitted. The names of the places which Deenbur remembered were Wygul, Gimeer, Cheemee, Kaygul, Minchgul, Ameeshdesh

Jamuj, Nishaigram Richgul, Deree, Kuttar, Camdesh, Donggul Pendesh, Villegul, and Savendesh. It is, however, believed that all the inhabitants of Dura i Noor, and other defiles of Hindoo Koosh, north of Cabool and Jullálábád, are converted Kaffirs, which their appearance and language seem to bear out.

The language of the Kaffirs is altogether unintelligible to Hindoos, as well to as their Uzbek and Afghan neighbours. Some of its sounds—soft labials—are scarcely to be pronounced by an European; but the specimens which I have given in Appendix IV. will best illustrate it. They are set down as spoken by Deenbur. The short sentences which follow the vocabulary bear, however, an evident affinity to the languages of the Hindoo stock. As the Kaffirs have no written characters, I give them in an English dress. When in the Kohistan of Cabool, near Punjsheer, I had an opportunity of meeting some of the people who speak Pushye, which resembles the dialect of the Kaffirs, as may be supposed from their proximity to them; and, as will be seen in the vocabulary, Pushye is spoken in eight villages named as follows: 1. Eshpein; 2. Eshkein; 3. Soudur; 4. Alisye; 5. Ghyn; 6. Doornama; 7. Doora i Pootta; and 8. Mulaikir;—all of which are situated among or near the seven valleys of Nijrow. The Pushyes are considered a kind of Tajiks by the Afghans.

I have stated the account which the Kaffirs give of themselves: I received the following additional particulars from a Mahomedan who had visited four villages, named Kutar, Gimeer, Deeos, and Sao, all of which are beyond the frontier hamlet of Koolman, which is inhabited by Neemches Mussulmans, and lies north of Jullálábád. He described the Kaffirs as a merry race, without care; and hoped he would not be considered disrespectful when he stated that he had never seen people more resembling Europeans in their intelligence, habits, and appearance, as well as in their gay and familiar tone over their wine. They have all tight clothes, sit on leathern stools, and are exceedingly hospitable. They always give wine to a stranger; and it is often put in pitchers, like water, at public places, which any one may drink. To ensure a supply of it, they have very strict regulations to prevent the grapes being cut before a certain day. My informant considered the country of the Kaffirs quite open to a traveller if he got a Kaffir to be his security. They have no ferocity of disposition, however barbarous some of their customs may appear; and, besides the mode of ensuring forgiveness already described, he stated that, if a

Kaffir has killed ten men of the tribe, he can appease the anger of his enemies by throwing down his knife before them, trampling on it, and kneeling.

Besides my Mahomedan informant, I met a Hindoo at Peshawur who had penetrated into that part of the Kaffir country which is about twenty-five miles beyond Chughansuraee, where he resided for eleven days. Some of his observations are curious. He was protected by a Kaffir, and experienced no difficulties; but he would not have been permitted to go among the more distant Kaffirs: had he attempted to do so, he would either have been killed or compelled to marry and live permanently among them. He was not however convinced of the impracticability of the journey, being kindly treated as far as he went, and admitted to their houses. He saw their dancing, and describes them as being a race of exquisite beauty, with arched eyebrows and fine complexions. These Kaffirs allow a lock of hair to grow on the right side of their head; and the Hindoo declared they were of his own creed, as they knew Seva. They had bows and arrows for defence: they pulled the string of the bow with their toes, and their arrows had heads like drooping lilies. Their country had many flowers, and much shade: numerous coins are found in it, resembling those to be procured about Bajour, and some of which have Grecian inscriptions. The worthy Hindoo insisted upon its being a fact that the Kaffirs sold their daughters to Mahomedans according to their size, twenty rupees per span being considered a fair valuation! There is certainly no difficulty in procuring Kaffir slaves; and the high prices which are readily given for them may have induced these poor people, who closely adjoin the Mahomedan countries, to enter upon this unnatural traffic.

But by far the most singular of all the visitors to the Kaffir country of whom I have heard was an individual who went into it from Cabool about the year 1829. He arrived from Candahar, and gave himself out to be a Gubr, or Fire-worshipper, and an Ibraheemee, or follower of Abraham, from Persia, who had come to examine the Kaffir country, where he expected to find traces of his ancestors. He associated, whilst in Cabool, with the Armenians, and called himself Shuhryar, which is a name current among the Parsees of these days. His host used every argument to dissuade him from going on such a dangerous journey, but in vain; and he proceeded to Jullálábád and Lughman, where he left his property, and entered the Kaffir country as a mendicant, by way of Nujjeel, and was absent for some months. On his return, after quitting

Kaffiristan, he was barbarously murdered by the neighbouring Huzárás of the Ali Purust tribe whose malik, Oosmán, was so incensed at his countrymen's conduct, that he exacted a fine of 2000 rupees as the price of his blood. All these facts were communicated to me by the Armenians in Cabool; but whether poor Shuhryar was a Bombay Parsee or a Persian Gubr I could not discover, though I am disposed to believe him to have been the latter, as he carried along with him a "rukum," or document from the Shah of Persia. The death of this successful sojourner among the Kaffir tribes is a subject of deep regret; but it holds out a hope that some one may follow the adventurous example of the disciple of Zoroaster, and yet visit the Kaffirs in their native glens. I know not what could have given rise to an identification of the Kaffir race with that of ancient Persia, unless it be the mode of disposing of their dead on hills without interment: but there are certainly traditions all over Afghanistan regarding the Gubrs, or Fire-worshippers; and one of their principal cities, called Gurdez, in Zoormut, south of Cabool, yet exists, and even in Baber's time was a place of considerable strength.

The country of the Kaffirs and the districts which adjoin it have also been entered and passed through by many wandering jewellers. One of these individuals had visited Cashgar, beyond Deer; and proceeded thence to the town of Shah Kuttore, under Chitral, and on to Budukhshan, habited as a fakeer, or devotee. He always received bread when he asked for it, but could not with safety have made himself known. The account of this man's journey, and of what he saw during it, is curious. Near a "zyarut," or place of pilgrimage, at Bajour, there is an inscription, of which I have given a sketch: I take it to be old Sanscrit. About

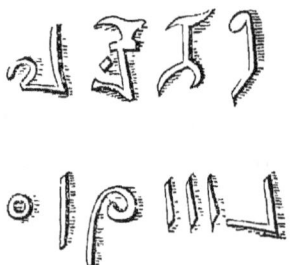

two miles beyond that place is another inscription; and between the village of Deer and Arab Khan, towards Cashgar, there is a third, at a point where the road is cut through the hill for some yards: it commemorates the fame of the engineer. Koteegiram is an ancient place, a day's march from Deer, and two days' journey from Bajour. There is a small idol cut in black stone, and attached to the rock: it is in a sitting posture, about two feet and a half high, and is said to have a helmet on its head, similar to what is seen on the coins from Bajour. It may be a Hindoo figure, for the tribe holds it sacred: but idols are frequently dug up in all parts of this country; and a small one, eight or nine inches high, cut in stone, was brought to me from Swat, which represented a pot-bellied figure, half seated, with crossed arms, and a hand placed on its head. Such idols are also found at a "tope" in the plain of Peshawur; and whether they represent Bacchus, or some less celebrated hero, antiquarians must determine. But to continue the jeweller's rambles. At Cashgar he purchased rock crystal (beloor) from the shepherds, who, in their simplicity, believe it to be the frozen ice of a hundred years! *In situ* a maund of it costs twenty rupees; and he doubled his outlay on returning by making it into seals and armlets. It is exported to China, as buttons for the caps of the Mandarins. From Cashgar he proceeded onwards to Budukhshan, for lapis-lazuli and rubies: on his route, after leaving Cashgar, he crossed the river that passes Chitral, here called Kooner. In three days he came to a hill called "Koh-i-Noogsan," or the hill of injury, down which he slid upon the frozen snow, on a leathern shirt, and came to a bridge, which however was not on the high road.

I was so much pleased with the account of this new and interesting journey, that I prevailed on the man to make a second, and to attend to such instructions as I should give him regarding copies of the inscriptions. One is already given, and I annex another, which he brought from Swat. It

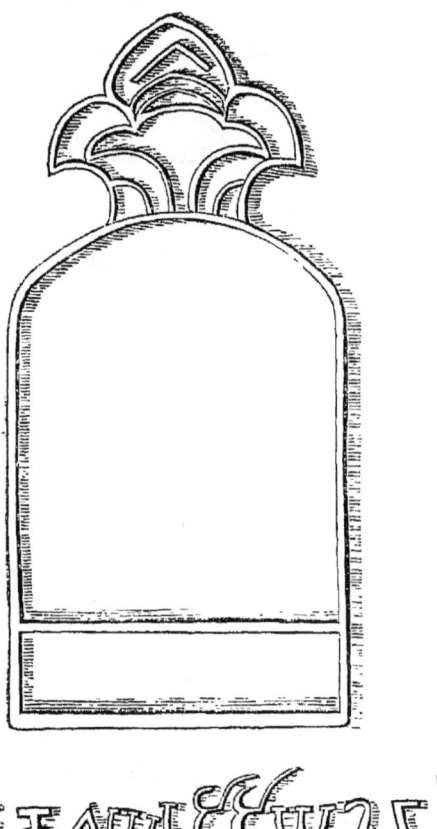

consists of only one line, and is in Pali. The inscriptions, however, of Kupoordeeguree, north of Peshawur, which he also brought, were by far the most valuable: they consisted of five lines; and I should have given a drawing of them had not Mr. Masson subsequently visited that place, cleared away much that hid the stone, and taken a perfect copy of a very extensive inscription which he will doubtless give to the public.

From these quarters, so full of interest, let me carry the reader beyond the mountains, and record a few particulars which were related to me regarding the more remote countries of Cashgar, &c., subject to the Chinese. The town of Cashgar is held by a detachment of Chinese, but the duties leviable at it are received by the Khan of Kokan, who has his Mahomedan officers stationed there. This arrangement has resulted from the late differences between the states; and it is not unlike the usage of the British in India towards their frontier states. The garrison occupies a separate fort, called by the Mahomedans Gool-Bagh, which I understand is a general name for forts similarly occupied. All traffic is carried on inside the Gool-Bagh, none being allowed outside; and each person on entering receives a small piece of wood, which is tied to his waist, and must be returned on coming out. If it is found in the evening that the number of sticks issued does not tally with those received back, the strictest search is instituted. All the houses have bells at their doors, which are rung by a customer before he can get in. The strength of the garrison is about 3000 Chinese, not Toonganees, as I have elsewhere erroneously called the soldiers, whereas such is only the designation of the people of the country, who are Soonees. They live in great fear of their Mahomedan neighbours, although ambassadors have been sent from and to Bokhara and Pekin. There seems, however, to be more communication between Russia and these countries than is generally imagined. Native Russians and Armenians pass through Cashgar to Tibet, and even lower down; but the Chinese arrest the progress of all eastward of Yarkund. Opium finds its way by this route to the centre of the empire, and the trade in it increases annually. It is sent in sticks, and brought, I imagine, from Turkey, through a line of communication that may be improved upon. While such jealousy of others exists, the greatest encouragement is held out to trade in all its branches; and even if a Mahomedan debtor, fleeing from his creditors, takes refuge with the Chinese, he is at once given up, on application to the authorities. The mode of punishing their own culprits is by placing a wooden collar round the neck of the offender, and labelling upon it his crime, and the period for which he is sentenced to wear it. The Chinese neither speak Persian nor Toorkee, and intercourse is carried on by means of interpreters. All dealings in money are made in yamoos or ingots of silver; but a copper coin is current, with a Chinese stamp on one side and a

Mahomedan one on the other. The people of Cashgar itself are composed of Turks and Uzbeks, and visitors also arrive from Tibet and Cashmeer. A Mahomedan acquaintance of mine, who had visited Cashgar, divided its people into three races. First: those who burn their dead; second, those who bury them; and third, those who put their dead in coffins and send them inland : but I imagine the good traveller's distinctions were somewhat fanciful. The climate is described as very dry: rain seldom falls. A phenomenon regarding the harvest, if correctly reported, is singular. Its productiveness, it is said, depends upon the clouds of red dust which always fall or are blown in this part of Asia. The soil is saline, and is said to be benefited by this admixture of foreign earth. The clouds of dust in Toorkistan are tremendous, but I had not heard of their existing to such an extent as here described, and the statement requires confirmation. Another object of curiosity in these parts is the hot sand, about ten miles from Aksoo, on which food can be cooked. I imagine it is the result of some subterraneous heat, such as at Bakou on the Caspian, and other places.

I could gather few particulars of the country of Khoten, lying to the eastward of Cashgar; but I have little reliance on the reports, lately brought from that quarter, of the existence of a Parsee race, flourishing under all the institutions of Zoroaster. I have already given an instance of the rambling propensities of these people, and their hopes of finding traces of their kinsmen among the Kaffirs; but I fear the Parsee community of India must seek for their progenitors elsewhere than in Khoten.

As I have hitherto spoken but briefly of Kokan, the country lying to the west of Cashgar, I will now mention a few particulars regarding it. The power of its chief or khan, Mohamed Ali, is on the ascendant, as he has established his influence over Tashkend, the town of Toorkistan, and all the cultivated country north of Kokan, and over many of the Kuzzak tribes between him and Russia. To the south, the small district of Durwaz is disputed by the Khan and the Mir of Koondooz. There is not much intercourse with Bokhara, but the communication between Kokan and Constantinople is more regular than that of the other states of Toorkistan. The political connection with China leads to an interchange of presents: the Chinese have hitherto sent more valuable gifts than they have received, and all the articles are given in sets of nine, a favourite number among this people. The government is well spoken of, though the Khan, like his brother of Bokhara, is dissipated. A colony of Jews has lately settled in the country, at the towns of Namghan and Marghilan: they pay a poll-tax as Hindoos, and are chiefly engaged in dyeing. Kokan itself, though not nearly so populous as Bokhara, is said to occupy as much ground, its gardens being extensive. Several new bazars and mosques have of late been built, and the town itself lies on both sides of the river Sir, which is fordable above Namghan. There is a very ancient city to the north of it, two days' journey distant, called Choost, which enjoys a fine climate, and from which many antiquities are brought. Kokan is celebrated in Central Asia for three things—a kind of ruby, which was discovered some sixteen or seventeen years ago, but is inferior to that of Budukhshan—the "sung-i-shuftaloo," or plum-stone, so called from resembling that fruit in shape, though its colour is white—and a kind of verdigris: coal also exists in its eastern districts. The country between Kokan and Cashgar is very elevated, and has pine-trees. The road leads by the Osh-i-Sooleeman or Solomon's throne, and the journey is one of twelve days.

Changing the scene of my inquiries, I shall now describe those small states north of Hindoo Koosh, and beyond Balkh, on which our information is defective. These are Maimanu, Andkho, Shibbergam, Siripool, and Akhchu, which are all noted for little but internal quarrels, and being active agents in the slave-trade. They are situated in a plain country, well watered by rills or canals, and having abundance of forage. Near the towns are many gardens: the houses are all of the bee-hive shape. Maimanu is the most important of the whole: the chief is Mizrab Khan, an Uzbek of the tribe of Wun, and his country extends from Maimanu to the Moorghab, and adjoins that of Shere Mahomed Khan Huzara. Maimanu itself is an open town, or rather village, of about 1500 houses; but the strength of the chief consists of his "ils," or moving population, who frequent Umar, Tankira, Sorbagh, Kaffir Khijrabad, Kusur, Chuchakkoo, Tukht-i-Khatoon, and other sites which can scarcely be called villages. He also numbers Arabs among his subjects, many of that tribe having been long settled there. With his whole adherents drawn out he could muster about 6000 horse and three small guns, but he could never quit his territories with half the number, as he is on bad terms with the chief of Siripool, who is much feared, though less powerful. Mizrab Khan is about forty years of age: he succeeded his brother about six years ago, whom he poisoned—a common mode of disposing of people in these countries, and a fate which his own father also met.

Andkho, or Andkhoee, is ruled by Shah Wulee Khan, an Ufshur Toork, who settled here with others of his tribe in the time of Nadir: they were then Shiahs, but are now Soonees. The "ils" of the chief, besides his own race, are Arabs, and he can furnish 500 horse, and is on good terms with Maimanu. Andkho has a larger fixed population than Maimanu, being on one of the high roads to Bokhara, but there is a scarcity of water in this district. It is here that the wheat is a triennial plant. Andkho is the place where poor Moorcroft perished. Shibbergam belongs to an Uzbek chief named Roostum, who has a character for moderation: he can muster 500 or 600 horse, and is on good terms with both Maimanu and Koondooz. Shibbergam is considered to be a very ancient place, being supposed to date from the days of the Kaffirs (Greeks), and is still the strongest fort in these parts. The ark or citadel is built of brick and mortar, and surrounded by other walls of mud. Killich Ali Beg, the late chief of Balkh, besieged it for seven years without success; but it must be understood that it is only strong against Uzbeks, who are badly supplied with artillery. Water is conducted to it from the rivulet of Siripool.

Troolfkar Shere, an Uzbek of the tribe of Achumüillee, governs Siripool, and is known as a brave and determined man. He is on bad terms both with Koondooz and Maimanu; and though he has only 1000 horse, he resists the attacks of both those chiefs, and plunders in all directions. His feud with Maimanu arose on account of his daughter, a wife of the former chief, being seized by Mizrab Khan. His "ils" are in Sungcharuk, Paogeen, Goordewan, and Dughdral; and if he can enlarge their number, which is not improbable, his power will become formidable. Siripool itself is as large as Maimanu.

Akhchu is a dependency of Balkh, and held by a son of Eshan Khoja, the governor of that once vast city: it is consequently tributary to Bokhara. The governor of Balkh, through fear, lately permitted Moorad Beg of Koondooz to establish himself on one of the canals of Balkh; but the king of Bokhara sent a force of 8000 men and dislodged him. Half of this body was raised in Balkh, and the rest from Bokhara. The Koondooz chief offered no resistance to the king.

South of these districts, and between Cabool and Herat, lies the hilly country of the Huzaras, or, as it is called, the Huzarajat. An obscurity* hangs over the settlement of this race among the Afghans; and, without hoping to clear it up, I will place before the reader my notes regarding them.

The Huzaras are distributed as in the following pages, giving the population in round numbers:—

* After all, as the Huzaras are of the Mongolian race and adjoin the Uzbeks, their location in their present site is not very extraordinary: their language, which is Persian, is a more remarkable feature in their history.

		No. of Families.
Dehzungee.		
Buchu Ghoolam	3000	
Yanghoor	4000	
Tukuna	1500	8,500
Sepa		4,000
Dih Koondee.		
Doulut Beg	5000	
Roushun Beg	2500	
Hyder Beg	1500	
Chaoush	1000	
Burat	500	10,500
Dih Choupan, or Zurdaloo, near Kara Bagh.		
Bobuk	1000	
Bihbood	1000	
Aldye	500	
Chardustu	1000	3,500
Tatar and Hubush		1,500
Fouladee, Do.		1,000
Kaloo		750
Toorkmun and Parsa, behind the Pughman Range		750
Shaikh Ali of Ghorbund, half Soonees, half Shiahs		5,000
Bulktiaree, near Ghuzni.		
Allahodeen	750	
Islam	500	
Eeshukee	500	
Kimloot	500	
Shukhu	250	2,500
Jaghoree.		
Boobuk	5000	
Culendur	4000	9,000
Carried forward		47,000

		No. of Families.
Brought forward		47,000
Malistan	2500	
Hoojuriston	2500	
Zoulee	1000	
		6,000
Chukmuk of Gizon, near Candahar		1,200
Paruka		1,200
Behsood, south of Bameean.		
Kulsitan	2000	
Sugpa and Doulutpa	1000	
Durweish Ali	2000	
Junglye	2000	
Bool Hussum	1500	
Boorjugye	1000	
Dihkan	1000	
Dih Murdagan	1000	
		11,500
Grand Total		66,900

The Huzaras of Dihzungee are nearly independent: those of Dih-Koondee altogether so. At Kara Bagh they come down upon the plains beyond Ghuzni, and are subject to Cabool, as are those of Jaghooree, Behsood, and Fouladee. The Tatar and Hubush Huzaras lie between Bamcean and Koondooz. All these are Shiahs, excepting the Huzaras under Herat, and half of those who live in Ghorbund.

The Huzaras state themselves to be descended from two brothers, Sadik Kumr and Sadik Soika, Sadik being a title among them. They are particularly mentioned in the annals of Jingis Khan's wars; and 3000 families are said to have been left by that conqueror, and 1000 by Timourlane. The Huzaras themselves claim descent from the Toghianee Toorks: some, however, of those who live at Dih-Koondee deduce their lineage from a Koresh Arab; others from the Kibtee, a race coeval with the Jews. The Fouladee Huzaras of Hoojuristan are said to be so called from a daughter of Afsariab. The Shekh Ali Huzaras, according to their own account, have been located there from the time of Burbur the Infidel.

The Huzaras are a race of good disposition; but are oppressed by all the neighbouring nations, whom they serve as hewers of wood and drawers of water. Many of them are sold into slavery; and there is little doubt that they barter their children for cloth and necessaries to the Uzbeks. All the drudgery and work in Cabool is done by Huzaras, some of whom are slaves and some free: in winter there are not less than ten thousand who reside in the city, and gain a livelihood by clearing the roofs of snow and acting as porters. They make good servants, but in their native hills their simplicity is great. A Syud, who had been much among them, tells me that, if he bared his head, they did the same. They are fond of music. Their chiefs are called Mirs, and, towards Toorkistan, sometimes Begs: the women of rank are addressed Agha: they go unveiled, and wear two or three loongees on the head, like a tiara. The report which has been spread of their giving their wives to their guests is not true of the race generally; but inquiries have established that it is the practice of some of the Jaghoorees, who are in consequence fast losing their Tartar features. Throughout this tribe a stranger may marry for a night or a week, and either leave his wife or take her along with him; but this is only according to Shiah usages. The property of the Huzaras consists of sheep; and they manufacture from their wool good carpets, and also the fabric called " burruk." Except in the warmer parts of their country, they have few gardens. They are without a chief: had this not been the case they might have become a powerful race, but of this there is now little probability, though they would, if under discipline, make brave and good soldiers.

NOTE.—The following tradition, for which I am indebted to Mr. Leech, is current in Afghanistan regarding the Huzaras:—

"In the time when Balkh, as well as the country now called Hazarajat, was under a Hindoo king called Burbur, (the remains of his imperial city of the same name are still to be seen near Bameean,) he bought a thousand Huzara (slaves), to throw a dam across the river which passed his city of Burbur, which is said to have been fed by 72 streams; but all his dams were carried away. Aly, the son of Aboo Taleeb, called by the Mahomedans Shah i Mardan (the king of men), was one Friday returning from prayers with his cousin Mahomed, the Arabian Prophet, when he was accosted by a beggar, asking for alms in the name of God; Aly answered he had no money, but requested the beggar to sell him. From this proposal the beggar recoiled with religious horror; but, on Aly insisting, he consented. Aly requested him to place his foot on his, and shut his eyes; in a moment the beggar was transported by the Imam to the city and kingdom of Burbur. The beggar took him before the king for sale, who consented to buy him for his weight in gold provided he would perform three acts: 1. Build a dam over the river; 2. Kill a dragon that infested the country; 3. Bring Aly, the cousin of the Prophet, bound before him. This being agreed to, the beggar bore away the enormous price of his benefactor. Hazrat Aly first applied himself to the construction of the dam. Taking with him the thousand slaves of the king, he examined the spot: the mountain through which the river flowed projected over the river; with one stroke of his sword he made a huge cleft, and with his foot precipitated the mass into the stream so dexterously that every drop of the river was stopped from flowing. The slaves fled in terror to the king, and told him of the miracle that had been wrought. The inhabitants, seeing that Aly had done more than they requested, as he had not only saved the city from floods, but had cut off the irrigation of their lands, entreated him to plan a remedy: this he soon effected by a stroke of his hand, the five fingers making five sluice-gates. He afterwards killed the dragon, by jumping on his stomach; and brought a strip of the back for Burbur, as a trophy. The king asked him then to perform the third agreement: Aly requested the attendants to bind him, and discovered himself to Burbur, who was extremely delighted, of course, as he had for some time been plotting a campaign against the same Aly in his own country. As he was about to order him to be conveyed to prison, Aly burst his chains, and, drawing his sword, called upon them to become converts to the true faith. His sword being, like the shield of Achilles, of immortal workmanship, it soon effected the conversion of Burbur and his people. Taking the beggar with him, he returned to Medina, and arrived there three hours after his departure from that city."

CHAPTER X.

Our occupations at Cabool—Visit to "a Country-Gentleman"—His estate—Our party—A Moollah—His ingenuity—Visit to the Mirza—Peculiar science—Summary marriage—Riches a proof of ability—Ladies of Cabool—Employments—Ameer's sisters—A murder and punishment—Courageous female—The Winter season—Lohanee merchants—Cruelty of the King of Bokhara—Horrid dungeons—Acquaintance of Mr. Elphinstone—The Ramazan—Opinions on death—Belief in dreams—Traditions—A Persian envoy—His adventures—Rejoicings—A Bokhara merchant's tea-party.

I turn from distant countries to relate our own occupations at Cabool. During our leisure hours, and when freed from the discussions on politics, which day by day became more energetic and more lengthened, in consequence of the Persians having invested Herat, we made many new acquaintances, and visited our old ones. Among the latter was my Peshawur friend, Naib Mahomed Shureef, who, although a Kuzzilbash, appeared regardless of the dangers which threatened all his tribe from the vicinity of the Persians; and not only regularly visited us at our quarters, but invited us to his country-seat at Kurgha, eight miles from Cabool.* On the 6th of November Lieute-

* The accompanying sketch of Cabool is by Captain H. Wade, of H. M. 13th Regt.

nant Leech and I, gladly escaping from the bustle of the capital, accepted his invitation, and the Nuwab Jubar Khan, an Afghan Moollah, and two or three other persons from neighbouring forts, joined the party. Our host was in high spirits and excessively amusing. He assured us that in winter his estate was the warmest situation in the country, and in summer the coolest: that the view which it commanded of Chardih and Dih Muzung, and the valley lying between it and Cabool, was unrivalled; and if we objected to visit him in spring, when the trees were in blossom, he would tempt us out by saying that in summer the white leaves of the poplar rustling looked like buds; and that in winter the snow, as it fell in flakes on the trees, was not to be surpassed in beauty even by the peach-blossoms of Istalif. The house, indeed, was very agreeably situated, and commanded a charming prospect, being the reverse of the one which is seen from the Tomb of Baber, as that celebrated spot terminates the valley. The broad acres of the proprietor, which he told us had cost him upwards of a lac of rupees, were spread out before us; whilst, equidistant from us and Cabool, lay, in our rear, the fine valley of Pughman. Our host placed before us an abundant breakfast of kabobs, nicely served up, to which we did the amplest

justice, and whiled away the rest of the morning in listening to his discussions on a vast variety of subjects, for he was a professed talker. He gave us a detail of his numerous ailments, and his unsuccessful search after a cure for them, until he found it in wine, which he pronounced to be a specific for all earthly maladies. The Moollah, in some long Arabic sentences, protested strenuously against the use of such unholy medicine: upon which Shureef quietly asked if he expected him to refrain from a remedy when he had one in his power, and such a remedy too!—and then launched out in praise of a particular vintage which he and his brother had gathered in some years before. He then, with many a sigh, related how he had broken all the bottles of this matchless wine, for grief on account of that brother's death; and how well it was remembered by every man who had partaken of it, "Since two glasses of it set one asleep!" As the Naib appealed to me for my opinion on the subject, I told him that "Our notions of good wine consisted in being able to drink much without experiencing any bad effects." "A bad plan," said he; "for a man then must drink till he is as large as a butt: no, no, ours is the best test." The curiosity of the Moollah being aroused by this discussion, he begged I would prescribe for him something to improve his digestion, which all the party forthwith construed into a wish for wine, and great was the mirth which this gave rise to. The Moollah, being put upon his mettle, now turned his batteries of religion upon us, and poured out quotation upon quotation in praise of temperance and water-drinking, until he fairly beat us out of the field. Dinner, or rather lunch, was spread before us at about three o'clock, and we returned to Cabool much pleased with our party. Naib Shureef I may fairly designate as an Afghan country-gentleman. He goes to his villa in spring and summer, feeds his own sheep, cattle, and poultry; has a small village on his estate peopled by Huzaras, who assist him in his agricultural pursuits; burns lime on his own ground to repair his house; and has enclosed a large tract of ground, and planted it with fruit-trees which now produce abundantly. In this garden is the largest willow-tree known in the country, called, *par excellence*, "Mujnoon bed," beneath which he often seats his friends.

At Kurgha I observed the sheep turned in upon the young wheat-fields, and allowed to crop them. The water is first let in upon the land to freeze, and the flocks then browse upon the leaves, without injuring the plants, which indeed are said to grow up stronger in spring in consequence of the process.

The orchards also were receiving their last irrigation, or, as it is called, "yuhkcheeab,"—ice-watering,—for by the first of November all the pools are frozen over.

On my return I had a visit from an acquaintance, Moollah Khodadad, who had been absent from the city for a short time settling the harvest revenue. He amused me by recounting the mode he had adopted to escape from being the political representative of Dost Mahomed Khan, an honour for which he had been singled out in consequence of his great abilities. It seems that, after the last battle with the Sikhs, Kooshal Sing, one of their officers, addressed the Ameer, suggesting the propriety of his sending a man of rank and knowledge to Peshawur to adjust their differences; and Khodadad was the fortunate wight selected, he not being in Dost Mahomed's service, nor knowing anything about it. A whisper reached him, he repaired to the Bala Hissar, and the friend who sat next him told him, in Afghanee, "that they had prepared a pannier (kujawa) for him," meaning that he was to be sent on a journey. Dost Mahomed conversed at large on what ought to be done; and, at length, looking to the Moollah, but without making any allusion to his having been fixed upon as his representative, said that some *proper* person should be sent. "You look towards me," said the wary Moollah; "shall I say what I think?" "Certainly." "Well, then," said Khodadad, "you have received a letter, and for it you propose to send an Elchee,—a reply to a letter should be a letter: besides, if any one is sent to Peshawur, the people will look upon it as springing from fear." Some of the courtiers loudly reprobated these arguments, declaring that they were founded in ignorance. "How many jars of water are in the fountain before you?" asked Khodadad. The courtiers all declared they did not know. "But I do," said the Moollah. The Ameer desired him to state how many there were. "That, my lord," he replied, "entirely depends on the size of the jar employed to measure it." This indirect allusion to the want of comprehension in his associates amused the Ameer and nettled them. The discussion was broken off, and the deputation to the Sikh camp postponed *sine die*. It was only a few months after he had got out of this dilemma that the Moollah was actually nominated as Elchee to proceed to the court of Moorad Beg of Koondooz. "Look at my fortune," said he, with facetious gravity as he told me the story: "first they were going to send me to a Hindoo, and then to a robber; to make up for it, however, they styled me, in my credentials, 'of high rank, great fame, place, wealth,' and heaven knows what. Well, I thought I could make something of all this, so I went once more to the Bala Hissar, to converse with the Ameer. I observed to him that, if such titles and rank and glory were assigned to me, I had better be provided with equipages, attendants, and rich clothing, suitable for so great a man: for, as to myself, I had none of them; and that, if I went without them, the wise men of Koondooz would soon find out the contradictions between what I was and what I was said to be. I should be deemed an impostor, and his Highness's business would fare but badly." Dost Mahomed, it appears, had no reply to make to the erudite Khodadad; and therefore sent a certain Kumber Ali Khan in his stead, who, being a Kuzzilbash Shiah, was but scurvily treated at the Koondooz court. I warned my friend the Moollah not to be too confident: he had twice escaped, but the third appointment might be fatal; and I predicted that, in spite of all his ingenuity, he would yet find himself his country's representative abroad. It will be seen from this long story that the honour of being an ambassador, so much sought after in Europe, has not the same attraction in Asia. If, as it has been said, envoys are but clever men sent abroad to lie for their country, we might be disposed to applaud the Moollah's modesty and unconquerable love of truth; but the fact is, that there is here little reward attached to the rank, and still less honour. An ambassador is, however, almost always certain of good treatment; and there is a proverb among the Afghans which enjoins it.

The Mirza of Dost Mahomed Khan, hearing that we had so greatly enjoyed our visit to Kurgha, invited us to pass the day at his fort, which was called Nanuchee, and was situated about three miles from Cabool to the north-west, and on the verge of the "chumun" or meadow of Wuzeerabad. The scene differed in all its features from the one which we had beheld at our good friend Shureef's villa. Above the fort are the remains of a garden laid out by the Begum or queen of Juhangeer, which commands a glorious view of the lake and the surrounding country, and is, perhaps, the most picturesque in the vicinity. From a hillock which is still higher than this garden, the eye commands at once the plains of Chardih and Wuzeerabad, which the Afghans call Goolistan and Bostan. A nobler and more enchanting position for a residence can scarcely be imagined. Its selection does honour to the Begum, whose name, however, is lost in history. From the tomb of Baber to this garden is a favourite ride with the *beau monde* of the capital, who are wont first to visit the one and then the other, drink wine at both, and return to Cabool by the "chumun." Our day with the Mirza sped merrily. We had Hafizjee, the son of Meer Thacez, Imam Terdi, a clever man, and several other Afghans; and there was much general conversation in a quiet way. As we sat at the windows and looked out upon the extended prospect, the sun every now and then was hid by clouds; and as their shadows moved across the distant hills, our friends repeatedly exclaimed, "What 'Sultanut!' what majesty in nature!" with an enthusiasm which would have done honour to European tourists. I must not forget to mention that on this occasion I was asked as to my knowledge and belief in a science, which is called "Kiafa" by the Afghans, and which seems to be something between phrenology and physiognomy: not only the eyebrows, nose, and features generally, but even the beard, form the discriminating marks, instead of the bumps of the skull, as with our sapient professors, and the result of experience is recorded in sundry pithy axioms, such as the following:—A tall man with a long beard is a fool. A man with a beard issuing from his throat is a simpleton. An open forehead bespeaks wealth and plenty. The science is further developed in various couplets, some of the most curious of which may thus be rendered:—

He that has red eyes is ever ready to fight: And who has thick lips is a warrior.

Hope for liberality from him whose arms are long: And fear not the courage of one with a thick waist.

Men of small stature are often deceitful: And so are those with deep-seated eyes and thin noses.

Those who have soft hair are of good disposition: But those whose locks are hard are otherwise.

Open nostrils are proofs of a tyrant: And large teeth of little wisdom.

Large ears give hopes of long life: And spare ankles of activity in the race.

The man who has the arch of the foot large cannot walk far: But the flattened sole tires not.

Having thus treated not only of the features of the face, but of nearly all the limbs of the body, I must lay aside the science of "Kiafa," trusting that no one of my readers will find any of the unfavourable symptoms applicable to himself.*

Not far from our residence in the Bala Hissar lived Syud Mohsun, a man of some influence among the Huzaras, who used frequently to visit us, and tell us strange stories of that simple people. The unexpected honour of marrying a Princess, and becoming brother-in-law of the Ameer of Cabool,

* A brief tract on this science seemed to me deserving of translation; and I have accordingly given it in illustration of the modes of thinking on this subject among the Afghans.—Vide Appendix.

had fallen upon him. Dost Mahomed, after he had allied himself to the family of Shah Zada Ablas, was afraid lest his wife's sister should marry any of his nobles, and determined that the lady should be united to a holy man: he accordingly sent for the Syud to his haram, whither he had already summoned the Cazee, and without previously informing either party, forthwith proceeded to join them in holy wedlock. The Syud at first refused, and declared that the honour was too great. This objection the Ameer removed by assuring him "That his fortune had predominated!" "But," insisted the involuntary bridegroom, "I am a poor man, and cannot afford to clothe a Princess!" "Never mind, never mind!" replied Dost Mahomed, "I will do that for you;" and married they accordingly were. And now the Syud sorrowfully declares that he is not master of his own house. Two slave girls from the Huzara country attend this fair scion of royalty; and the poor man declares that he himself is but an upper servant. Such marriages are common in these countries, since Syuds and other ministers of religion, when allied to females of royal blood, can do less political harm than other persons. At all events there was not much regal dignity in some of the occupations of Syud Mohsun and his illustrious wife, seeing that they prepared the best jelly which I tasted in Cabool, made from the sour cherry, or gean.

Talking one day with Jubar Khan, the name of Hufa Begum, the celebrated queen of Shah Shoojah, who had just died, was mentioned, and a remark was made that she was a very clever woman, and had left a good deal of money behind her. "That," said the Nuwab, with grave emphasis, "is the clearest possible proof of her ability." I fear this is a standard by which the ladies of the Western world have no wish to be tried. Both the Nuwab and his brother the ruler have, however, credit for managing their ladies economically. The Nuwab, generous to a fault to Christian, Jew, or Mahomedan, is blamed for denying to his wives liberal pin-money, or, as it is amusingly called in this country, "Soorkhee-sufeedee," rouge and white paint allowance, with both which cosmetics the ladies here adorn themselves.

But I must not thus lightly pass over so important a part of the population of Cabool as the ladies. Their ghost-like figures when they walk abroad make one melancholy; but if all be true of them that is reported, they make ample amends when withindoors for all such sombre exhibitions in public. There, during the long winters, they gather round the "Sundlee," a kind of low square table, covered with cloth, and heated from below by charcoal, and tell stories and make merry. They have a saying that the indoor joys of Cabool in winter make every one regardless of the enemy without. Among the Afghans, women exercise considerable influence at least: Dost Mahomed Khan, at a time when he was very anxious as to the conduct of his brothers at Candahar, addressed a letter to his sister, who was there also, and urged her to keep them in the proper course; thus proving that even in important matters of state their judgment and discretion are resorted to. A circumstance, however, occurred while we were at Cabool, which proved that one at least of Dost Mahomed's sisters was not a paragon of virtue. Sudoo Khan Barukzye, to whom she was married, was shot through the body on returning home at night. The assassin was secured; and, horrible to relate, confessed that the Chief's sister had bribed him to commit the deed. The princess fled to the house of a relation, and unblushingly justified her conduct, on the ground that she had been long barbarously used by her husband. The truth of this was not doubted, for he was well known to be a most depraved wretch: still nothing could justify so inhuman a retribution. The wounded man lingered for a day, and his murderer passed into eternity a few hours after him, having been cut in two pieces, one of which was gibbeted at the Gate of the Bala Hissar, the other in the great Bazar. A butcher was the executioner. The lady, whose guilt was at least equal, escaped without punishment; for the Mahomedan can only shed the blood of him by whom man's blood has been shed. There are, however, women in these countries who have pre-eminently distinguished themselves by their conjugal devotion; and I should do wrong were I to pass over in silence Aga, the lady of Yezdan Bukhsh, a Huzara chief, whom Dost Mahomed Khan detained at Cabool as a hostage for her lord. The separation was painful to both; but particularly to the husband, who was accustomed, in all his difficulties, to be guided by the counsel of his wife; and he secretly sent messengers to her, urging her to make her escape. This she effected by changing her attire to that of a man, and dropping from the window of her prison. She then mounted a horse and fled to the Besoot country, between Cabool and Bamecan, pursued by two of the Ameer's officers, accompanied by some of her husband's enemies. She was overtaken; her companion was killed, but she herself escaped, and reached the first fort in her own country, from the walls of which she defied her pursuers, proudly exclaiming, "This is the land of Yezdan Bukhsh!" This noble woman's husband was afterwards, as Mr. Masson has related, barbarously strangled by Hajee Khan Kakur. The simplicity of his disposition ruined him, as it has done many of his countrymen; and, after having conducted the Afghans through a dangerous campaign, his life was basely taken.

I have already stated that the water froze so early as the beginning of November, and that snow fell on the hills; but on the 11th of December, after it had gradually stolen upon us, inch by inch, it at length fairly covered the ground in the city, and dusky grey clouds hid the sun. The cold became severe, and the whole of the population appeared clad in sheep-skins. It was a serious affair to our Hindoostanee attendants, and two of them fell victims to the folly of persevering in their Indian habits, and cooking their food outside the house in defiance of the rigours of the climate. They died of pneumonia, a disease which is very prevalent in Cabool, and from which, without very active treatment, few recover.

With the snow came the last caravan of merchants from Bokhara, principally composed of Lohanees. A party of these men paid me a visit, and after telling me all the news of that quarter, implored me to use my influence in their behalf, as they had most inconsiderately involved themselves in a serious difficulty. It appeared that after passing Bameean they had struck off from the legitimate route, if I may so term it, and made at once for Ghuzni, which lay on the direct road to their homes. But a poor government cannot afford to lose its taxes; and they were arrested at that town by the Ameer's son, who seized all their property, amounting to 6000 ducats and 4000 tillas of Bokhara. On this the government had a claim of one per cent., but the whole was confiscated; and Dost Mahomed quoted, in his defence for so doing, the usage of the British and Russians, who seize upon all smuggled goods. This argument by no means satisfied the poor merchants; and although I exerted all my personal influence in their behalf, it was only after long and vexatious delay that they obtained restitution of a quarter of their money, and orders on the custom-houses, payable in the ensuing year, for a further portion, which latter, I fear, they never received. The cash which the ruler had thus possessed himself of again changed masters in a few days, being stolen by his treasurer, whose line of argument, in defence of his conduct, was that his pay was in arrear. Dost Mahomed, however, did not relish this imitative spirit; and the treasurer was apprehended and about to be put to death, when the Nuwab, ever active on the side of mercy, said he ought to be pardoned; that so bad a man as he was ought never to have been trusted, and that great part of the blame rested upon those who had employed him. This reasoning had its effect, and he was dismissed with a sound drubbing.

The Lohanees described the king of Bokhara as having become tyrannous and headstrong: he had degraded his minister, the Koosh Begee, and had refused the Hindoos leave to burn their dead, because, on being asked their creed, they had said they were "Ibrahamees," or followers of Abraham. He had also, without any show of reason, caused all Mahomedans trading with Hindoo partners to be doubly taxed. Having discovered an intrigue between a baker's daughter and a Hindoo, he ordered both parties to be baked in the oven, although in his own person he held out the worst possible example to his subjects. It is, however, to be doubted if he is altogether in his senses. His acts of tyranny are so audacious and so numerous, that I have never ceased to congratulate myself at having passed so successfully through his kingdom. In espionage he appears even to surpass the Chinese. From these men I received an account of the horrid dungeons in Bokhara, known by the title of "Kuna-Khanu," Kuna being the name of the creatures which attach themselves to dogs and sheep (Anglicè, ticks), and which here thrive on the unhappy human beings who are cast in among them. The dungeons abound also in scorpions, fleas, and all kinds of vermin; and if human subjects happen to be deficient, goats or the entrails of animals are thrown in to feed them: so that the smell alone is in the highest degree noxious. One day suffices to kill any criminal who is cast into these horrid dens, and a confinement of a few hours leaves marks which are never effaced in after life. The situation of the dungeons is below the ark or citadel in which the king resides.

One of the traders to Bokhara was the Moollah Nujeeb, an old friend of Mr. Elphinstone's, and to whom, through the influence of that gentleman, a pension has been granted by our government. I had many conversations with Nujeeb, who was never weary of enlarging on the talents and virtues of his patron, or in expressing his admiration of what he denominated "the greatness of the English nation." It appears that when his pension was first conferred upon him he wrote to Mr. Elphinstone, to know "what kind of political information was expected from him in return." Mr. Elphinstone told him in reply, that "he wished occasionally to hear from him as to the state of his eyes, and that he hoped the spectacles he had given him enabled him to see better."

This indifference to passing events, and still more, this renunciation of what throughout all Asia is considered as the grand and legitimate mode of obtaining political information, had sunk deep into Nujeeb's mind, and again and again did he advert to this *surprising* proof of " the greatness of the English nation." There is certainly a striking difference between the avowed system of morals of the Afghans and the Europeans. The former seem to consider anything that is done amiss in secret as nothing; and it is only when discovery follows crime that they regret its commission. Their standard of morality would appear to consist, not in avoiding error, but in avoiding its discovery; and it is a common expression with them, that " Such a one was my friend: he did not take the screen from my misconduct." It was not wonderful, therefore, that the Moollah should consider it the acmé of morality in his patron not to ask him to offend even secretly against the state under which he was living.

The Ramazan, which had commenced with December, was rigidly kept. A gun was fired long before dawn, to rouse the faithful from their slumbers, that they might eat before the crier announced the hour of prayer. This fasting had blanched the cheeks of many of my visitors; and observing this, I asked one of them, a Moollah, "If it was not a severe penance?" he replied, "No: I am a mere worm, addicted to food; and hence the change which you remark in my countenance." Having upon this incidentally observed, that "All of us would shortly become food for worms," the holy man expressed his unbounded admiration of this trite truth. I, in my turn, was pleased with an expression which he used when I asked him if he had any children. "Two," was his reply; "the rest have gone before me." There was a tranquil sorrow and a simplicity in his manner of saying these few words which struck me greatly.

Death and futurity form a frequent subject of conversation among the Afghans, as indeed they do with all nations. On one occasion I was much interested by the discourse of an old merchant, who visited me shortly after he had lost his daughter. In the failure of all medical treatment, he had, a few days before her dissolution, removed her from her husband's house to his own, in the hope that the air and the climate in which she had been born and reared might restore sinking nature. It was the will of God that it should be otherwise, and the spirit of his child fled whilst she was repeating some lines from "Musnumee," a philosophical poem, which he had taught her in early youth. The last lines she uttered related to eternity. The parent assured me that many circumstances which had occurred subsequently to her death had afforded him consolation and reconciled him to his loss. One of his neighbours had dreamed that this beloved daughter was remarried, and in great prosperity. He himself had dreamt that his forefathers had sent for his daughter, and were overjoyed at receiving her. Other circumstances had occurred of a soothing nature: the shroud in Mahomedan countries is tied at the head, and when the body is deposited in the earth it is opened, that the relatives may take the last look and turn the head towards Mecca. In the case of this young woman, it was found that the face was already turned in the right direction. The priest who had been reading the Koran over the grave had fallen asleep, and dreamed that the deceased had declared herself overjoyed at the happy change. I found that the narrative of all these circumstances received the most serious attention, and thus dreams and omens working on the father's mind had yielded him consolation; and why should we deny peace of mind to an afflicted parent by seeking to destroy their effect?

The Afghans place implicit reliance on dreams. A Moollah of Cabool once told me that "Dreams are the soul in flight without the body; and," added he, "physicians may say, if it please them, that they arise from digestive derangement, but no such paradise could spring from causes so material. It is in dreams that we find the clearest proof of an Omnipotent Providence."

There are many other superstitions among these people, and almost every hill in the country has its legend attached to it. A village near Cabool bears the name of "Chihil-Dookhteran," or the Forty Daughters; and tradition runs that, on one occasion, when the Kaffirs from the mountains made an inroad on the plain, forty virgins were preserved from violence by being transformed into stones; and that the identical forty stones are visible to this day. Eastward of this same village lies the "Koh-i-Krook," or hunting preserve of the kings of Cabool: a miraculous tale is connected with this ground. The story goes, that in days of yore a certain king pressed a herd of deer in this very preserve so closely that they rushed straight to his seraglio, where his lovely queens and ladies were adorning themselves in fine apparel, and putting rings into their ears and noses, and set them all running wild over the country. The Afghans, it will be perceived, are not deficient in the imaginative faculties, and they may be quoted as a proof that invention precedes judgment.

But to return to the things of the earth and its inhabitants as we now find them. On the 14th of December I received a visit from my quondam fellow-traveller, Mahomed Hoosan, who had since been the Elchee from the chief of Cabool to the king of Persia; from which country he had returned, bringing with him a Persian ambassador, whom he had left at Candahar, whilst he himself came on to Cabool to report progress. The Elchee had gone to Persia to sue for an alliance, but he had experienced nothing but disappointment and neglect. I laughed heartily at the man's adventures, which, although they had been very far from agreeable, he detailed with infinite gaiety and humour. He narrowly escaped death at Soonee Bokhara, merely because he had sought to bring about an alliance with Shiah Persia: at the court of the Shah the ministers had tried to poison him for telling the plain truth, that an army and guns would be useless in opposing the roving Toorkumuns, against whom his majesty had proceeded; and at the capital the royal favour was altogether denied him because he had gone to the English ambassador's quarters, instead of those tardily assigned to him by an unfriendly minister. In

Persia difficulties had beset him at every step. Once before he had been obliged to leave the country, and now, after a nine years' absence, his enemies again rose up against him, but here his ambassadorship saved him. In his journey back to Afghanistan he had been exposed to many perils, whilst pursuing the unfrequented route through Bum-Nurmansheer and Seistan to the river Helmund, down which he was carried three fursukhs by a flood, and was left for two days without food. Near Herat he was threatened by Kamran, as well as by robbers; at Candahar the Sirdars slighted him; and, the unkindest cut of all, Dost Mahomed would send no one to conduct the ambassador whom my unfortunate friend had brought with so much trouble and difficulty from the "centre of the universe." Such was the tissue of complaints which he poured forth, calling the chief of Cabool a knave, his courtiers no men, and the whole nation a mass of Afghan stupidity. He said that at the Persian court Mirza Aghassee was supreme, owing to his having made some lucky guesses, during the youth of the present Shah, regarding his accession to the throne.

The worst of all poor Mahomed Hoosan's misfortunes was, that, having once been an Elchee, he did not deem himself at liberty to walk as a common man in the bazaar; and thus his dignity had destroyed his comfort. I told him that he had nothing else for it but to follow the European model, and write his travels; or, in Indian phrase, "Take walk and write book." He took my advice, and some time afterwards presented me with a small volume full to overflowing of unique adventures. He had ample leisure for his literary labours, as he was all but confined to his house by the Ameer; and although he declared positively that he would perform no further service, nor have anything more to do with embassies, he still lived in perpetual terror of being called upon to *accept office*, and punished, he knew not to what extent, if he refused to do so. He told me a story of a man whose misfortunes, he said, resembled his own. A certain king quarrelled with his vizier, and ordered him to be kept in confinement; to cheer his solitude, however, he sent him a companion. The vizier began to read the Koran aloud, with great gravity and emphasis, and his visitor began to cry. "What may be the particular passage," asked the minister, "that excites you so much, my good friend?" The simple-hearted man replied, "Oh, my Lord, when I look at you reading, and see your beard moving, I think of a favourite goat I have got at home; and then I remember that I am obliged to attend on your highness, and am shut out from all my domestic comforts." "Thus," said the Elchee, "it is with me and the Afghans. I am amongst them against my will; and it would be less irksome to me to pound the nine mountains in a mortar, or to circumambulate the globe a dozen times, than to continue here."

On the 29th of December the "eed" terminated at midnight. A man ran in from the Kohistan, and swore, before the Cazee, that he had seen the moon twenty-nine days ago, whereas this was but the twenty-eighth day of its age. Not a moment was lost in proclaiming the joyful news and the end of the fast; salutes were fired at the dead of night, the people yelled and shouted, and I started out of bed, believing, at the very least, that the city was sacked.

During the festivities that followed, Budro Deen, the great Bokhara merchant, invited us to dinner, and entertained us with singers, and with the "suntoor," a triangular musical instrument with innumerable wires, an importation from Cashmere which I had not before seen. The Nuwab Jubar Khan was present, as well as several other persons. The dinner was well arranged and excellent, and we had songs in many languages. The Pooshtoo is softer when sung than when spoken; but Hindoostanee is the favourite language with the Afghans, having, to use their own phrase, "more salt in it."

After dinner the hospitable Bokhara merchant dilated on the good qualities of his tea, and insisted on giving it to us in the real orthodox style. He accordingly commenced operations, stirred the fire almost out, and placed the kettle upon it, but for a long time he could not manage to make it boil. At last, when he had succeeded, he put the tea into the pot, covered the lid with a cloth, and, not satisfied with this, planted the teapot itself in the fire, as he had done the kettle, and finally produced a beverage which certainly was of a superior quality, and which we all drank of, and praised to his heart's content. The Nuwab drank away at a great rate, and declared that he had never before taken so much. The man of tea, however, urged us on to further indulgence, telling us that at Bokhara, which is the fountain of tea, the repast always concluded with "tulkh chah," or tea without sugar. The good Nuwab declared "He would not drink tea without sugar; that it was impossible for him to drink any more with it, and doubly impossible for him to drink any more without it." We all laughed loud and long at this sally, and returned to our homes at a brisk trot, through the quiet city, under a clear sky and frosty night, much pleased with our party and with our host.

CHAPTER XI.

Russian agent, Lieutenant Vilkievitch—Distribution of our party—Vicinity of Cabool—Pillars of Chukreea—Mr. Masson's researches—Ancient history of Cabool—Idols and Hindoo remains—Gurdez—Geographical memoirs—Dialects—Herat—Major Pottinger—Delay in Indian courts—Kuzzilbash secretaries—A Moollah's tenets—Mode of lighting houses—Mild Winter—Early Spring—Idle habits—The Ameer's position—Change of policy—My departure from Cabool—Arrival at Jelálábád—River of Cabool—Our rafts—The Shutee Gurdun—Peshawur—Arrival at Lahore—Runjeet Sing—Join the Governor-General at Simla.

In the midst of these amusements the arrival of a Russian officer produced a considerable sensation at Cabool: almost immediately on his entering the city "le Lieutenant Vilkievitch Polonois" paid me a visit, and on the day after his arrival, which happened to be Christmas-day, I invited him to dinner. He was a gentlemanly and agreeable man, of about thirty years of age, and spoke French, Turkish, and Persian fluently, and wore the uniform of an officer of Cossacks, which was a novelty in Cabool. He had been three times at Bokhara, and we had therefore a common subject to converse upon, without touching on politics. I found him intelligent and well informed on the subject of Northern Asia. He very frankly said that it was not the custom of Russia to publish to the world the result of its researches in foreign countries, as was the case with France and England. I never again met Mr. Vilkievitch (or, as I see it written, Vicovich), although we exchanged sundry messages of "high consideration;" for I regret to say that I found it to be impossible to follow the dictates of my personal feeling of friendship towards him, as the public service required the strictest watch, lest the relative positions of our nations should be misunderstood in this part of Asia.

The state of affairs at Candahar rendered it advisable for me to depute Lieutenant Leech to proceed to that city; and he accordingly set out on the 28th of December, taking the route of the far-famed Ghuzni, and was one of the first who beheld the tomb of the Sultan Mahmood, and the two lofty minarets of that fallen city. He performed the journey to Candahar without difficulty in about fourteen days. I now found myself alone in Cabool, all my companions being scattered in different directions, and all favourably situated for increasing our knowledge of the country, and furthering the objects of the mission. I felt that I had cause to rejoice at the good fortune which had placed it in our power to accomplish so much. In addition to our own labours, I had, with a view to increase our antiquarian stores, despatched a messenger, a Syud, into Toorkistan, with directions to proceed by Balkh and Shibargam to Bokhara, thence to Samarcand, Kokan, and Cashgar, and to return, if possible, by Pameer and Koondooz. The first portion of this journey he performed with success; and transmitted to me some valuable coins of Bactria, which now, under Professor Wilson's guardianship, occupy a place in the Museum at the India House, and I yet hope to receive the result of the Syud's further labours.

But the vicinity of Cabool itself, now that we could ramble about it with safety, afforded many objects of interest. On the further side of the Logur River, and about seven miles S.E. of Cabool, are the topes which Dr. Honigberger opened in 1834. These I visited, and saw the two pillars, or, as they are called, minarets, of Chukreea, which I believe have not hitherto been described. One of these is built on a spur of rock, in a ravine immediately over a "tope," the position of which it may be supposed to have marked. Another stands on the crest of the mountain, about two miles distant, and is an object so conspicuous, that it may be seen with the naked eye from the city of Cabool. The lower one is about forty feet high, and built of solid stone, without any access to the interior. These buildings are evidently not minarets, but more probably of a monumental nature. The whole ravine in which the lower one is situated is marked with the ruins of Kaffir forts, and three hundred yards higher up than the pillar is an unopened "tope." Mr. Masson has done so much for this branch of discovery, and has exhumed so many gold boxes, cylinders, and coins, that I will not trouble my readers with any crude speculations of my own on a subject which is now undergoing so strict a scrutiny in Europe. Beyond the greater pillar is an old town called Aeenuck, of which tradition has many tales.

The ancient history of Cabool itself is unsatisfactory. The people themselves refer you to Noah's two sons, Cakool and Habool, as the founders of their race, who, they say, quarrelled about the name of the place, and at length agreed to form it by taking a syllable from each name,—hence Ca-bool. The Hindoos assert that the ruler who was overthrown by the Mahomedans, and known by the name of "Urj," was fourth in descent from Vikramjeet, but no history brings Vikram so near our time as this. Urj is said by some to have been a Gubr, or fire-worshipper, and to have had two brothers, Silur and Toor: he is also sometimes named Cabool Shah. At Cabool I met with the following passage in a work * which treats of its conquest by the Mahomedans, who state it to have been under their rule for 1240 years:—

"The army marched and encamped before Cabool. Cabool Shah, also well known by the name of Urj, came out to meet the Mahomedan force, commanded by Abdool Ruhman, and, having fought a very severe battle, returned to the city and never again left it. Abdool Ruhman fought with the besieged for a whole year, and encountered great hardships in taking the citadel (hissar), but at last took it by the sword, slaying many soldiers and capturing their wives and children. Cabool Shah, the king, was brought a prisoner before the general, who ordered him to be put to death on the spot; but he read the Mahomedan Creed (Kuluma), and became a Moslem, when Abdool Ruhman honoured him highly. Abdool Ruhman then ordered all the booty of Cabool and Sejistan to be brought forth: one-fifth of this plunder he sent home by his servant Ameer, with a letter announcing his victory." Oriental historians further describe Cabool as one of seven cities built by Hushung, son of Syamuk, son of Kyamoors; the other six being Tabris-

---

* Rid wu ruwafiz.

tan, Isfahan, Old Merve, Babool, Candahar, and Mudayar. The extract I have given goes to prove the Hissar, or Bala Hissar, of Cabool, to be a far more ancient edifice than the time of the Chaghties or their Mahomedan predecessors. Modern Cabool is given to the days of Sultan Mahmood, but the ancient city is said to have stood on the same hills as those on which the present one is built, only to the south of the citadel, and where the Armenian and other burying-grounds now are. In a country where earthquakes are so frequent we need not be surprised at finding no remains of ancient architecture: there are not four substantial houses in the present town, and, if any accident happened to it, few traces would remain to later ages. In the locality pointed out as that of the ancient city, many colossal idols are dug up: they are of mud with a coating of red paint, and fall to pieces on the touch; bits of them were frequently brought to me. These relics carry us back, without doubt, to the Hindoo age. The coins found in and about Cabool have Hindoo devices on them, yet, in the face of this evidence, many of the modern inhabitants of that caste will tell you that their emigration from India took place at no very remote date. Whilst we were in Cabool an earthen vessel filled with silver coins, all of one type, was disinterred at

Shukurduru, in Koh-damun. Mr. Prinsep calls these coins Indo-Sussanian, and he deciphered the Pehlevi Sanscrit legends upon them.* But throughout all this country there are Hindoo remains. At Ali Musjid, in Khyber, when they were erecting a new fort, they dug up a small tablet of red stone three inches square, on which was sculptured a group of four persons and two deer, surrounding a seated figure: the style of its execution was good. I imagine that the principal personage represented is Boodh, a scarf being thrown over the left shoulder, as in the figures at Bamiàn: the ears were pendent and the tiara large. Gurdez is always referred to as a place of antiquity in Cabool, and is still of some importance, the fortification being built of huge stones, with a deep ditch. Between it and Ghuzni there are the ruins of a large town, called Khurwar, which seems to have stood on an extensive plain, like Begram, and from this place also many coins were procured.

I was not fortunate enough to find any written records regarding Cabool, nor does it appear that any such exist. In my search, however, I obtained some curious works on the geography of this and the neighbouring countries. One of these, styled

* Vide Mr. Prinsep's Journal for May, 1838.

"Moosalik ure Moomalish," had twenty-one manuscript maps in it, accompanied by chapters containing detailed descriptions. Another called the "Juma ool insab," and which was brought from Balkh, gave a minute and curious account of that ancient city. A third, the "Ujuib ool tubukat," was compiled from eight other works, chiefly relating to subjects of geography. All these I forwarded to the Geographical Society of Bombay, an institution which from its position is peculiarly calculated to follow out such inquiries; but, indeed, it is impossible that any Oriental society, whatever its specified objects may be, should be indifferent to the literature of men "whose emulation diffused the taste and the rewards of science from Samarcand and Bokhara to Fez and Cordova."

In the absence of historical truth we sought, with redoubled interest, to obtain a knowledge of the language and dialects of this country. To these a very valuable and detailed memorandum sent by General Court, and, I believe, received from the lamented M. Jacqueb, at Paris, directed our attention and assisted us greatly. Of the specimens of the Kaffir and Pushye dialects I have already spoken. Lieutenant Leech undertook the preparation of vocabularies and grammars of most of the languages to the west of the Indus, the Brahooee, Beloochee, Punjaubee, and Pooshtoo, together with the Burukee, Lughmanee, Cashgaree, &c. The language of the Brahooees was found to differ essentially from that of the Beloochees. The Burukee or Kanigramee, spoken by the people of Logur, has an affinity to Persian, although those using it claim a descent from Arabia, and assert that they entered the country with Sultan Mahmood. The dialects of Lughman, Cashgar, and Deer, as well as the Pushye, are found to be cognate with languages of Sanscrit origin and Hindoo stock. The Arabs of Cabool have altogether lost their native language: this is also the case with the Calmucks introduced from Northern Asia, although the kings of Cabool at one time gave great encouragement to that race, and were accustomed to make them a present of a sum of money on the birth of each child.

But to proceed to other matters. The gallant struggle made for the independence of Herat by the Afghans, guided by our able and courageous countryman, Lieutenant Eldred Pottinger, now a Major and Companion of the Bath, produced good effects for a time at Cabool, but these unhappily were not lasting. If I had become a convert to the Afghan belief in dreams, I should have had, during every week of my residence, proofs of our ultimate success and supremacy in the country; and it will not, perhaps, be now read without interest, that, on the 17th of January, 1838, the "Moojawar," or guardian of the tomb of the Emperor Baber, waited upon me, and stated, with much solemnity, that "he had, on the preceding night, seen in a dream the Firingees seated on Baber's grave, receiving the salutations of the Afghans." The ulterior results of our dominion he, however, could not precisely tell, as he was unfortunately awakened by the call of the crier to morning prayers. Another Afghan from Candahar, who called upon me one day, said, " You stand aloof from us, but you will be unable to continue this course : our country is good, but it is without a head; and, like a beautiful widow, it voluntarily avows her attachment to you, and you cannot refuse to accept her as a wife." All my visitors, however, were not so complimentary. An Afghan who had seen India was speaking of our administration of justice; and I endeavoured to gather from him what he considered to be the defects of our Indian rule, as far as they affected his own class, which was that of a merchant. He answered me, according to the Asiatic fashion, by a proverb : " Give us a new life, and the patience of Job, and then all will be well." This satire on the tardiness of our courts of justice, coming as it does from *far* Cabool, may, perhaps, not be entirely without its effect.

If, however, an Afghan complains of endurance being necessary to those who are so unfortunate as to be *embayed* in legal proceedings, what would an Englishman think of the trials of patience which the Kuzzilbashes of Cabool have voluntarily imposed upon themselves, and of which I had excellent opportunities of judging at this crisis? Nearly all the secretaries of the country are of this persuasion, so that the whole of the correspondence is in their hands. In all their written accounts the defence of Herat, although the siege was conducted by the King of Persia himself, was described as the resistance of men true to God against wretches. The Persians were styled infidels and heretics, and the slaughter of a few of them recited as a triumph, while prayers were offered up for their destruction, and joyful expectations expressed that they would be annihilated. The letters containing these opinions are not only read in Cabool by Persian secretaries, but are answered by them in the same style, although it is perfectly known that they are of the very class on whose devoted heads so much obloquy is poured by the Soonee Afghans. The situation of the Kuzzilbashes of Cabool seems a good deal to resemble that of the Copts in Egypt: they lead much the same sort of life, and hold a similar station in society. Power and influence console both races for the hard words and rough usage of their employers.

An Afghan Moollah asked me if we had any distinction of Soonees and Shiahs in our creed? I told him that we had various sects, and explained the difference of opinion between Roman Catholics and Protestants. He at once observed that "It was not a stock or a stone that was an idol: it was what man worshipped, be it money or be it flesh." I had not expected such sentiments from a Mahomedan. I must also mention an observation of the same man as to the professors of Christianity. He said, "We were called 'Nussaree,' or 'Nazarenes,' because we had given *assistance* ('nusrut') to Christ." I ventured to tell him that our Saviour dwelt at Nazareth; and that a much simpler explanation of the term could therefore be given: but it is not an easy matter to convince a Mahomedan doctor of an error in his opinions, founded as they are on the prejudices of education.

I was agreeably surprised by the mildness of the winter at Cabool, after all that I had been told of its severity; but it appears that this year the weather had been unusually temperate. The people have no knowledge of lighting their apartments, except by means of oil-paper or cloth; and it was not without great surprise that they saw me cause the quicksilver to be rubbed off mirrors which we purchased in their bazar, and the glass fitted into window-frames. Although this glass had been brought all the way from Moscow, it cost little more than half a rupee for a large-sized pane. The comfort which I thus so cheaply obtained led some of the Khans to imitate my plan for keeping out the cold. By the 26th of February, the willow, or "bedee mishk," had blossomed; on the 11th of March, the first flower of spring, or the "sosun," a kind of small sweet-smelling iris, made its appearance; and on the 1st of April the apricots showed their blossom. Nevertheless, it snowed on the 27th of March; and tradition states that Ghuzni was destroyed by snow, nine days and a half after the vernal equinox. The cold was not so intense, even in the depth of winter, as to prevent me from riding out, my horse being ice-shod; but experience has since proved to me that the severity of the winter in Cabool differs very greatly in different years.

During winter the bazars are well filled; but in the country the people literally do nothing. They sit outside their forts wrapped up in sheepskins, and basking in the sun, which is always warm and agreeable. If there were any manufactures in the country, the people might employ themselves well and usefully during the cold season; but at present their days are unprofitably passed in relating stories and adventures. From so much idleness, one is disposed to infer favourably of the natural resources of the country, and of the mildness of its government. I remember to have met with the remark in a late number of the 'Westminster Review,' "that a despotic nation can only be great during a career of victory:" but, however true this may be as an abstract principle, in Afghanistan at least we see that a cessation from conquest has not been followed by ruin; and that, if greatness has left this people, they still retain a large share of comfort and enjoyment, although the splendour of their monarchy be no more.

The Afghan invasions of India were not made by open warfare: they were as the prowling of wild beasts after their prey; and, like them, the invaders were contented secretly, and by surprise, to obtain their spoil and drag it back into their dens. Happily, neither the Afghan, nor his neighbour the Tartar, any longer dares to ravage the land. British supremacy now hems them within their own limits; and the vast power which we have established brings these nations as suitors for our alliance, instead of invaders of our territory. It will compel a restless people, and in a degree it has already done so, to fall back upon their own resources, and must in time lead to the development of many elements of power and happiness which have long lain neglected in their fine country. The impatience of an Afghan is proverbial. He has a homely expression, " Not to use the wager of the knife" (shurt i karud), that is, to seek to cut his melon before he buys it; but his conduct is at variance with his proverb: greater reforms have, however, been made in society than that of weaning an Afghan from his evil habits; time and circumstances have rendered them familiar to him, and time and circumstances may also efface them.

The ruler of Cabool, Dost Mahomed Khan, partook at this time of the impatience common to his nation; and, some may perhaps say, not without sufficient cause. Herat was closely besieged by Persia. Should it fall, the danger to Candahar and Cabool was apparent: should it be successful, and repulse Persia, that danger still existed to Cabool. The British Government, confident in the success of its measures in Persia, placed no value on an Afghan alliance. Fear, therefore, overtook Dost Mahomed, and it was seconded by appeals to his interest; and thus two of the most powerful motives which influence the human mind inclined the chief to look for support to the west instead of the east. Having clearly ascertained that such were his views, there was no room for doubt as to the line of conduct which it was expedient for me to adopt; and I accordingly intimated to him my intention of returning to India. He expressed great regret at my decision; and when, on the 26th of April, I finally quitted Cabool, he was profuse in his professions of personal friendship and regard. Mr. Masson accompanied me, as he conceived that his position in Cabool would not be safe after my departure, and under the circumstances which led to it. We reached Julálábad on the 30th of April, and were hospitably received by the Ameer's son, Akbar Khan, and by whom, as I have before mentioned, I had been received with great pomp and splendour on entering Cabool, on the 20th of September.

I was anxious to examine the river of Cabool, and resolved, therefore, to descend it upon rafts: two days were spent in their preparation. More pains were bestowed to effect this than I had anticipated. About eighty skins were used for each raft; but only a fourth part of these were inflated; the rest were stuffed with straw, spars were placed across, and the whole bound together by a floating frame-work. When the paddles are used, the motion of the raft is circular, the great object being to keep it in the force of the stream.

On the 3rd of May we set sail, and reached Lalpoor, which is half-way to Peshawur, in seven hours: here we halted for the night, and were hospitably entertained by the Momund chief. Next day we prosecuted our voyage, and in eight hours reached Muttee, in the plain of Peshawur, where there were elephants, palanquins, and horses, waiting to convey us to the hospitable mansion of General Avitabile.

The excitement in descending the river of Cabool is greater than the danger; nevertheless, considerable care and dexterity are required to avoid the projecting rocks, and the whirlpools which they form. We were caught in one of them, called Fuzl: one raft revolved in it for two hours; and it was only extricated by the united exertions of the crews of the other rafts. The Camel's Neck, or the far-famed "Shoothur Gurdun," presented an appearance, as we approached it, so grand and impressive, that it will never be effaced from my memory. We had dropped down the river for half an hour, under heavy clouds; precipitous rocks rose some thousand feet high on either side;

before the public. I have appended, however, a view of the city of Umritsir.

A short month's stay at Lahore served to accomplish the ends which Government had then in view. The ulterior measures could only be matured at Simla, whither I proceeded by invitation, to wait on Lord Auckland, to whom I paid my respects on the 20th of July, accompanied only by Dr. Lord, Lieutenant Wood having again returned to the Indus. And thus terminated my mission to Cabool.

the 16th of May, having reached Cabool four days after I had left it; and having, like myself, descended the river. Our meeting was one of unmixed satisfaction. Prior to my departure from Cabool I transmitted instructions to Lieutenant Leech to leave Candahar and proceed by Kelat-i-Nusseer, and one of the great passes through the hills, to Shikarpoor. He performed the journey in safety, and I joined him at that place in the October following.

Towards the end of May an express arrived from Government, directing me to repair with all convenient speed to the court of Lahore, to consult with Mr. (now Sir William) Macnaghten, who was then on a mission there, on the critical state of our affairs westward of the Indus. We lost no time in obeying the summons; reached Attock by water on the same day that we left Peshawur (the 31st), and joined the party at Lahore on the 17th of June, having performed the journey chiefly during the nights. I hastened to pay my respects to the Maharaja; and found him changed in all things but his kindness. Runjeet Sing was now tottering on the brink of the grave. It is unnecessary for me to give any details of the mission then at his court, as the Honourable Captain Osborne has already laid an able account of it

CITY OF UMRITSIR.

before the public. I have appended, however, a view of the city of Umritsir.

A short month's stay at Lahore served to accomplish the ends which Government had then in view. The ulterior measures could only be matured at Simla, whither I proceeded by invitation, to wait on Lord Auckland, to whom I paid my respects on the 20th of July, accompanied only by Dr. Lord, Lieutenant Wood having again returned to the Indus. And thus terminated my mission to Cabool.

APPENDICES.

APPENDIX I.

Report of the Establishment of an Entrepôt, or Fair, for the Indus Trade.

Fairs common in Asia—Lohanee Afghan merchants—Their routes—Positions on the Indus—Kala Bagh not adapted—Dera Ismael Khan—Mooltan—Bhawulpore—Mittuncote—Dera Ghazee Khan preferable to all—January the best season—Site to be neutral—A small military force—A British superintendent necessary—Booths and warehouses—Duties to be levied—Remission of toll on vessels returning—Rock salt of the Punjaub—Grain, probable exports—Articles of traffic—Russian fairs—Banking establishments at Shikarpoor—Effects of the Mission to Cabool.

In the following Appendix will be found, in a collective and condensed form, the result of my inquiries and observations regarding the most convenient place for the establishment of a mart, or entrepôt, with reference to all the branches of trade proceeding up, down, or across the Indus: also, as to the means best suited for the institution of an annual fair, in furtherance of the plan of the British Government, for promoting commerce by way of this river, and for providing at the same time for the security of the merchant, and establishing a system of moderate duties.

It may be observed, at the outset, that, in the foundation of a periodical fair in these countries, there would be no innovation on established usage: the system is known to most Asiatic nations; it has been followed up with eminent success in Russia; it exists in full force to this day in Toorkistan, north of Hindoo Koosh; it is not unknown in some parts of the Cabool dominions, and has long been familiar to the natives of India. The celebrated fair at Hurdwar will immediately occur to the reader's recollection; besides which, numerous "melas," or assemblages, take place in different parts of the country. The performance of a religious ceremony, or the casual collection of a body of people for any purpose, would naturally suggest to the merchant that the opportunity was favourable both for the sale and purchase of goods; and to causes such as these we owe, no doubt, the first institution of this system of traffic, which was at one time universally followed in our own country and all the other kingdoms of the West. In the altered state of society in Europe, which has brought people to congregate in towns, where every necessary and luxury of life can daily be procured without difficulty, fairs have become less generally useful than they formerly were: but in Asia everything yet contributes to render them important, and they flourish accordingly, being, in fact, the only means by which nations distant from each other, and the population of which is widely spread, can be readily supplied with articles of either home or foreign produce. Although there has not been hitherto any such establishment on the Indus, the materials exist ready for the purpose; and, had it not been for the political state of these countries, we should long ere this have had a flourishing and important fair on the banks of this river. The merchants, who carry on the trade from India to Cabool, are principally Lohanee Afghans, whose country lies westward of the river, between Dera Ismael Khan and Cabool; and they now make an annual journey to and from these places, bringing with them the productions of Afghanistan, and taking back those of India and Europe. Being a pastoral race, they are their own carriers; and being brave, they require no protection but their own arms. They leave the rugged mountains of the west at Derbund, and assemble at Dera Ismael Khan, where some of them dispose of their property: others proceed lower down the Indus to Dera Ghazee Khan, or cross over to Mooltan and Bhawulpore; where they are sometimes enabled to obtain a supply of goods for their return trade. Failing this, the Lohanees pass into India, and even to Calcutta and Bombay. Their resort to these distant marts results solely from their inability to supply their wants nearer home; and whilst the establishment of a fair would enable them to effect this, the site of it is clearly indicated by the names of those four places above mentioned, Dera Ismael Khan, Dera Ghazee, Mooltan, and Bhawulpore.

Other localities, Mittun, or Mittuncote, on the south, and Kala Bagh on the north, also suggest themselves; and I shall now proceed to state the comparative eligibility of these different localities, as an entrepôt of trade. The whole of them have been particularly described in the official Reports which I have rendered to the Indian Government, any repetition of which, on the present occasion, I deem to be unnecessary.

The highest point to which the Indus is navigable throughout the entire year is Kala Bagh, above the latitude of 33° north, about eighty miles from Attock, and the same distance from Dera Ismael. There is no doubt that boats can ascend to Attock for eight or nine months of the year, and even to Peshawur; but the Indus between Attock and Kala Bagh is at all times narrow, and during the swell it is rapid and dangerous: the downward navigation, however, is never interrupted. Kala Bagh, therefore, is the highest point to which this river can be ascended with ease and safety; and thus a natural limit is fixed, beyond which a commercial emporium cannot be advantageously placed. The town of Kala Bagh is one of considerable importance in consequence of its salt-mines, but is situated in a barren country, and remote from the great caravan-roads, though there is a line of communication from it, or rather from Micud, twenty-eight miles higher up, by Jajee and Teera, to Cabool, through the valley of Bungush, which is now frequented. Light duties and safety from the Khyberees compensate for the inconvenience of an unfrequented road. This line can only be considered as a partial outlet from the Indus, and Kala Bagh, in consequence, not adapted for our purpose.

Dera Ismael, which is the next place of any note in descending the river, has an advantageous position, and is also the market-town of the Lohanee merchants. It is, however, a small place, and subject to alteration from the inundations of the river, which, a few years ago, swept away the entire town. It is nearer to the great commercial city of Umritsir than any of the other places on the Indus, and lies on the road between it and Cabool. This tract, however, is not much frequented, except by the merchants who carry on the extensive export trade in the native fabric of Jung and Mangana, which consists of coarse white cloth.

European goods are not in general sent by this road, for the merchant seeks to avoid the desert tract between the Jelum and Indus; and in addition to this, the marts from which he obtains his supply of goods for Cabool and Toorkistan are situated below Umritsir. Though Dera Ismael covers the road from that city, it does not on that account possess any paramount advantages; for, the object being to promote a trade by the river, and the present supply of goods being procured from the towns lower down, they possess superior advantages. Without casting Umritsir out of the line, Dera Ismael Khan must yet be considered one of the most eligible sites on the Indus.

The town of Dera Ghazee Khan is, however, the first in importance on the Upper Indus. It is itself a manufacturing place, and it leads to the commercial towns of Mooltan and Bhawulpore, which are near to it and to each other, and which now furnish many articles for the Cabool market. It is also about equidistant from Umritsir and the opulent town of Shikarpoor, in Sinde: so that it embraces not only the trade of the Punjaub and India, of Candahar and Cabool, but of the more remote capitals dependent on them, Herat and Bokhara.

The goods of India may be sent to it by river-carriage as far as Mooltan and Ooch; and the narrow neck of land which lies between these places and Dera Ghazee may either be crossed by camels, which are both cheap and abundant, or the Indus itself may be used as the channel of transport for articles that are bulky, and which do not require to be conveyed with particular expedition.

From Bombay to Dera Ghazee the water communication is open; and from the Upper Indus the intercourse is equally available.

In former times many roads led down upon this town from the west: time and peace will, in all probability, again open these now forsaken lines; and thus will be concentrated in one point all the desirable means of approach.

In addition to all this, Dera Ghazee in itself is a populous and thriving town, agreeably situated amidst a grove of date-trees, and not liable to be flooded by the Indus. In consequence of its fertile soil, and the open, airy neighbourhood around it, the necessaries of life are to be purchased here cheaper than in any other place on the Indus, and the supply may be increased from the adjacent districts.

Of Mooltan and Bhawulpore I do not speak as sites for an emporium, since they do not lie on the Indus. They both stand on rivers which can be approached from the north and south, and are very near Dera Ghazee Khan, the one being distant but forty-five and the other eighty miles. Their vicinity confers further advantages on Dera Ghazee; and, indeed, were Mooltan situated on the Indus, it would certainly be a preferable locality to any other; but, standing as it does, it is destitute of the advantages enjoyed by the lower Dera.

There is yet another position, and one which, at first sight, appears the most favourable of all the towns on the Indus,—Mittuncote. This was my impression when I entered on the investigation which I am now reporting, for Mittun stands at the confluence of the Indus with the five rivers of the Punjaub. An examination of this locality, however, led me at once to abandon every hope of its suiting the purposes intended. The place itself stands about two miles from the Indus, on an elevated spot; but the country around is flooded by the inundation, and is either under water or a mere marsh for half the year, during all which period it is both hot and unhealthy. Mittun is a small town, with a population of about 4000 souls; and although a site not far from it to the west, and much preferable, might be found, still the objections of being unable to bring boats close up to the town, as well as the humidity of the soil around it, are invincible, and exclude Mittun, however well adapted it may be in a geographical point of view, from being the selected spot.

It will be thus seen that Dera Ghazee Khan has advantages above all other places as the site of the entrepôt of the Indus trade, and that the only other locality which can at all be placed in comparison with it is Dera Ismael Khan, which has certainly an important advantage over it in being situated higher up the river.

The season of the year at which the bazar should be held must next be considered. The Lohanee and other traders descend from Bokhara and Cabool about the month of November, and set out on their return towards the end of April. This therefore indicates that the time of assembly should be between these months, which will fix the cold weather as the season, and the whole of January as the month. A later date than this would be advantageous in the upper navigation of the river, which, from the nature of the winds, is most readily accomplished in spring and summer: but it is necessary that the merchants should reach Cabool in June; and, besides the importance of their taking advantage of the season and avoiding the extreme heats in the valley of the Indus, all procrastination which would interfere with established usage is to be avoided. A month or two earlier, or the fall of the year, would suit the inclination of the western merchants even better than January, for it would relieve them from their anxieties as to procuring their goods, since they might still, if disappointed, go into India and return in time for the caravan to Cabool.

The delay after purchase is to them no very great inconvenience, for their families and flocks are with them, and they feel themselves at home: still January is probably the healthiest time of the year, and would insure, in consequence, a regular communication with Shikarpore, and all other places.

The interest which the Government of India has always felt for the improvement of commerce by the line of the

Indus has been made known to the mercantile community; but the British must come prominently forward, and act in concert with the natives, before any fair or bazar can be established with success. The superintendence of a British officer on the spot is imperatively necessary. Dera Ghazee Khan is in a foreign territory, but the rulers of Lahore, if they continue to be actuated by the spirit they have already evinced, will certainly make no objections to allow the same system which has been pursued in the Lower Indus being followed up here. The place should be made neutral ground, and the agent will then be invested with powers which will prove of the highest benefit. The protection of property, the police of the bazar, the regulations for its location, cleanliness, and supply, the collection of the duties that may be fixed, should all be managed by him, and a competent establishment under his orders.

A military force, probably a regiment of infantry, would be quite sufficient to insure confidence; and it is immaterial whether the Sikhs or the British Government furnish it, provided its services are placed under the control of the British Superintendent. It should also form an especial part of his duty to adjust all disputes that may arise between the traders; and, in the event of any of them dying without heirs, to take possession of the property, and account for it, according to usage, when those entitled to it may make their appearance. A regulation of this description in Russia has given great popularity to the system pursued in that empire.

It might be considered premature to enter upon any arrangement for the erection of booths or sheds for the accommodation of the merchant; but in the event of success attending this measure, it will certainly become necessary to do so. This duty must be confided to the

Superintendent, who will also have to arrange all the details as to their being put up and removed, to receive the rents leviable for them, and to settle the distribution of merchandise in different quarters, according to the usage in Asiatic countries. It will also be necessary to erect warehouses of a substantial nature, in which to house such property as the merchant may leave behind him, either from inclination, inability to transport it, or death; and this establishment will likewise require the vigilant superintendence of the British agent. The neighbourhood of Dera Ghazee presents many places adapted for the purpose, but it will be expedient that the site should be between the river and the town, and as near the former as possible.

The style of building in these parts is with sun-dried bricks and a wooden frame-work; so that an arrangement might easily be adopted which should combine economy and utility with sightliness of appearance.

The residence of the Superintendent should, on every account, be permanent throughout the year, and his undivided time devoted to the subject. All references sent to him, from any direction, would thus be promptly and satisfactorily answered; and in the end he might become the means of communicating to the whole of the merchants the nature of the probable demand, and the necessary supply, so as to insure to them a good sale and secure them from loss. A watchful foresight such as this would materially forward the interests of commerce, and tend more than anything else to put an end to the petty quarrels which now perpetually arise among the chieftains, such as that which exists at the present time between Bhawulpore and Mooltan, regarding indigo. The principle of reciprocity would then become general; and the very circumstance of the officer's presence would produce the most happy effects in the neighbouring countries. He would have it in his power to induce the hill tribes, the Muzarees and Boogtees, to open a safe road through their country to Shikarpore, which might be done without difficulty, for they are friendly to the British Government, and ready to meet its wishes. They and the mountaineers to the west might, in time, if properly managed, supply the place of regular troops: for it is found that a prudent degree of reliance on these half-civilized tribes is almost always rewarded by faithful service; and the Muzarees, once so notorious for their piracies on the Indus, may yet become, like the Bheels of Southern India, a protection against plunderers and lawless brigands. And even should these expectations not be fully realized, it is at least certain that the near residence of a British officer will tend greatly to deter them from acts which are at variance with the tranquillity of the country and the well-being of society.

The advantages of a resident Superintendent have thus, I conceive, been rendered manifest; and it further seems most desirable that he should be relieved from all that portion of the business which is connected with the navigation of the river, or wants of those proceeding by it, except as to the issue of the necessary papers. Passports should be granted by him as well as by the agents at the head and mouth of the river; but the river-duties should be intrusted to a distinct officer, who should, if possible, be a nautical man, and charged with the superintendence of the navigation, as the military officer is with that of the fair. This is a matter of the highest importance; for, notwithstanding the arrangements that have already been made, I myself was applied to by the same individual at three different places, Khyrpore, Bhawulpore, and Mittun, for a passport before he could move his cargo, and this in consequence of the present British agent having been withdrawn to perform a necessary duty near Lodiana.

This River Superintendent should have free permission to proceed from Attock to the sea, and ought to act in concert with the Superintendent of the Fair, both of them being under the guidance of the agent of the Governor-General; and all the native officers along the river should be directed to attend to the orders of the River Superintendent. If it were deemed advisable, and it certainly appears to be so, this officer could organize an establishment of pilots along the Indus, which would cause no expense to Government, and be hailed as a boon by the community, which would readily contribute to its support. All regulations, also, regarding the hire of boats should rest with him, as well as full permission to examine their condition and reject those which were not river-worthy. The merchant would thus be secure against imposition and loss, and the boatman would take a pride in his vessel, since regular employment and his lawful hire would be insured to him. By these means we should, in process of time, acquire a complete influence over all the people on and near the Indus, together with such an accurate knowledge of the river itself as would lead to those improvements which experience never fails to point out.

The treaties already made provide for the levy of duties on the Indus, from the sea to Mittun. The navigation from that place to Attock should at once be arranged, which would be much less difficult than the adjustment of the duties at the fair: for the first few years these should be trifling, if not altogether remitted; but a scale must be fixed for their ultimate levy. At present goods pay a tax at Dera Ghazee Khan, according to weight, which averages, on cloth and indigo, an *ad valorem* duty of from $1\frac{1}{2}$ to $2\frac{1}{2}$ per cent. This is, however, a mere transit duty, and differs materially from what the state would be entitled to if the goods were disposed of. In Russia the duties leviable are 4 per cent. on entering the fair, and 1 per cent. on quitting it; and the same rates might be introduced as the standard at Dera Ghazee Khan, if no reasonable objections presented themselves.

Since it would be an object of high importance that the merchants proceeding to this emporium should have the means of procuring return goods, so that they may avail themselves of the spare tonnage of their vessels, it would be well to consider how far the British Government can afford to admit into its territories the rock-salt of Kala Bagh and the Punjaub. This is a point on which it does not fall within my province to express a decided opinion; but it certainly appears to me to be feasible, and even consistent with the regulations under which the monopoly is maintained, to admit mineral salt into India, provided similar duties are imposed upon it. The prime cost of salt at the mine, or on the seashore, is a mere trifle: but the former article is far superior to the latter; and in course of time we might see vessels sailing from Bombay with cargoes partly made up of Punjaub salt for the London and Liverpool markets, instead of storing mud and stones to be cast away at the harbour's mouth, or at best employed in road-making at Blackwall and the docks. Salt, being a valuable commodity, would hardly appear to require any remission of toll.

Grain is an article which the fertile banks of the Indus and the Punjaub rivers would afford in large quantities for export; but the present treaties grant no privileges to encourage the transport of this bulky article beyond sea, and they are consequently tantamount to a prohibition. An arrangement should immediately be entered into with all the powers to free grain of every description from all but a nominal duty. So long as the rate of duties prevents a profit being derived from grain, none, of course, will be exported, except from one section of the river to another, whilst a revised system would be productive of advantages alike to the community of Western India, and to the proprietors and cultivators of land on the Indus and its tributary rivers.

Grain, particularly rice, is now extensively exported from the Delta of the Indus, and a light toll, never exceeding twenty-four rupees per boat, is levied; so that it would only be in unison with the already established usage to extend this benefit throughout the course of the river. One per cent. *ad valorem* would suffice to check irregularity, and would be a fair tax on this necessary of life; but even this might be reduced according to the distance from which the grain is brought, as for instance in the case of the harvest of the Punjaub, which would have to be transported to the Delta of the Indus, before it could compete with that which is raised so much nearer the market. If an article of value cannot be found, a coarser description furnishes a return, which, though it be inferior, promotes the good of trade. This is apparent in the commerce which America now carries on with India.

Without instancing other articles in which it would be advisable to lighten the duties, it has occurred to me, as a general proposition, that it would be expedient to remit, on the return voyage, one-half the toll to vessels which had already paid the full amount in ascending or descending the Indus. This would place the parties at both extremities of the river on a par with each other, and would encourage them, instead of breaking up or selling their boats at the termination of a profitable trip, to set out upon another, even though it were less advantageous. If some such arrangement be not made, many of the boats will return empty, and no duty can be then leviable on their passage, which would not only subject the rulers to loss, but would prevent the scheme coming to maturity. It might, however, be provided that the upward and downward voyage must be performed in the course of one year,—that is, in twelve months,—to entitle the merchant to the remission suggested.

Whatever plans or arrangements may be finally adopted for the removal of obstacles to this trade, it will be necessary not only to promulgate them by means of the Gazettes in India, but to have them translated into Persian, Punjabee, Shikarpooree, and Sindee, and extensively circulated in the countries themselves. A lamentable ignorance exists among the native merchants regarding the intentions of Government on the important subject of opening the Indus. Some few individuals who have had intercourse with European officers are aware of the real object in view, but the bulk of the community are uninformed, and are inclined to consider the regulations which have been established as intended for the benefit of foreigners, to their exclusion. The natives of Sinde, in particular, fear to embark capital, believing as they do that they would not be entitled to, or rather could not insure, the same protection as a strange merchant from India or the Punjaub. This impression would be removed by having the regulations which are fixed upon made public, under the authority of the rulers themselves, followed up further by personal explanation from the agents of the British Government. The Ameers of Sinde and all the other powers are guaranteed by treaty from any interference with their usages regarding internal trade; but they are not, on that account, at liberty to prevent the merchants of their country, should they wish it, from profiting by the opening of the Indus. If this were so, it would certainly be an exclusion of the natives, to the sole benefit of foreigners. This is a subject which requires to be clearly and fully explained, particularly in Sinde.

The free navigation of the Indus will be productive of two distinct advantages:—the first, a more ready supply of the productions of its own region, from one part of its banks to another; the second, a means of transport, by water, for a considerable distance, of the goods of India and Europe towards Cabool and Toorkistan. The first branch of this commerce, or the internal trade, will probably continue in the hands of those resident on the river; and the speculations which have been entered upon already show it to be a profitable traffic.

The second is, however, by far the most important, and to encourage it is of course our principal object. To form a more perfect idea of the articles in demand, three lists are annexed to this Appendix. In the first (No. 1) are enumerated the goods which at present reach the city of Cabool from Russia, by way of Bokhara, distinguishing those which are sent on to India; the second (No. 2) details the articles which are now brought to Afghanistan from India and Europe; the third list (No. 3) those which are sent from the Afghan country to India. These lists are, I believe, complete as the commerce now exists; but it cannot be doubted that in due time it will be extended to many new, and probably some of them important articles. Descriptions and specimens of the present articles of traffic, together with the probable profit upon them, have been prepared for the information of the community.

In the various propositions which I have suggested, it has been my endeavour to avoid all unnecessary interference with the merchant. The principles of trade are in these days too well understood to admit of any useless interposition on the part of the state. We may aid it without giving it undue or unnecessary support, and we shall best advance its interests by removing obstructions, and leaving it to run its own course. If the success of similar schemes elsewhere is an encouragement, such encouragement is certainly afforded us by what is now passing in the Russian empire. Fairs have been founded there within the memory of men now living, at which business to the amount of two hundred millions of roubles, or about ten millions of pounds sterling, is now transacted, and even this sum is on the increase.* The removal of the great fair of Maccaire to Nejnei has only served to give commerce a greater impetus; and if Dera Ghazee Khan shall ultimately prove not to be an eligible situation, another site may easily be found. With light duties for the first few years, this fair cannot fail to prosper, and goods will even desert the natural track, if their owners perceive that they can obtain by it a more secure and a more ready sale, although the rate of profit should be smaller.

The continental system of Napoleon led to Russia being supplied with English goods by way of India, Cabool, and Bokhara. This fact is supported by the authority of a Russian writer and the concurring testimony of native merchants. The channel is therefore not new; and as some of the fairs of Russia are in a great degree supported by the trade with Central Asia, a part

* Vide the statements of M. Levean and Captain Cochrane.

of that trade will certainly be drawn to the nearer mart on the Indus, and contribute to the success of the undertaking. A banking establishment may be said to be at hand to aid it; for Shikarpore is at this day the focus of all the money transactions of Western Asia, and it is but 300 miles distant from the site of the proposed bazar, and is situated between it and Bombay, the great mart of Western India. Above all, the interest now exhibited by the British Government in encouraging this commerce must prove of the highest advantage. The effects of its mission to Cabool have already become apparent, and no less than five caravans with shawls have arrived from Cashmeer since our reaching Cabool, a briskness of trade which has been unknown for years; and, what is still more remarkable, the merchants have come with a knowledge that the duties have been raised sevenfold. They all express themselves ready to meet this additional duty; and publicly declare that the arrangement of our Government in deputing an agent to encourage commerce has inspired them with this renewed confidence.

In conclusion, it is desirable to recapitulate the contents of the foregoing report; and to state briefly the several propositions contained in it, which are as follows:—

I. The establishment of a fair on the Indus is agreeable to the usage of Asiatic nations; and therefore a very desirable measure.

II. That the best site for such a mart, with reference to all the branches of trade, is Dera Ghazee Khan.

III. That the season most suitable for holding the fair is the month of January; during which, or part of it, the assemblages should take place.

IV. That the site should be made neutral ground; and the fair managed, in all its branches, by an agent of the British Government, who should be appointed Superintendent, and by whom all duties should be collected, places of accommodation erected, and arrangements made for the security of the property of the traders absent, as well as present.

V. That the superintendence of the navigation of the river, and the due execution of all the regulations regarding the craft upon it, should be vested in a different officer, who should, if possible, be a nautical man, and by whose exertions a pilot establishment might in time be formed.

VI. That the Indus should be thrown open to Attock, on the principles already acted upon; and the amount of toll and duties fixed according to a given scale.

VII. That if, consistent with what is due to the state, the mineral salt of the Punjaub should be permitted to enter into British India under certain limitations, its export would contribute to the public good as a return trade.

VIII. That the toll on boats laden with grain should be revised, and a lighter assessment made with the same end.

IX. That only half toll should be levied on return boats, which would place the merchants at both extremities of the river on an equal footing, and also promote commerce.

X. That all the arrangements entered upon, besides being published in the gazettes of India, should be translated into the languages of the country, and made known to the native merchants, first through the rulers on the Indus, and then through the agents of the British Government; as a lamentable ignorance now exists of all that is going on or intended.

XI. That the three annexed lists will enable the mercantile community to judge of the existing state of the trade, of the articles in demand, and of those which are procurable in return; the nature of the profit and other particulars being furnished elsewhere.

XII. That the state of the fairs in Russia, and the progressive increase in the business done at them, hold out encouragement to the merchant, that, with the existing facilities and a bank at Shikarpore, a portion of that commerce will be diverted to the Indus. This is illustrated by a striking instance of the effects already produced in Cabool, from the interest which the British Government has now exhibited in the encouragement of trade.

No. 1.

LIST of ARTICLES, mostly Russian, found in the Bazar of Cabool and brought to it from Bokhara.

No.		No.	
1	Ducats, tillas, sooms, and yamoos.*	19	Kunson, a kind of leather.
2	Gold-dust.*	20	Kirmiz, or cochineal.*
3	Pistols and muskets.	21	Bluestone or sulphate of copper.
4	Gun-locks.	22	Iron trays.
5	Padlocks.	23	Kullabuttoo, two kinds.*
6	Knives and razors.	24	Sungot.*
7	Wires of iron and brass.	25	Broadcloth.
8	Copper.*	26	Chintz.
9	Russian boxes, snuff-boxes.	27	Velvet.
10	Needles.	28	Attas (satin).
11	Glass spectacles, mirrors.	29	Khoodbaft.
12	Porcelain.	30	Shija.
13	Flints.	31	Koitan, or muslin.
14	Beads and corals.*	32	Nanka.*
15	Fishbone.*	33	White cloth.
16	Paper.	34	Handkerchiefs (silken).
17	Tea.	35	Chuppun Kord.
18	Saleb Missree.	36	Silk of Bokhara and Koondooz.*

Note.—The Articles marked thus * are passed on to India along with the productions of Cabool, given in List No. 3.

APPENDIX I.

No. 2.

LIST of EUROPEAN and INDIAN ARTICLES brought to Cabool.

No.
1 Jamdanee.*
2 Muslin

No.
34 Badal Khanee and Hazeani.
35 Loongee of Mooltan.*

APPENDIX I.

No. 3.

List of the Productions, &c. of Afghanistan, sent into India.

No.
1. Madder.
2. Assafœtida.
3. Dried fresh fruits.
4. Koosoomba dye.
5. Drugs.
6. Tobacco and snuff.

No.
7. Wool and Doomba sheep.
8. Silk, raw.
9. Lead sulphur, zak or zinc.
10. Horses and ponies.
11. Bactrian camels.

Those Articles which pass in transit from Russia, Bokhara, and India, are stated in List No. 1.

APPENDIX II.

Report on the River Indus, by Lieut. John Wood, Indian Navy.

General View of the Indus—The Navigable Character of the River—The Soundings in Indian Rivers—The Mode of Navigating the Indus—The Winds and Weather in the Valley of the Indus—The Boats upon the Indus—Steam Vessels—Remarks on the Steam-boats of the Ganges—The Fuel for Steam-boats—Report by Captain Johnson on the relative Value of Wood and Coal—The Inundations of the Indus—Its Fords, and Site for the proposed Fair—The Indus and Punjaub Rivers—Concluding Remarks.— Tables:—1. Comparison of Chronometers—2, 3, 4. Longitudes and Latitudes of Places in the Line of the Indus—5, 6. On the Soundings of the River—Tonnage—8, 9. Cost and Hire of Boats.

I.—*A General View of the Indus.*

This report is confined to the navigable Indus, or that portion of the river lying between the sea and Attock.

Throughout the whole of this distance the river is known as the Sinde; sometimes indeed it is called the Attock, but this latter designation is local in its application. I have retained both, and apportioned them as follows:—

The Lower Sinde, or Indus, extends from the Sea to Bukkur.

Upper Sinde, or Indus, extends from Bukkur to Kala Bagh.

Attock, from Kala Bagh to Attock.

By dividing the river into these sections, each is

made to mark certain important alterations in the navigable character of the stream.

It may here be premised, that of the course of the river north of Attock our knowledge is confessedly superficial. A few miles above that fortress the Indus ceases to be navigable; but not before it has received, in the Cabool river, a tributary that further extends the advantage of water-carriage to the west—the most important of all directions.

Source.—To what Lieutenants Burnes and Macartney have written on the subject I have nothing to add: unless Moorcroft's travels settle the question, the source of the Indus is still a problem to be solved.

In the plain above Attock the Indus is divided into many branches, but abreast of that fort they all unite. One deep, narrow, clear, blue stream shoots rapidly past, and, at once entering the hills, disappears from sight. Among hilly groups it winds to Kala Bagh. At Mukkud the channel widens, and the expanded river flows quietly forward with a lessened velocity and a reduced depth. On escaping from its rocky bed the river enters a level country, through which it winds onward to the sea. Its boundaries are now those of the valley; the Soliman mountains are on one side, and the Indian desert on the other.

Length of Course.—From the sea to Attock the distance in a straight line is . . . . 648 miles.

By the river it is increased to . . 942 miles.

Breadth of the Stream.—The width of the surface-water in the dry season varies from 480 to 1600 yards; the usual width is about 680 yards.

Depth.—When the river is in full freshes, twenty-four feet; but in an opposite season of the year, nine, twelve, thirteen, and fifteen feet are the usual maxima of its soundings. The greatest depth of water in the Indus occurs between Kala Bagh and Attock: one hundred and eighty-six feet has been here sounded.

Velocity.— Seven knots an hour in the freshes, and three when the river is low. It is scarcely necessary to remark that the three last items are very inconstant. At no two places are the measurements exactly alike, nor do they continue the same at one place for a single week. A more particular account of these will be found under the next head.

Fall per Mile.—From Attock to Kala Bagh 20 inches.
    Ditto Kala Bagh to Mittun 8 ditto.
    Ditto Mittun to sea,* . 6 ditto.

Discharge per second.—Cubic feet maximum
in August, ... 446,080
 Maximum in December, . . . 40,857

Annual Discharge.—5,383,600,934,400— or 150,212,079,642 tons avoirdupois.

Power of Transport.—Rolled pebbles do not occur in the bed of the Indus below Chandia-ke-kote, a village five miles south of Kala Bagh. Above Kote, though not below it, the sand of the Indus is searched for gold. The precious mineral is also found at Dera Ismail Khan; but not in the river. It is washed down by the rains from the Soliman mountains. Pebbles also occur at a certain spot in the river below Hyderabad, in Lower Sinde; but they can be traced to hills in the neighbourhood.

Height of the River's Banks.—Assuming for the purpose of explanation that the source and the embouchure of the Indus are upon the same level, the river in its long course may be said to have two maxima of rise.

---

* The fall of the river from Mittun to the sea is from Captain Burnes' Memoir of the Indus.

APPENDIX II.

These are shown in the following sketch, where the measurements are those of the stream when in full flood.

See Rise at Hyderabad 15 feet, Mittun 8½ feet, Kala Bagh and Attock 48 feet.

The rise between Kala Bagh and Attock cannot be called natural: it is caused by the contracted bed into which the stream is here thrown among the mountains. The rise at Hyderabad is the result of a carefully kept register daily; but at the other places this item has been reduced from an examination of the river's banks, and the best information I could procure.

Colour and Temperature.—To Dera Ismail Khan the water of the Indus is of a lead colour; below that town it becomes of a dirty-whitish yellow, tinged with red. In the freshes the red tint is heightened, but the general colour continues the same.

Between Attock and Mittun all the streamlets that fall into the Indus are of a bright red; save the Hurroo and Toe, which have pebbly beds and clear water.

TEMPERATURE OF THE RIVER.

MONTHS.	AIR.		RIVER.		REMARKS.
February	69°	2′	64°	2′	Noon observations
March	90°	0′	75°	0′	in the parallel of
April	97°	0′	81°	0′	24° 0′ North.
May	100°	0′	84°	0′	
June	101°	0′	87°	0′	
July	95°	5′	88°	0′	
August	95°	7′	88°	0′	
September	94°	5′	86°	0′	

II.—*Navigable Character of the Indus.*

Between the sea and Attock the facilities for navigation are not everywhere equally great; they vary with the state of the river's bed. As an acquaintance with the one may contribute to a knowledge of the other, I shall apportion the river into sections corresponding to its capabilities, and afterwards indicate the character of the present method of navigating the stream.

The Delta.—As high as the influence of the tide extends, there will always be an ample depth of water for even vessels of a greater draft than those elsewhere described as the best and only boats suited to the river under all circumstances.

It reaches to Nooroo-kanood, a village on the left bank of the river below Tatta. But above this navigation is intricate, nor does it materially improve till beyond the *delta*.

This is owing to the great expansion of the river's bed, where, among the numerous channels that present themselves, it is not always an easy matter to select the right one. No great inconvenience is felt on this score by the vessels now upon the river; for whether they ascend it laden or in ballast, dragged by the track-rope or propelled by the breeze, their progress is so slow that they may be said to feel every inch of the way.*

From the Delta to Sehwan.—This is the best portion of the river, and the *pulla* fisherman, as he floats down the centre of the stream, proclaims the fact. The pole to the lower extremity of which his net is fastened measures from sixteen to twenty-two feet, and, according as this may be in March or August, either eight or fifteen feet of its entire length is immersed in water.

---

* See Table V. for the soundings of this and other sectional divisions.

Two rocky ledges occur in this section; both project from the right bank of this river, and are found, one under the village of Jerkh, and the other at the north end of the Hilaya reach. Both are under water in the swell.

Sehwan to Roree, or Bukkur.—As the character of the last section was determined by the avocations of the fisherman, so may be that of this one. The fishing-pole is no longer in general use; but among the shallows in the middle of the stream, men armed with creels, shaped like inverted cones, may be seen busy at work ensnaring the *pulla*-fish. Here, then, it may be presumed, the depths are too irregular for the employment of the former method. Such is the cause; and thus does the practice of the fisheries on this river become an index to the state of its navigation.

Bukkur to Mittun.—A great change here takes place in the character of the river. The stream at Roree, though at some places it may be found in a single bed, is more often divided into two or more parallel branches, from 400 yards to four miles apart. Where the former is the case, (at Mittun-kote and for some distance below it, for example,) the channels are more mazy and intricate than where its volume, as in the latter instance, is apportioned among a number of branches. These changes in the configuration of the river are met by a corresponding alteration in the build of the boats. A new description of vessel, called a *zohruk*, of a less draft than the *doondah*, is now the common cargo-boat. Where the other is retained, its size is reduced. *Doondahs*, it will be afterwards shown, requiring five feet and half an inch to float them, are in use upon the river below Bukkur; but above that fort I have not met a single boat of a draft exceeding three feet nine inches.

Mittun to Kala Bagh.—The Indus in this section, as high as Dera Ismail Khan, is equally well suited to navigation, though not better than that last described. It also in some degree resembles that section in its parallel branches and broad bed. Between Dera Ismail Khan and Kala Bagh the difficulties of the navigation increase.

Kala Bagh to Attock.—The downward voyage may be made throughout the year; but from April to October the passage is hazardous, and rarely attempted. Boats at all seasons may ascend as high as Sharkee, a village on the right bank of the river, a few miles above Mukkud, but between that and Attock the upward navigation is restricted to the winter months, and even then a boat must have a double crew, and be of a build that does not obtain below Kala Bagh, called a *duggah*. For a description of this vessel see the 7th article in this Report.

III.—*Of the Soundings in Indian Rivers.*

After having sketched the greatest capabilities of the Indus, from the draft of its boats, it will not be necessary to enlarge, in this place, on the nature of its soundings. South of Muttun-kote I have inserted, under sectioned heads, specimens enough to show the characters of the channels* referred to. A table marked maximum, minimum, &c., is quite the thing for a thermometrical register; but such a formula for soundings, when applied to an Indian river, mars its own object, unless, indeed, it be based on the accumulated experience of years. That I do not therefore crowd these pages with figures,

* See Table V.

is from a firm conviction of their inutility. They are, in fact, positively injurious; for when a practical man at a distance casts his eyes over the contents of a table purporting to give the soundings in a river's channel, and finds the least depth to be two fathoms, he very naturally concludes that a boat constructed to draw only nine feet will navigate the said river. No conclusion could be more erroneous; the reasoning is suited to the equable streams of the New World, but not applicable to the ever-changing channels of our Indian rivers. To what other causes can we attribute that crude digest of a prospectus for introducing steam upon the Indus for commercial purposes that lately reached this country from England, authenticated by names of the first rank and respectability in the mercantile world? One of the articles in the proposed Joint Stock Company provided for stationing a ship of one thousand tons (an old East Indiaman) as a dépôt inside the river. Such a vessel could hardly come in sight of the Sindian coast. Lieutenant Carless's survey of the mouths of the river has made us acquainted with their actual condition; and in another part of this report it is shown what should be the draft of the Indus steamers;* and this decision is the result of a most careful examination of the river, both in its dry season and during its freshes.

IV.—*Of the Mode of Navigating the Indus.*

The diagram on the following page represents a reach of the river below Sehwan. The better to illustrate the figure, I shall suppose a boat deeply laden at

* See the 7th Article in this Report.

the village Y is about to start on the downward voyage, and that her "*meerbar*," or man in charge of the boat, is a stranger to the river. Leaving the village, he would doubtless take the large channel indicated by the feathered arrows, without regarding, if indeed they had been seen, the numerous offsets on the right hand; when abreast of the shoal S, a decrease in the depth of water would for the first time apprise him of his having lost the fair channel, and shortly after this intimation had been received the boat would ground on the bar G. Now, by inspecting the sketch, it will be seen that between the villages X and Y the deep channel has shifted from the left to the right bank of the river. The alteration has been effected by the silent drainage of the lateral channels O, P, E, and D, and by the unperceived departure of a large body of water over the bar extending from S to G into the back-water F. E is the passage the boat should have pursued; but this knowledge

Sketch of a Reach below Sehwan.

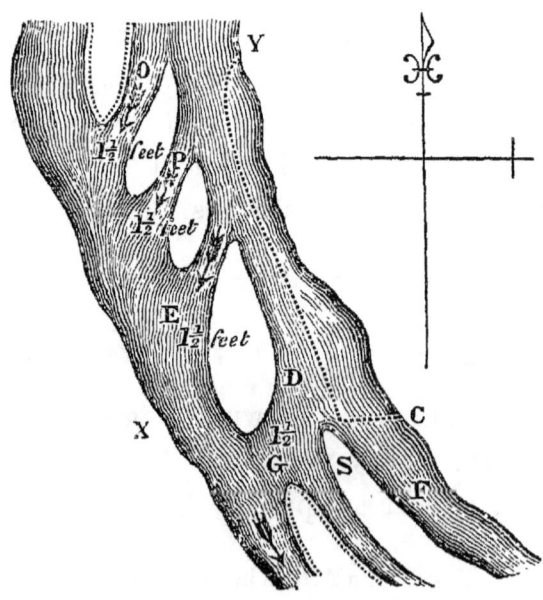

APPENDIX II.   313

could only have been the result of a previous careful examination, appearances at starting being decidedly in favour of channel D. The nature of these changes will be rendered still more evident by inspecting a section of the river's bed. Take for example the following:—

First Channel.—3. 4. $4\frac{1}{4}$. $4\frac{1}{4}$. $3\frac{1}{2}$. $2\frac{1}{2}$. 2. $\frac{3}{4}$ $\frac{3}{4}$ $\frac{3}{4}$ $\frac{1}{2}$ $\frac{3}{4}$ $\frac{3}{4}$ $\frac{3}{4}$ 1. 1. 1.
Second Channel.—$1\frac{1}{2}$. $1\frac{1}{2}$. 2. $2\frac{1}{2}$. $2\frac{1}{2}$. $2\frac{3}{4}$. 1. 1. 1. 1. $\frac{3}{4}$ $\frac{1}{2}$ $\frac{3}{4}$ $\frac{3}{4}$ $\frac{1}{2}$ $\frac{3}{4}$ $\frac{3}{4}$ $\frac{1}{2}$ $\frac{3}{4}$
Third Channel.—$1\frac{1}{4}$. $1\frac{1}{2}$. $1\frac{1}{2}$. 2. 2. 1. $\frac{1}{2}$ fathoms.

Such a line of soundings is not uncommon, though this one differs from the usual section in having an additional channel, two being the more usual number. The junction of these is not effected at a particular spot, but is, on the contrary, the result of a parallel course of many miles, during the whole of which distance the change is gradually being effected. They thus imperceptibly glide into each other; and should the channel selected by a boat descending the river be that which the stream is in the act of abandoning, she must be moved into the new-formed channel as soon as a decrease of soundings gives warning of the fact. Now it is deserving of remark, that, when the necessity of change first becomes apparent, there is seldom more than three-quarters of a fathom water on the spot separating the channels. Whether alterations in the channels of other large rivers are brought about in a similar manner, I am not aware: but this peculiarity, if it can be so termed, is familiar to the boatmen on the Indus; and with a description of the manner of their meeting it, and of the precautionary measures to which it gives rise, I shall conclude this notice of its navigation.

No vessel with cargo on board makes a downward voyage unaided by a pilot-boat: it is called here *sooee*, or guide. These are small cheap skiffs, managed by a couple of men, one of whom standing on a platform in the bows gives the depth of water, while the other, with his scull over the stern, steers the boat. Cheap as the services of a pilot may be had, the protracted length of the voyage makes it a burden too weighty for a single cargo to bear, and the custom therefore is for boats to drop down the river in fleets, or by divisions, when *sooees* become so multiplied, that to every two or three large boats a tender is attached. Grain being the only freight, all shipments are made at a stated season of the year; and as the quantity of corn produced on the banks of the Indus in autumn far exceeds that cut down in spring, the winter fleet outnumbers in an equal proportion that which takes its departure about midsummer. In February, 1837, when the river was at its lowest level, I counted forty-two grain-laden boats pass Sehwan on their way to Hyderabad, whither the surplus of the Upper Provinces is yearly exported.

The largest of these boats drew five feet and half an inch of water, and the manner of conducting the fleet was as follows:—When the day's stage had been fixed, a detachment of *sooee* went ahead to sound, into each boat there being, besides her own small complement, two or more of the *doondah's* men. On their arrival all is bustle and noise in the fleet. The fastenings of the boats are cast off, the oars are plied, and the huge hulk, preceded by her guide, sheers out into the stream.

If the *meerbars* have confidence in the channels, and the wind be fair, a large square sail is set, and the unwieldy *doondah*, deep though she be, outstrips her tender, and seems to skim the surface of the water;— such a fleet in motion is worth seeing. First, the large white sail of the headmost boat is discovered at the top of the reach, then another, and another, until the surface

APPENDIX II.

of the river becomes studded with those uncouth yet really interesting objects. As may be supposed, this mode of navigation is tedious, the daily stages not averaging more than from ten to twenty miles. Delays too are not unfrequent in the dry season, but never exceed fifteen days, and rarely extend to half that number.

When there is a prospect of a long detention, it is customary for large boats to transfer a portion of their cargo into smaller ones, and take it on board again when the shoal water is passed. In high wind, the boats remain fast by the bank of the river. The two following Tables are inserted in illustration of the above remarks:—

TABLES showing the Cargo-draft of the largest Boats upon the Indus, with the least Water in the continuous Channel, during the dry Season of 1837.

Class of Boats.	Draft of Boats.		Channel.	
	Cubic Draft.	Gunwale above water-line.	Places.	Depth.
	Ft. In.			Ft. In.
1st Class	5 0½	10 Inches.	Gooloo	3 8
2nd ditto	4 9	9 ditto.	Lillong	4 4
3rd ditto	4 3	9 ditto.	Mycotta	4 8
4th ditto	3 3	7 ditto.	Bulalpoor	4 1
5th ditto	3 0	5½ ditto.	Kaira	4 8

The places in the above Table are all situated between Schwan and Roree; but they furnish a good example of the depth in other places.

Boats descending in the freshes proceed as above described. In this season the length of the voyage is much shortened, though attended with considerably more risk. A pilot is still required; but a previous examination of the channel is not always considered necessary.

The following Table gives a statement of the downward voyage at opposite seasons of the year. It embraces the whole navigable extent of the river, and includes pilotage where such a custom prevails. The voyages are such as are rarely performed even by Sinde boats, even when the river is clear, and other circumstances favourable.

The Downward Voyage.

Stages.	Dry Season.	Freshes.	Pilotage.
Attock to Kala Bagh	1½ Day.	1 Day.	—
Kala Bagh to Dera Ismail Khan	7 ditto.	2 ditto.	6 Rupees.
Dera Ismail Khan to Dera Ghazee Khan	10 ditto.	3½ ditto.	6 ditto.
Dera Ghazee Khan to Mittun	4 ditto.	2 ditto.	3 ditto.
Mittun to Roree	6 ditto	3½ ditto.	a boat 18 Rs.
Roree to Sehwan	7 ditto.	4 ditto.	ditto 16 ditto.
Sehwan to Hyderabad	3 ditto	2 ditto.	ditto 12 ditto.
Hyderabad to sea	2½ ditto.	2 ditto.	ditto 12 ditto.
Total	41 Days.	20 Days.	

The upward voyage is performed by the aid of the wind and track-rope. This last mode of procedure is slow but certain; and averages about eight coss, or thirteen miles, a day. With a strong favourable breeze the daily progress is increased to twelve and eighteen coss. The prevailing winds during the year, and their consequent influence on the navigation of the river, are given under the next head, and it will there be seen that the freshes, far from presenting any obstacle to the upward voyage, are more favourable to it than otherwise. During their continuance a south wind blows from the sea to Kala Bagh; and though less steady on the Upper Indus than in the lower part of the river, it is a great service to navigation, since the time consumed by an up-river voyage, in the dry season, may be stated as one-half in excess of that required to perform it in the swell. Annexed is a Table, showing the relative time occupied by the voyage at opposite seasons of the year:—

The Upward Voyage.

Stages.	Dry Season.	Freshes.
Seaport to Hyderabad	15 Days.	7 Days.
Hyderabad to Sehwan	8 ditto.	4 ditto.
Sehwan to Roree	11 ditto.	7 ditto.
Roree to Mittun	14 ditto.	6½ ditto.
Mittun to Dera Ghazee Khan	10 ditto.	4 ditto.
Dera Ghazee Khan to Dera Ismail Khan	11 ditto	10 ditto.
Dera Ismail Khan to Kala Bagh	12 ditto.	7 ditto.
Kala Bagh to Attock	15 ditto.	Impracticable.
Total	107 Days.	45½ Days.

Of the foregoing Tables it may be remarked, that, under a different management, the number of days occupied in performing the voyages, especially up river in the dry season, will be much reduced. At present, *time* is no object to the Sindian; and, besides, he loads his boat so deep, that the ripple caused by only a moderate breeze endangers her safety.

V.—*Of the Winds and Weather in the Valley of the Indus.*

The prevailing winds of the Indus conform to the direction of the river, blowing for six months up the stream, and as many down it. From April to September the breeze is southerly, and during the other months of the year it comes from the north. An east wind of twelve hours' continuance is rarely felt. When a change in the prevailing direction takes place, the wind veers by the west from 10 P.M. till noon of the following day; the wind is usually fresh. The evening and afternoon are too often oppressive, for want of the usual breeze. This last remark is, however, more especially applicable to the weather on the Upper Indus.

In Lower Sinde it is often just the reverse, the breeze there freshening up about 3 P.M. However warm the days may have been, the nights, with few exceptions, are cool. A more particular account of the prevailing winds will be found in the annexed Table:—

Prevailing Winds.

Months.	North.	South.	Calm and Variable.
January	29	2	0
February	22	6	0
March	17	13	0
April	7	15	8
May	1	29	1
June	0	28	2
July	0	28	3
August	6	27	4
September	0	24	0
October			
November			
December			

The South Wind.—It reaches Kala Bagh at the entrance of the mountains, and last year was as fresh and steady upon the Upper as on the Lower Indus. This wind is believed by the boatmen of the latter to cease at Sehwan, and in my Report on the inundation in 1836 I mentioned the circumstance. Such, however, is not exactly the case. South of Sehwan, a spur from the Hala mountains comes down upon the Indus, which intercepts the breeze, and turns it off from the river, so that above the town for many miles calms and sultry weather are characteristic of a season remarkable at other places for the steadiness of the prevailing wind: yet, though this peculiarity is thus shown to be local, another circumstance leads me to think (contrary to my own experience) that the south wind is less fresh upon the

Upper Indus than lower down the river. Above Roree the boats have but a single reef-band in their sails, while at Hyderabad it is no uncommon thing to see them scudding before the breeze with their sails double and even triple reefed.

The north wind is not so steady as the south, but is often more violent while it lasts; clouds of sand darken the air, and compel the trackers to bring their boat to the bank. This wind is cold in November, December, January, and February: the thermometer at sunrise is often but a few degrees above the freezing point. During the season that northerly winds prevail, gales from the south are not infrequent. These are always severe, and usually last three days. The change is marked by cloudy, rainy weather, lightning and thunder.

Variable Winds.—During those sultry breezes that follow the daily lulling of the prevailing wind, the calm is often agreeably broken by light breezes off the river. These are seldom sufficiently strong or lasting to benefit navigation, but in tempering the heat of the atmosphere, and conducing to the health of the numerous tribes that dwell on the banks of this river, they serve an important purpose.

Storms.—Plenty of warning is always given, and ample time afforded to secure the boat, which should be done either under the weather-bank of the river, or the lee side of an island or sand-bank. An unsheltered position in deep water, with the open river to windward, generally settles the fate of an Indus boat. If loaded, she at once fills and goes down, and, if empty, the shaking produced by a short chopping sea soon opens the seams of a vessel that has no beams to hold her frame together.

In a river danger from this cause may appear slight; but when the stream and wind are opposed to each other, a short breaking sea is formed that will swamp a six-oared cutter at a grappling. Most of the boats that are lost on the Indus are wrecked in the manner here described. Gales of wind are experienced throughout the whole line of the Indus. They are more frequent near the mountains than in the neighbourhood of the sea.

VI.—*Of the Boats upon the Indus.*

The boats upon the Indus are of simple construction, and their figure is perhaps the best that could be given, considering the kind of navigation in which they are employed. They are easily constructed, not very expensive, and for stowage of cargo no form could be better devised. Their proportions, though not elegant, are pleasing, and when tracking or under sail their appearance is pretty.

The employment of the Indus craft is confined to harvesting the crop, serving the ferries, and keeping large towns in fuel. For these purposes the supply is ample. Secondly—Between the sea and Attock two kinds of vessels are in use, the *zohruk* on the Upper, and the *doondah* upon the Lower Indus. In boats belonging to the latter class a slight difference in the build gives rise to a further classification, and of this description of vessel the *moohanah* (boatman) enumerates more than one variety. But before particularizing each, a description of the *doondah* is necessary: her good and bad qualities are shared alike by them all, and the following notice of this boat is therefore applicable to every vessel on the river:—

Form and method of construction.—The hull or body of the boat is formed by the junction of three detached pieces, namely, two sides and a bottom—at variance with our ideas of naval architecture: the three parts are first separately completed, and then brought together as a cabinet-maker does the side of a box. The junction is thus effected: when each of the three parts that are to form the whole is completed in itself, the sides are carried to the bottom of the boat, and at once secured by crooked pieces of timber to the flat future bottom of the *doondah*. To bring the bow and stern up to the corresponding parts of the side is more difficult; and to effect this many days are necessary. Where the bow and stern are to rise, the planks are lubricated with a certain composition, which gives them a tendency to curve upwards, and this is further increased by the application of force. The extremes thus risen, a tackle is stretched between them, and by a constant application of the heating mixture, and a daily pull upon the purchase, they rise to the required angle, and are secured to the side, while an advantageous curve is imparted by this process to the plank in the boat's bottom. The bow of the *doondah* is a broad inclined plane, making an angle of about $20°$ with the surface of the water. The stern is of the same figure, but subtends double the angle.

Advantages of this construction.—To the slight curve in her bottom planks she is indebted for the following advantages:—In descending a river, should she strike upon a sandbank the boat turns like a top, and presents no stationary point for the stream to act against. A merely flat-bottomed vessel would probably show her broadside; and the stronger the current was running, the greater would be the difficulty in getting such a boat again into deep water. Thus in a situation where the *doondah* experiences but a little inconvenience, and occasionally, it may be, a few hours' detention, a boat of another and but a slightly altered form would be very awkwardly placed, though her safety might not be actually endangered. In passing through eddies, the common or wedge-shaped bow dips considerably, while the form of the *doondah's* prow has a tendency to lighten her draft; and the more rapid the current or the greater her velocity, the more buoyant she floats. When forced out or against the river's banks—an accident which the defective steerage of the *doondah* renders of frequent occurrence in tracking, the form of her bow, where the bank is not too high, parries the violence of the shock. A greater defect in the common wedge-shaped bow for river navigation (at least in those of the Indus, where the current is very irregular) is the surface it presents for currents or cross-currents to act against: these force the boat from its course, and deprive the helm of its power. In tracking this is often seen; and I can remember rather a ludicrous instance which occurred to the *Indus* steamer, whilst coming up the river to Hyderabad, in 1836. The day to which I allude, it was necessary to second the power of the engine by a tracking party on shore, and a number of Hindoo countrymen were employed for the purpose. All went on well, till the bow of the boat got inclined to the direction of the current, when out she shot like an arrow into the stream, and with her dragged the trackers. Casting off the drag-rope prevented accident; but the situation in which it left the Hindoos was not a little grotesque. Between the firm ground and the river lay a strip of recently placed alluvium, and in this the Sindees were planted at various depths from the middle downwards.

The present great defect in the form of the *doondah* is bad steerage. By rounding her quarter, and making other judicious alterations, this could be improved. To fit them for conveying merchandise, they require to be stronger built, and, for the convenience of the merchant, to have better accommodation: in fact, to be restored to the state in which an early traveller, Captain Hamilton, described them when trade flourished by the Indus, and its arrangements were such as to attract the notice of an intelligent European.

Rig of the Boats.—The masts are poised upon strong beams resting athwart the gunwales. Moving on this *fulcrum* their management is easy, and the masts can be lowered down or placed upright at pleasure.

The sail is hoisted behind in preference to before the mast for several reasons, the principal of which is, that as the boat sails only with a favourable wind, it is never necessary to brace or haul up the yard, and fewer hands suffice to manage the boat.

The *jumptee* is the state barge of the Sinde Ameers, and is used by them and their principal officers on all occasions, whether of business or pleasure. Perhaps the appearance of this boat, as she approaches the capital, is more characteristic of the Indus and of Sinde than anything else to be seen in the country. On this day her *meerbar* puts on clean clothes, and the national cap received from the Ameers on a recent river excursion. The bright hues of the cap formed by the gaudiest coloured chintz, vie with those of a Kilmarnock bonnet or a Paisley tartan. The crew are dressed as becomes the occasion; and as they bend to the track-rope the breeze distends their ample robes, and a further character of stateliness is imparted to the *jumptee*. Large red flags wave over her stern, and from the raking mast streams a long party-coloured pendant, that anon skims the water, as the breeze lulls and freshens. In the bow of the boat is a small crimson pavilion, in which royalty reclines, and in the other extreme of the vessel a roomy cabin of elaborately carved work, for its numerous attendants.

The steersman, on an elevated platform, stands in bold relief, and while he guides the boat encourages the trackers. The *jumptee's* crew are a noisy set; but, for aged men, wonderfully good humoured. They are divided into two gangs or watches, and are as partial to a cup of good *bang* as sailors are to grog. These boats are decked, and of considerable tonnage. One which I saw at Hyderabad measured one hundred and twenty feet over all, with a beam of 18½ feet; her draft of water was two feet six inches; she pulled six oars, and had a crew of thirty men. They are built of Malabar teak, chiefly at the ports of Mughribee and Curatchee. *Jumptees* are seldom lost; the only danger to which they are liable is that of having their bottom pierced by sunken trees. Their more substantial build keeps the frame of the boat together in situations where the poor-pieced shell of a *doondah* would fall asunder. The *doondah* is the cargo-boat of Sinde, her principal and almost her sole employment being the transport of grain.

The Cowtell.—This again is the ferry-boat of Sinde: her construction adapts her for this service, and for conveying horses up and down the river. From her great beam and draft of water, she is a faster boat than the *doondah*. In all their excursions on the river, the Ameers are accompanied by many boats of this description. The class is not numerous, and most of the boats are the property of government.

The *doondah* is common from the sea to Mittun, and

the boat most generally used in the fisheries, both upon the river and its *dunds* (small lakes). It is the smallest description of vessel upon the Indus, and at the same time one of the most useful. Two men are ample to its management; but a man and wife are its usual crew.

The Zohruk.—What the *doondah* is in Sinde, the *zohruk* is upon the Upper Indus, namely, the common cargo-boat of the country. The planks of this vessel are held together by clamps instead of nails, and the junction is often neatly enough executed. This class of boats is not so strong as the *doondah*, but they sail faster and draw less water. They are more roomy than the *doondah*, and though less adapted for the conveyance of goods, are much superior for transporting troops.

The Duggah.—This is the clumsiest, and, at the same time, the strongest built boat upon the Indus. She is confined to that rocky and dangerous part of the coast between Kala Bagh and Attock. The form of the boat differs but slightly from that of the *doondah*. The *duggah* has neither mast nor sail. Her name is the Sindean word for cow, and the awkward sluggish motion of this boat shows that it has not been misapplied. If the *duggah* drops down the river to Mittun, there she must remain, and be sold for whatever sum she will bring; for to drag her up against the stream to Kala Bagh would cost more money in the hire of men than the boat is worth.

Management of the Boats.—Under sail, the very best of them will not be within eight or nine points of the wind. Dropping down the river with a contrary wind, the mast is unshipped, as also the rudder, and the latter is replaced by two sculls. Should the wind blow strong, a boat without cargo can make no progress, and the safety of one laden is endangered by the chopping sea it raises.

Tracking is performed as follows:—The boat is provided with a track-rope at least a hundred fathoms long: it is rove through the uppermost sheave-hole at the mast-head, and the inner end fastened to the rail or platform on which the steersman is standing. On the hauling-post before the mast is a guy, called a "*lagh*," the lower end of which passes through a ring-bolt in the bow of the boat. This guy is of as much utility as the helm itself. Before the boat starts, the track-rope is middled, and the inner half coiled down under the feet of the steersman: one man is stationed by the guy, and the remainder of the crew toggle on to the shore part of the line. Thus yoked, they march at the rate of two miles an hour up to the knees, often higher, in water or in mud. Whilst thus advancing the foremost walker calls out "Shoal water!" on which the inner end of the clog rope is let go, the guy eased off, the helm put to one side or the other, as the case may be, and the boat, thus relieved, avoids taking the ground by shooting out into the stream. The shoal passed, the guy is shortened, the line again middled, and the crew advance at the same slow pace as before. Boats should have two track-ropes, and when turning the bend of the reaches both should be on shore. They should also be provided with a heavy grapnel to drop, in the event of accident to the track-ropes.

The steep banks in bends of the river should be avoided, for under them circles a current in a contrary direction to that of the main stream, the quick gyratory motion of which is constantly exerted, to the destruction of the bank, and that of such boats as frequent it.*

Boat-building, materials, suggestions.—Boats are constructed according to established usage, which has fixed

---

* See an example of this in Table VI., headed Irregularities in the Bed of the *Indus*.

a proportion between the beam and length of each boat. The tonnage is calculated on the boat's bottom, from the point where the stem and stern rise. The angle at which it takes place is matter of taste: a high projecting stern improves the steerage, and a low bow gives speed. The banks of the *Indus* are deficient in almost every article used in constructing the boats on the river. The Lower Sinde is supplied with plank and spars from the Malabar coast, and with coir and cordage from the same quarter. The Ameers of Hyderabad are, however, the chief, almost the sole purchasers. The *Moohana*, unable to give the high price asked by Cutch boatmen for teak plank, exhibit both skill and ingenuity in building boats of timber of their own country's growth: for this the orchard is robbed, and the country for miles round laid under contribution. In the bottom of a single boat, teak, baire, fir, babool, and the curreel tree are sometimes seen together; and in the same extent of workmanship six hundred and seventy-three patches have been counted.

The Upper *Indus* is principally supplied from the banks of the Chenaub, where the talee tree, the sissoo of Hindostan, is seen with a trunk measuring twelve feet in circumference. Three such trees furnish plank enough to build a large-sized *zohruk*.

The Attock boats are built of good fir, brought down the Cabool river, and from the forest of the Lower Himalaya.

Iron-work.—The Lower Indus is supplied from Bombay, and the upper portion of the river from the mines of Bunnoo and Badjour. It is customary to purchase the latter in the matrix, and to allow a percentage to the blacksmith who smelts the ore, and works it up into nails.

Cordage.—Upon the Upper Indus the rope is either of hemp, or formed from the culm of certain tall reedy grasses, very plentiful on the banks of this river.

The tools of the Sinde carpenter are as little diversified in form as those used by the same class of artificers in India. The absence of good material to work upon sharpens his inventive powers, and gives a manual dexterity that improves the execution of whatever he may have to do, when really good timber comes before him. If a curve is to be imparted to one or a dozen planks united, chaff moistened with water is the Sinde carpenter's store; or what answers the purpose still better, the dung of animals, and more especially that of sheep.

Teak-built boats are much prized by the *Moohana*, as are those of cedar and fir construction, which come from Pind Dadun Khan, on the Jelum. Such boats, when well put together, will run forty years: but from seven to ten is the duration of those patched up with the jungle wood of the country; and if care has not been used to see that the wood employed in her construction was originally well seasoned and selected, a less number of years brings on the decrepitude of age, when to delay a thorough repair is to lose the boat.

Adaptation of the Indus Boats for the transport of Military Stores.—They are not calculated to bear the weight of ordnance, such as a battering train; and at the present moment there is not a boat upon the river which a committee would declare efficient for the transport of these heavy guns. For this purpose, the boat should have a perfectly flat bottom, that the weight of metal may be equally distributed over the immersed portion of the hull. The sides, too, require to be fixed to the bottom in a more secure manner than is at present customary. The knees which connect them should be formed of iron, in preference to wood. If shot is to be carried, the bottom of the boat should be planked over the beams, as well as under them. The latter is all that is done at present; but if this is not guarded against, the nails will draw, and the shot fall through.

Should it become desirable to increase the amount of tonnage upon the *Indus,* boats could be built at Bombay, Hyderabad in Sinde, or Pind Dadun Khan in the Punjaub. If at the former place, it would be desirable only to prepare the frame there; but to build the boat, that is, to put her together, in the river. Good artificers are to be had in the country; but the introduction of a few superior workmen from the dockyard, with a clever native foreman or overseer, would be necessary. A smith is an indispensable accompaniment; and when steamers are introduced, this establishment should, to be efficient, be possessed of science, material, and skill. If Hyderabad were to be selected for building boats, still all the material must come from Bombay. If Pind Dadun Khan had the preference, a small supply of cedar plank might be there calculated upon, and the services of better workmen than are to be procured in Sinde.

Boat-hire.—In this charge there is some incongruity; yet it does not appear to exceed the rate of hire that prevails upon the Ganges.*

VII.—*Of Steam Vessels for the Indus.*

Naturally solicitous to be acquainted with the present state of internal steam navigation upon the Ganges, on presenting Government with the result of my experience

---

* See Tables VII, VIII., and IX. for the tonnage, price, and hire of Indus boats.

on this river, I addressed a letter, forwarding a list of queries on the subject, to Mr. C. B. Greenlaw, of Calcutta; and through the kindness of that gentleman, I have been favoured with the accompanying valuable Report from the pen of Captain Johnston, comptroller of Government steam vessels,—an officer more conversant with these matters than any man in India. In submitting this document to his Lordship the Governor General in Council, I will only remark, that in every essential point the class of vessels described by Captain Johnston seems well suited to the Indus, and the economy that pervades the steam establishment upon the Ganges is worthy of imitation here.

Towards the close of the year 1835, when the *Indus* steamer arrived off Hyderabad, one of the Sinde Ameers expressed a wish to be possessed of a similar, but a more powerful vessel. Captain Burnes, who was then at that court, requested my opinion on the description of vessel best suited for the Indus, and from the reply to his communication the following paragraph is an extract, from which it will be observed that I had then fixed for the draft of an Indus steamer the exact number of inches which boats upon the Ganges draw.

Paragraph 11th.—" In a preceding paragraph I stated that powerful vessels were required on the Indus; the reason is this: In some parts of the stream the current has a velocity of five and six knots an hour.* It will, therefore, be wise to possess a sufficient power, since steam is now so under control, that in the downward voyage, where accidents are more liable to occur, it can be reduced at pleasure; but if the engines be originally too weak, a new boat is a costly remedy. Two feet six

---

* I had not, when this was written, seen the Indus during its freshes.

inches is a good draft of water, and ought not to be exceeded: the boat to have great beam, not much length, and no keel."

Remarks on the Steam-boats of the Ganges, furnished by their Comptroller, Lieut. Johnston, R.N.

"Four iron steam-boats are now employed in inland communication; each steam-boat is 125 feet long over all, 22 feet broad, and tows an accommodation boat of the same length, and 20 feet broad, with a hold of 5 feet deep, capable of stowing 4000 feet of cargo, weighing 40 tons, the boat's draft when so loaded not exceeding 30 inches. The iron sides of the boat are 5 feet deep; above that is a light superstructure of wood in the accommodation boat; between the deck, which forms the hold, and the deck on which the crew and passengers walk, the height is nearly 7 feet; and the included space from one end of the vessel to within 20 of the other, or fore end, is divided into cabins and dining rooms, &c. Fourteen cabins are available to passengers: four of 12 feet by 9; four of 9 by $8\frac{1}{2}$; and 6 of $8\frac{1}{2}$ by $6\frac{1}{4}$; a dining-room, 20 by 12; two bathing-rooms; two pantry or store-rooms, a butler's-room, guard-room, and two cabins for officers. Each cabin has a water-closet: the windows or venetians are 4 feet deep by $2\frac{1}{2}$ wide. In the steam-boat the iron side is continued up in the centre to the height of the beams which carry the paddle-shafts, and the light paddle-boxes are of wood. The engines are double, of 60-horse power, oscillating: they consume of Burdwan coal about ten pounds per horse power per hour, and carry, at a draft of 30 inches, about 450 maunds. In the steamer there is a large cabin abaft the boiler, not habitable by Europeans in warm weather, but very comfortable in the cold. Before the engines there are two cabins on each side, 8 feet by 5, with a space between that forms a mess-room. There is also a very light cabin on the deck, of ¾-inch board, 8 feet by 10; the engines are before the boiler; the steamers have one mast and topmast, on which they set square sails when the wind is fair. The boat (a good stout cutter) is always towed close up to the stern of the accommodation boat. The anchors are 4 and 5 cwt., besides stream and kedge anchors, grapnels, &c. They are well furnished with ground tackle: chain-cables are alone used. The diameter of the paddle-wheel is 16 feet, the breadth 6, the board 6 feet long, 8 inches deep, and 18 on each wheel: they are preferred of fir, and are 2 inches thick. The centre board, when the vessel has her coal on board, is three inches below the water surface. The greatest speed of the steamer, when alone, is nine statute miles an hour; with the accommodation boat in tow, seven miles.

"The contractors have their coals in dépôts on shore, and send it in boats to the steamers when they cannot lay alongside the bank. Coal is taken by weight, and one hour allowed for the delivery of one hundred maunds.

"In the bow of the accommodation boat, and in the stern of the steamer, are fixed strong posts well secured, and at the same height a saddle is bolted on each, and protected by an iron plate. An iron hoop, 6 inches deep, is on the post, also above the saddle, in contact with it: a beam of 18 feet long, 14 inches broad, and 5 inches thick, with jaws at each end, connects the boats, by resting with its two ends on the saddles, and is secured round the posts with a chain, with a hook and lever, so as, by letting go the end of the lever, to detach the chain in an instant, and allow the boats to separate. There are also hawsers from each bow of the accommodation boat to the paddle-boxes of the steamer, which serve to guide the boats, and assist the steering; the following boat acting as a powerful rudder to the preceding one.

"Progress is more easy and safe up the Ganges during the dry season. There is little danger at any time in ascending the streams, but much in coming down; most during the dry season, when the channels are all defined, and the commanders are instructed to come with great caution, dropping through the difficult reaches with the head of the boats up the stream. They are instructed to consider the preservation of the boats the first consideration; speed a secondary one. In the dry season, the voyage downwards frequently occupies sixteen or seventeen days; in the swell five, six, seven, and ten: the upward voyage, during the greatest strength of the current, occupies from twenty-five to thirty days; at other times nineteen to twenty-three, and twenty-five in the swell. The current of the Ganges is seven miles in the dry season.

"The boats in the swell can generally evade the strength of the current by running over or on the edge of sands: in the dry season they must generally encounter it in full force.

"There is an establishment of pilots (native fishermen). The distances vary from eighteen to twenty-six miles, through which they are required to be acquainted with the channels; nevertheless, a boat seldom makes a voyage without grounding, and the principal injury the boats sustain is coming in contact: under these circumstances it is nearly confined to the superstructure. On one occasion only a pair of boats suffered under water, being thrown against rocks by a strong eddy when descending under steam: each boat had a hole forced through the bottom; they were easily stopped, the injury being confined to the portion of metal actually in contact with the rock. A wooden boat would have been shattered by the concussion.

"It would not be possible to construct wooden boats to retain their forms as the light draft iron boats do; and I can conceive no means of improving on the boats we have, limited, as by the nature of the rivers we are, to length and draft of water. I believe that, for the Ganges above Allahabad, it will be in my power to fix a steam-boat not to draw more than 22 inches, with 24 hours' fuel: the economy of weight will be confined to the superstructure, the iron hull being the same in point of form and dimensions as those now plying, the metal a little higher.

(Signed)   "JAMES H. JOHNSTON."

There is one point in the above report where I conceive a different arrangement must be made upon the Indus to what prevails on the Ganges. Most of the fuel dépôts on the Indus must be afloat. If wood firing is used, there is no alternative; for otherwise the time lost in taking it on board will cancel all the other advantages of steam.

The banks of the Ganges are high, substantial, and, compared to the banks of this river, permanent. Towns overlook the river; ghauts, or landing-places, are constructed on the banks; and the steam-boat at most of the stations has only to shove alongside the ghaut and receive her fuel.

It is very different with the Indus. Towns stand within two miles of the river, and the banks are ever varying their outline. I would therefore recommend that large

APPENDIX II.

manageable flats be used for this purpose, and anchored at such distances apart as subsequent experience may suggest: their draft should be restricted to three feet six inches, and each should have a small boat attached, by which means the crew of the flat would be able to keep the floating well supplied from the shore store.

I am further of opinion that were the *zohruk's* defective steerage overcome, steamers built upon her model will be efficient boats.

VIII.—*Of Fuel for Steam-boats.*

The jungle on the banks of the Indus contains the following trees:—

1. *Mangrove.*—Found in the Delta, is plentiful, and burns well.—Though it attains no great height, it has sometimes a circumference of 12 feet.

2. *Kundie.*—Rarely exceeds 9 feet in height, and is found, though not confined to the locality under the Lukkee mountains, between Chandkote and Sehwan. In Lower Sinde this wood is scarce; but twelve miles south of Mittun, on the west bank of the river, is an extensive jungle, in which this is the most common tree; the hardness of its fibre and the crookedness of its grain make it in great request among the boat-builders.

3. *Baun.*—Little of this wood is seen below Hyderabad; but between that capital and Sehwan the tree is common. As fuel it is useless.

4. *Jall* or *Pello.*—This tree is found in every part of the river's course. Between the river and desert two descriptions of trees prevail. Tamarisk fringes the river, Jall or Pello the desert; the latter as a fuel is not superior to Baun.

5. *Tamarisk.*—From the sea to Kala Bagh this wood

is more or less plentiful; almost any quantity of it is procurable: but the large wood is distant from one to twelve miles from the Indus, and considerable expense and delay must necessarily be incurred in transporting it to the river. Tamarisk is the common firewood of this country.

6. *Kurreel.*—It is plentiful in Sinde, but makes an indifferent fuel: it gives out volumes of smoke, but emits no flame. This wood is generally crooked, and its fibre being hard, it is advantageously used for knees of boats, and wherever curved lines, strength, and durability are sought to be combined.

7. *Loohera.*—Between Lake Munchur and the mountains grows a tree of this name, of a dwarfish size, and very common; as a fuel it is even worse than the last described.

8. *Tallee.*—This tree is not common on the banks of the Indus, and the few that do occur are found near villages, in single trees. It attains a large size, and is much in request amongst the boat-builders. It burns well, but the tree is too valuable to be cut down solely for firewood.

9. *Babool* or *Bubber.*—This tree is plentiful in Sinde, but becomes less as we ascend the river. It makes an excellent fuel.

Shikargahs or *Hunting Forests.*—They are numerous below Sehwan, but above that town they are not found. The trees they contain are mostly Tamarisk and Babool. These forests at some places fringe the river for three and four miles, but their medium width seldom exceeds one. In a few of them are trees of a large size; but far the greater number are merely extensive thickets, containing saplings of sorts, tall grass and reeds, the spontaneous offspring of a rank inundated soil.

In December, 1835, I made several experiments with the *Indus* steamer to ascertain the relative strength of wood and coal fuel. The result was as follows:—Tamarisk, when newly cut down, would not generate enough steam to feed the engine, though working only one-half power. If the billets were large and thoroughly dry, it answered the purpose better; though I consider this wood at best but a very indifferent fuel. Mangrove and the Babool trees are much superior: burning equal proportions of the two last, the furnaces were replenished once in seven minutes; with coal (not however of a very good quality) every fifteen. Coal has thus an advantage over wood fuel, in something more than the proportion of two to one; and when the superior performance of machinery driven by the former is taken into account, it is doubtful which is the more economical plan, to navigate the Indus with coal from England, or the jungle now growing upon its banks.* The question resolves itself simply into one of expense, for there is wood enough on the banks of the Indus to keep two or more steamers constantly plying for years to come.

On this subject, Captain Johnston, the Comptroller of Government Steam Vessels, has made several experiments with steam-boats on the Ganges. The result is already before Government; but, having obtained, through the kindness of that officer, a copy of his report, the nature and value of its contents are my apology for introducing it here.

Report on the relative Value of Wood and Coal, by Captain Johnston, the Comptroller of Government Steam Vessels.

On Friday the 27th instant, I ordered the steam to be

* Coal has been discovered on both banks of the Indus; the locality is the salt range, in the parallel of 32° North; deposits extending in a longitudinal direction, but not in a north and south one. Ten specimens from the west bank procured by Captain Burnes have been analysed by Mr. Prinsep, and four of them pronounced to be the purest form of mineral coal. Those forwarded by me, and which were discovered on the east bank, have not yet been examined.

got up, on board the *Experiment Flat*, and ran for two hours on the ebb tide between Fort William and the Reach below Budgebudge, and consumed nine and a half maunds of coal, making, on an average, 29 revolutions. I then returned with a flood tide, and in two hours consumed $11\frac{1}{4}$ maunds of wood, making on an average 21 revolutions. I also noted the time we were running the same distance under coal and wood steam; the periods were 90 minutes with coal, and 112 with wood: great care and persevering attention were required in the stocking with wood to keep the steam up, and twice the engines were nearly at rest from the steam failing. Admitting that the revolutions of the wheel on the strokes of the piston in the cylinder measure the steam expanded in any given time,

The coal would have supplied the cylinder 6960 times,
The wood 5040
———
Making a difference of . . 1920

measures, which, at 42 per minute, would have required $45\frac{1}{2}$ minutes longer of the consumption of wood to have completed, which, at the rate of $11\frac{1}{4}$ maunds in 240 minutes, would have required $4\frac{1}{4}$ maunds nearly, which, added to $11\frac{1}{4}$, would make $15\frac{1}{2}$ maunds of wood to produce the same quantity of steam as $9\frac{1}{2}$ maunds of coal; but it has been seen that, owing to the weakness of the steam provided by the consumption of wood, to perform the same distance, required $\frac{22}{120}$, or one-sixth more time nearly—a detention most injurious to the interest of internal steam navigation.

30*th October*, 1837.   (Signed)   J. H. JOHNSTON,
Comptroller.

IX.—*Of the Inundation.*

Like all other large rivers, the Indus is subject to a periodical increase of its waters, during the continuation of which it inundates a large tract of country. The river rises in March, and falls in September. From Mittun upwards, I have delineated the flooded district upon the chart; but in tracing its boundaries between that district and the sea, I labour under the disadvantage of having to draw my material as much from hearsay as personal observation.

It may in this place be observed, that the valley of the Lower Indus owes its crops entirely to the yearly swell of its river.

The soil of Sinde is naturally poor, yielding spontaneously the products of the desert; but, save within the belt of inundation, neither grain for man nor grass for cattle. Even here grass is scanty and coarse; a turf is a thing unknown on the banks of the Indus, and the islands in the stream below Bukkur are nothing more than naked sand-banks. Two consecutive crops exhaust the soil, unless manured. The natives, it is true, liken it to gold; but the comparison would be more just if applied to the river, the cause of all its fertility. On the banks of the Upper Indus the soil improves; and, were such a subject not irrelevant to this report, I might proceed to adduce the proof of this assertion, and to investigate the cause of so apparent an anomaly.

In some respects the annual swelling of the Indus is attended with peculiar phenomena. One year the country on its right bank is so deluged, that towns and villages, though protected by strong dams, are threatened of irrigation. In thus distributing its favours, the stream exhibits more of constancy than caprice, for, when once it has taken to either of the banks, it adheres for a series of years to the favoured side. Another circumstance merits notice. The Mississippi, when in flood, as we learn from Audubon, the talented American ornithologist, inundates the valley to a large extent; at that season the squatter and a lumber river canoe pierce the thickest depths of the forest, while flat boats of great burden, and steamers of noble dimensions, are seen moored to stately trees overhanging its banks. The Ganges, in the lower part of its course, overflows its banks in a similar manner to the Mississippi. During the S.W. or rainy monsoon, when the former river is in flood, the whole of its Sunderbunds, or delta lands, are, according to Rennell, submerged. With the Indus it is different. Inundation here is more often partial than general, and at the height of its freshes the Persian wheel may be seen watering fields on the verge of its banks. The *Kurreef* and *Rubbee* (autumn and spring) harvests afford the most conclusive evidence in this case. The crops of the first are produced from an irrigated, and those of the latter from an inundated soil; while the weight of the *Kurreef* harvest is to that of the *Rubbee* nearly as two to one.

On inspecting the accompanying chart of the Upper Indus, it will be seen that the river has double banks, or inner and outer ones. The first of these is as changeable as the navigable channels of the Indus, the latter as permanent as the river's course: the inner banks form its bed in the cold season, when the water is low and permanent, and hem in the floods and freshes of an opposite season. The following Table will further illustrate this interesting feature of the Indus, though I believe it is one common to all rivers flowing through plains:—

APPENDIX II.

Outer and Inner Banks of the Indus.

Parallel of Latitude.	Dry Season Surface Water.	Width of the Dry Flat.	River's Bed. Surface Water in the Freshes.
26° 28′ N.	1456 yards.	788 yards.	2244 yards.
26° 44′	658 do.	1560 do	2218 do.
27° 18′	850 do.	3004 do.	3854 do.

The double banks accompany the Indus after it has left the mountains at Kala Bagh for the remainder of its course. Were these banks continuous, the inundation would be restricted to narrow and defined limits; but as this is not the case, I will endeavour to point out where this barrier is broken or wanting.

From Attock to Kala Bagh.—No inundation.

From Kala Bagh to Mittun.—It may be generally remarked that in the northern part of the Upper Indus there is no inundation, while in the south, or lower part of its course, the flooded districts are of considerable extent, as a reference to the chart will show.

Mittun to Bukkur.—Neither on the east nor west banks of this division is there an outer bank, and the consequence is, that the country here is largely inundated. In the Mozarry districts, the floods of 1837 fell twenty miles back from the river; but in ordinary seasons twelve is the more usual measure of their width. On the opposite bank the inundation about Subzalkote reaches to the edge of the desert.

Bukkur to Sehwan.—Though the permanent banks may be traced in this section, their outline is broken, and the low districts behind them overflowed in the freshes. South of Schwan inundation of the west bank is general, though the quantity of uncovered land exceeds that submerged. Chandkote, the most valuable province in Sinde, is situated here; and its exuberant crops are to be attributed to its great command of water. Upon the opposite bank, between the river and the desert, is a strip of alluvium, the medial width of which is four miles. This belt marks the extent of the flooded districts; but for some years past there has been scarce any inundation upon this side of the river.

Sehwan to Efflux of Fulailee.—The Tela mountains for some distance below Sehwan prevent the river from expanding in a westerly direction, and a creeping hilly ridge serves the same purpose farther south. On this side of the river the inundation is confined to a very narrow belt: on the opposite side the desert opposes any outlet to the east; and here, though the inundated belt is wider than that upon the west bank, its breadth cannot be estimated at more than three miles.

Efflux of Fulailee to the Sea.—The delta of the Indus may be said to commence from the efflux of Fulailee. The lower portion of it only is under water, and the inundation here, as in the upper course of the river, is partial: the submerged part is a belt fringing the sea, measuring in width about twenty miles.*

X.—*Fords of the Indus.*

There are, properly speaking, no fords on the Indus below Attock; that is, there is no spot in its course where their annual occurrence is so certain as to warrant a dependence on their existence in any subsequent military operations of which the banks of this river may become the scene.

But that the Indus is at times fordable is certain; and in the course of my inquiries on the subject I have met

---

* These observations on the inundation of the Indus south of Mittun are given with much deference, as I have not had proper opportunity of inquiry. This does not apply to any remarks on this subject above Mittun.

with many individuals who assured me of having done it. What may be done once may be performed a second time; and when a solitary unassisted *Moohanu* can cross, it is just as possible that a regiment of infantry may follow. A ford open to a foot-soldier would present no difficulty to horse. The practicability of fording the river being once admitted, becomes a subject of importance; and, viewing it in this light, I shall devote more space than I otherwise should to its consideration.

The months in which the river is fordable are December, January, February, and March. No instance is on record of its having been done either north of Mittun or south of Hyderabad in Sinde. The Indus does not, within the excluded track, run deeper than in that portion of its course where the river is known to be fordable; but, being less frequented by the boatmen, its capabilities are not so generally known.

The fords are discovered by the annual fleet of grain-boats which descend in the cold weather from the Upper Provinces to Lower Sinde. Some boats in this fleet are of so large a draft, that their safe navigation calls for the most minute survey of the river's channels, and it is whilst so employed that the boatmen sometimes find they have crossed, almost unknown to themselves, from one bank of the river to the opposite, without once having had to swim.

During the dry season of 1836-37 I had frequent intimations of fords; but was not fortunate enough personally to discover one, for it so happened that, by the time I had got to the spot, they had always disappeared. The following sketch is taken from a trustworthy person whom I had sent to report on a suspected locality :—

Ford in the neighbourhood of Halá.

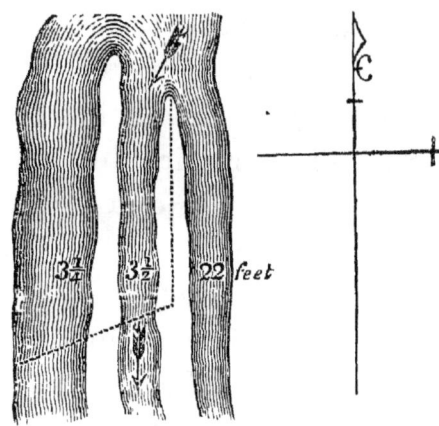

The centre channel is here the continuous one; that on the east side was, however, the deepest, and discharged the most water; but its mouths were closed up by shoals. Forty-two boats were lying above the ford, waiting for the channel to open: this was on the 27th of February. The dotted line shows the ford. On this subject I am glad to have the testimony of Dr. Gordon, the officer who went from Loodiana to Bombay with the Maharajah's (Runjeet Sing's) mercantile speculation. He tells me that, some distance north of Hyderabad, he came upon a shoal stretching completely across the river, when many grain-boats, unable to pass over it, were lightening their draft by transporting a portion of their cargo into smaller boats. Dr. Gordon, finding more water above the shoal than the boats in his charge drew, held on his course.

The custom of bridging the Indus by boats at Attock has prevailed since the days of the Greek invasion, and it appears to me that the same might be used with equal success to cross an army much lower down the river.

APPENDIX II.   345

The place most adapted for this purpose, whether viewed merely with reference to the river itself, or to the Afghan passes that lead down upon it, and which have not been unaptly termed the Gates of Khorasan, is Bukkur fort. Here we have a permanent channel, both banks of the river being faced with hard flint hillocks, while in the middle of the stream are some islets of the same material, on one of which is the ford; and contiguous to it, or rather adjoining it, another, containing the tomb of Peer Khaja Khizr. At no other spot below the mountains does the Indus present similar facilities for bridging. The channel here is as follows:—

Above the fortress the river widens to   1244 yards

In a line with the fort it is less, say . 1000 do.
The channel between the fort and the
    west bank of the river is, by measurement . . . . . . 98 do.
Ditto ditto on the opposite side of the
    fortress, estimated . . . 400 do.
Width of fortress and isle of Khaja
    Khizr . . . . . 502 do.

                                  1000 do.

Depth of the Channels.

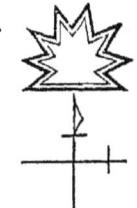

West Channel 98 yards measurement.
Current 2·9 knots.
5,6,7,9,12,15,9,3 feet.

East Channel 400 yards; estimated Current 3·7 knots.
7,7,9,9,12,12,13,15,18,30,24, 12 feet.

A spit projects from the north-west end of the fortress,

and extends to within 50 yards of the west bank. In this gut the current is four knots an hour, the depths were 6 6 7 7 6 6 6 5 5 feet: at the time these measurements were made the river had 12 feet more to rise. In fact it was when at its lowest level.

Last June I had an opportunity of examining this bridge of boats at Attock: it contained thirty-six boats, and the river, where they were moored, had a width of 540 feet; its depth by measurement taken the preceding year was 10 fathoms, and the current about 6 knots an hour. By comparing this account of the Attock bridge with the details of the river at Bukkur, it is evident that circumstances are greatly in favour of the former; but surely, if a few untutored boatmen succeed so well at one place, we ought not to despair of our success at Bukkur.

The chief, in fact the only, difficulty is, mooring the boats; and to effect this, the Seiks use an anchor of a form the very worst that could be imagined, and which has no other recommendation than its antiquity, and perhaps the ease with which it can be dropped from the boats. The figure is pyramidical, a skeleton of wood filled with stones. These uncouth things, when once let go, cannot be recovered; and as the strength of the bridge is not proof against that of the current in June, July, August, and September, a new set has to be made as often as the bridge is required to be constructed. Now, were a line of mooring anchors once laid down in place of these wooden baskets, and beyond chain bridles attached to them, a bridge of boats could be put together in about as many hours as days and weeks are now consumed in preparations.

The number of boats required to form a bridge would be built of a form the best that science could propose, and always kept in a state of readiness to haul out to their several berths, numbered, as the buoys would be, 1, 2, 3, &c. A bridge so formed would be a very solid construction, and able to brave, under proper superintendence, the strongest freshes in the Indus, whether abreast of Attock, or under the fort at Bukkur. Should it become necessary to destroy it, one end of the bridle chain has only to be slipped, and the mooring anchors are useless to an enemy. But little weight is due to the opinion of men who, not conversant with military affairs, cannot be expected to have clear ideas on such a subject. But still I venture to hold the opinion, that bridging the Indus at Bukkur is a practicable question.*

The difficulty would be to moor boats in the eastern channel; but, this once accomplished, the bridge might be made permanent, as the small western channel might serve for the navigation of the river.

XI.—*Of a Site for a Fair.*

While Government has it in contemplation to establish an *entrepôt* for trade on the banks of the Indus, it will not be irrelative to the subject of this report briefly to say a few words on the locality of those towns where the mart is likely to be fixed.

This question will, perhaps, be ultimately decided more by the existing foreign relations of the different towns, at the time when this selection is made, than with reference to their geographical position or their local site. Shikarpoor has hitherto been excluded from the

---

* I need not observe that this was written before Capt. Thompson (Bengal Engineers) threw his noble bridge across the river, by which the British army crossed in 1838, with their baggage and battering train.

list of places best adapted to answer the purpose of Government; but in the turn which current events may give to the political relations of Afghanistan, that town may yet become one of the *entrepôts* for the trade of Central Asia.

Shikarpoor is not destitute of collateral advantages. The large money transactions of its bankers, the extent and skilfully organised agency which they have diffused, are known to all interested in these matters; though the advantages of such an establishment can be duly appreciated only by merchants themselves. With steamers upon the Indus, the proximity of the town to Bombay, the market for European goods, is favourable to its site as a mart; and were Bukkur fort in our possession, the British flag upon that fortress would win confidence by guaranteeing security.

The *Zeearat* of Khaja Khizr, a *peer*, alike worshipped by Mahomedan and Hindoo, adjoins the fort of Bukkur, and on the anniversary of a certain day in April multitudes of both creeds flock to this shrine. Opposite, in the town of Roree, is a place of pilgrimage of still greater sanctity; for here, say the faithful, is preserved a lock of the prophet's hair.

The distance of Shikarpoor from the river operates unfavourably to its becoming a commercial mart: it lies eighteen coss inland of its port of Shukur. From May to September inclusive boats can come up to the town by means of a fine canal, called the Sinde; and were this work deepened and connected with the Larkhana canal or the Noroab canal of the Indus, we should have an inland navigation throughout the year, between Sehwan and Shikarpoor. It would traverse the richest portion of the Sindian territories, and evade an intricate passage of 100 coss upon the main river. So admirably is the

APPENDIX II. 349

country adapted for this means of transit, that throughout the entire line not a single lock is necessary, save for occasionally cleaning the canal. The returns would be great, and the outlay very moderate compared to that of similar works in countries where natural obstacles have to be surmounted, and where labour is a more valuable commodity than in Sinde.

The country around Shikarpoor is subject to inundation; but west of the town, and contiguous to the suburbs, is a dry plain, where buildings to any extent could be erected.

I do not believe there is a healthy spot on the banks of the Indus: in this respect there is little choice. Some towns have ailments peculiar to themselves; but from the day the river begins to fall in September to the end of November, asthma and fever are common, from the mountains at Kala Bagh to the sea.

Bukkur fort and Roree are built upon hillocks of flint, which, though not high, render both places more healthy than towns in the plains. The first is a fortified islet amid channel; and Roree overhangs the left bank of the river, with a depth of four fathoms water under the walls. As a *depôt* for military purposes, or an *entrepôt* for commerce, much could be written in favour of both these places.

Mittun.—The geographical position of Mittun is superior to that of any town upon the Indus. In addition to commanding both the Indus and Punjaub streams, it stands midway between the Gates (as the natives term them) of Khorasan, namely, the passes of Bolan and Sakhi Surwar, while immediately behind it are the entrances of the former pass by the auxiliary routes of Assui and Hurrund. The town is built upon a small artificial mound, and when the freshes are in the river it is surrounded on three sides by water: it is two miles distant from the Indus; but from the middle of June to the 22nd of September boats can discharge or take in cargo immediately under the town, by means of a fine natural watercourse navigable down the Bangalah and Omerkote. South of Mittun is a dry plain that fringes the above nullah; and should this town be preferred for the site of a fair, it is on the bank of this stream that booths and other buildings should be erected. During the inundated months, camels cannot travel north or west of Mittun. The inhabitants prefer well-water to that of the Indus. When the river has been falling for four or five successive days, to drink the nullah water is almost certain to bring on an attack of illness: this the natives attribute, and I think very properly, to the vegetable matter which must be brought into the watercourse by the drainings of the inundated districts. Mittun, and the village of Chatchur upon the opposite bank, can, taken together, supply forty boats, of from one hundred maunds burden to one thousand.

I ought before to have said that cutaneous eruptions trouble the inhabitants of Mittun: the sores frequently become ulcerated, but, though difficult to heal, the disease does not appear to affect the general health.

Dera Ghazee Khan.—This town has been more than once endangered by the inundation: when Nawab Jubber Khan, the brother of Dost Mahomed Khan of Cabool, was governor of the province, a wall that surrounded the town had to be thrown down to keep the water out, nor is there within a circle of many miles a spot exempt from its effects. Dera Ghazee Khan is situated about four miles from the river; but in the swell, like most of the other towns upon the Indus, it has a large navigable canal, by which it may be approached by boats for some months. Dera Ghazee Khan has, however, advantages that it will be difficult to set aside: the town lies at the foot of a pass in the Soliman mountains, that leads both to Cabool and Candahar, while it is equally central with respect to the Indian routes. It is the largest town upon the Indus, and, even under the Sikh rule, it wears an appearance of increasing prosperity. Its merchants, though they do not speculate largely, have an extensive agency and a considerable command of money. The country around yields heavy crops of grain, and the staples of cotton and indigo; while its home manufactures of silken stuffs, such as gool buddens, timorees, &c., are only equalled by the manufacturing marts of Bhawulpoor and Moultan. When to the above recommendations are added the fairs at Peer Adul and Sakhi Surwar, I believe that, everything considered, Dera Ghazee Khan, or rather some spot in its vicinity, will at once be considered the most eligible place to lay the foundation-stone of an Indian St. Macrea. By a reference to the map, it will be seen that Sakhi Surwar and Peer Adul are towns in the district of Dera Ghazee Khan: at each of these places a large *Mela*, or fair, is annually kept; that of Sakhi Surwar occurs in the Indian month Visukh, answering to our March. It is held in honour of the *peer*, after whom the place is named: the fair lasts five days, and pilgrims from India's farthest shores come to prostrate themselves at the tomb of Sakhi Surwar. Few come from the countries west of the Suliman range; and the followers of Brama outnumber those of Mahomed: the aggregate of both cannot be much under 100,000 souls. Though commerce is not neglected, there is but little business done.

A Khorasan or Afghan horse-dealer may now and then exchange an animal of his stud for the productions of India or the manufacture of Europe; but this *Mela* is essentially an assemblage for devotional and pleasurable purposes. With such materials, and the example of the holy Mecca, it is easy to foretell that (when the fair is established) many individuals in this annual concourse of devotees will become as enterprising merchants as they are now zealous and bigoted *fakeers*. Sakhi Surwar is twenty-four coss nearly direct west of Dera Ghazee Khan: it is a considerable town, situated in the mouth of the pass. Firewood is abundant, and a mountain rivulet supplies the town with water. At Peer Adul Zeearat, seven coss in a N.W. direction from Dera Ghazee Khan, a fair is held in February, similar to that of Sakhi Surwar.

Dera Ismail Khan is never inundated from the river, but is yearly flooded by mountain torrents. The present town lies about a mile back from the river, and was built about eight years ago, when the old Dera was washed into the Indus. Dera Ismail Khan is well planned, and, when its skeleton streets are filled with occupants, they, for width and cleanness, will match with those of most Eastern towns. The houses are of mud or sun-dried brick, terrace-roofed, and rise from a ground platform of from one to two feet high. Few are of more than one story. When I passed through it in the middle of summer, the bazar was well frequented; but in the winter months it is much more thronged. The town is a sort of nucleus or rallying point for those pastoral tribes of Afghanistan who prefer a clement winter in the valley of the Indus to the severity which characterises that of the mountain districts of their own land. Carriage is thus almost unlimited, as some of the tribes rear camels for no other purpose than to put them out to hire. The *Lohanas*, who from before the time of Baber have been the great carriers and traffickers of these countries, still frequent Dera Ismail Khan. The transit trade of India and Afghanistan is already fixed here; and if the routes radiating from the town are considered merely in reference to Cabool, then is Dera Ismail Khan better situated for a commercial mart than towns lower down the river.

These are all the places that present themselves as eligible spots for the establishment of commercial *depôts* west of the Indus; but should it ever become an object to Government to have the mart within their own frontier, then Leia, upon the Indian bank of the river, lying between the two Deras, is its proper site.

But to give full effect to these fairs, it is desirable that two be established, one for the Lower Indus and one for the Upper: the latter will supply, besides the markets of Afghanistan, those of Central Asia beyond the Parapamisan chain. The other, by the roads of Kandahar and Kelat,* will draw from Beloochistan, the districts around Herat, and the southern provinces of Persia, their staples of wool, assafœtida, and madder; while in return, it can supply the whole of this extensive region with the growth of India and manufactures of the British Isles, at a cheaper rate than can be done by any other route. Thus, should a general war in Europe exclude England from the Black Sea, an outlet equally good for the staples of her trade is offered by the Indus, with an *entrepôt* at Bukkur, and another in the Derajat.

---

* The port of Sonmeeanee seems by recent accounts to be most favoured by importers; and I understand that merchants are only awaiting the pacification of the country to commence carrying thence, *viâ* Biela and Kelat.

XII. *Indus and Punjaub Rivers.*

Travelling over the Punjaub, in a westerly direction, when its rivers are in flood, a little above the parallel of Kalabagh, no less than five streams are crossed, each occupying a large bed, and seeming to the eye a more important river than the Indus.

The Punjaub rivers, as are well known, fall into the Indus in one stream; and if we call our attention to the confluence of the united volume with the latter, the result is strikingly at variance with appearances and pre-formed opinions.

About the middle of May I examined both, when the relative size of the Indus and its Indian feeders stood as follows:

Indus, or Sinde.—Width 608 yards, max. current 4.8 knots, $\frac{3}{4}$. 1. 1. 1. 1. 1. $\frac{1}{4}$. $1\frac{1}{2}$. $1\frac{1}{2}$. $1\frac{3}{4}$. 2. 2. $2\frac{1}{4}$. $2\frac{1}{4}$. $2\frac{1}{2}$. $2\frac{1}{2}$. $2\frac{1}{2}$. $2\frac{1}{4}$. $2\frac{1}{4}$. 2. $2\frac{1}{2}$. 2. $1\frac{1}{4}$. 1. $\frac{3}{4}$. $\frac{1}{2}$. $\frac{1}{2}$ fathoms. Discharge per second 91.719 cubic feet.

Chenaub, or Punjaub.—Width 1766 yards, current 1.8 knots, $2\frac{1}{2}$. 2. 2. $1\frac{3}{4}$. $1\frac{1}{2}$. $1\frac{1}{4}$. $1\frac{1}{2}$. 2. $1\frac{1}{2}$. $2\frac{1}{4}$. 1. $1\frac{1}{2}$. $1\frac{1}{2}$. $1\frac{3}{4}$. 2. 2. $2\frac{1}{4}$. 2. $1\frac{1}{2}$. 2. 2. $\frac{1}{4}$. 2. $1\frac{1}{2}$. 2. $2\frac{1}{4}$. $2\frac{1}{2}$. 1. $\frac{1}{2}$. 1. $\frac{3}{4}$. $\frac{1}{2}$. $\frac{1}{2}$. $\frac{1}{2}$. $\frac{1}{4}$ fathoms. Discharge per second 68.955 cubic feet.

Here the principal cause of the disproportionate size of the Indus is the early commencement of its freshes. Indebted for its periodical rise principally, if not solely, to snow-clad mountains, an increase is first perceived in its stream when the sun comes into our northern latitudes at the vernal equinox in March; but the Punjaub rivers depending for their rise upon another and less constant source, namely, the rainy season of Hindostan, have their freshes later. At the time of my examination in May, the Sutlej, the most eastern of the Punjaub rivers, was at its lowest level; while the Jelum, the most western of the five rivers, and the one which has its source nearest to that of the Indus, had already shown signs of rising; from which I am inclined to think that measurements made in July would give, if not an entirely different, a less disproportionate result in the amount of water discharged by the Indus and its Punjaub auxiliaries.

But that the Indus is a superior river to the Punjaub seems very clear; and amongst the collateral proofs of this which may be urged is the direct nature of its course, compared with those of the Punjaub streams. Also the dread in which the river is viewed by the *Mohanas*, who, were the choice left to themselves, would prefer dragging their boats twenty coss up the Chenaub, to half that distance upon the Sinde.

Another circumstance connected with these two rivers is worthy of notice: in the Doab, or country lying between them, all canals are cut from the Sinde: in the month of July, when both rivers are in the flood, the surplus water of the Sinde pours down into the Chenaub, proving that though their beds for a distance of sixty miles are not more than ten miles asunder, yet that in their relative level there is a considerable difference.

It appears to me that Captain Burnes must have erred in giving so large a fall as twelve inches a mile to the Punjaub streams, and but half that quantity to the Indus. In the dry weather, the latter river has most decidedly a much stronger current than any of these streams; and even in the freshes, their current, as far as I have been able to observe the Punjaub rivers, is not so strong as that of the Indus. On the 27th of June this year, the current of the Ravee at Lahore was not more than three knots an hour, and neither that of the Jelum nor Chenaub exceeds four.

XIII. *Concluding Remarks.*

It has been matter of regret that so noble a river as the Indus should have no port accessible to vessels of burden.

The disappointment is, however, more imaginary than real. If indeed the merchant is necessitated to employ ships of 400 and 500 tons burden, such a class of vessels cannot enter the river, and he must land his goods at Curachee, the only port in Sinde open to vessels of this description; but if, on the contrary, he prefer water carriage to land-portage, why not avail himself of tonnage? In the fair season, hundreds of boats frequent the mouths of the Indus: they are the common coasting vessels of Cutch, and none of them exceed, when laden, a draft of nine feet. The average draft is six and seven. I believe that the principal mouth, namely, one that discharges the greatest body of water, will even be found the least navigable; and that the port of the Indus, though it may fluctuate between the Luckput creek and Curachee, will always be situated in a secondary branch, discharging little or no fresh water, but connected with the main stream by a creek or navigable channel open only to the flat boats of the river. But even admitting that a vessel drawing seven feet water could get upon the main trunk, nothing would be gained, as no other description of vessel but the light-drafted steamer already noticed will be found to answer upon the Indus, and such vessels will be able also to keep up the communication between the sea-going craft and the main river. If then a portage is thus shown to be unnecessary merely to give free access to the river, it is equally useless by way of avoiding the difficulties of navigation in any particular part of its course. In my former report I did indeed advocate the plan, but

I did so then from hearsay. Now I give the result of my own observations. The navigation of the Delta is certainly intricate; but the difficulties are not so insurmountable as to render a portage desirable, nor does the river improve so much above it as I was at the time given to understand.

In one respect, the authorities on the river have it in their power to confer a considerable boon on the navigation of the Lower Indus. The only obstacle in the river, from which danger is to be apprehended, and which no attention can effectually guard against, is sunken trees. Now the river brings down none of these from the mountains. All come from the *shikargah*, or hunting preserves of the Sinde Ameers. The supply might be cut off without material injury to these forests, or interfering with their highnesses' amusements. Let the Ameers but give an order, that between the *shikargah* and the river a clear belt of twelve yards wide be left, and in a few weeks their numerous foresters will have cut down a twelvemonth's fuel for our steamers, and insure a path for the trackers.

As these forests do not extend north of Schwan, the operation would not require to be carried above that town, the jungle wood there being too small to affect the channels of the river.

TABLE, No. 1.

Comparison of Chronometers.

	Chronometers.		Differences.	
Date.	No. 256.	No. 257.	1st.	2nd.
1836.				
Dec. 27th	4 18 00	4 31 05	13 ″05	2·0
28th	4 13 30	4 26 37	13 ″07	2·0
29th	4 26 50	4 39 58·5	13 ″08·5	1·5
30th	4 11 15	4 24 25·5	13 10·5	2·0
1837.				
Jan. 1st	4 12 35	4 25 49	13 14	1·7
2nd	4 36 05	4 49 21	13 16	2·0
10th	4 45 35	4 58 06·5	13 31·5	1·9
11th	4 42 35	4 56 08·5	13 33·5	2·0
12th	4 48 20	5 01 55·5	13 35·5	2·0
Feb. 15th	11 51 35	12 06 23·5	14 48·5	2·0
20th	11 18 30	11 34 31·0	15 01·0	2·5
26th	10 49 15	11 04 28·5	15 13·5	2·1
March 1st	10 48 00	11 03 19	15 19	1·8
5th	11 09 50	11 25 16	15 26·0	1·9
9th	4 38 00	4 53 32·5	15 32·5	1·8
April 9th	4 18 30	4 34 59	16 29	0
14th	4 02 21·5	4 19 00	16 38·5	1·9
17th	4 24 14·5	4 41 00	16 45·5	2·3
18th	4 00 12	4 17 00	16 48	2·5
19th	3 49 10	4 06 00	16 50	2·0
20th	3 54 37·5	4 11 30	16 52·5	2·5
27th	3 34 49	3 52 00	17 11·0	2·6
29th	4 00 14	4 17 30	17 16	2·5
May 19th	3 35 56	3 54 00	18 04	2·4
20th	2 51 53·5	3 10 00	18 06·5	2·5
1838.				
July 16th	9 59 00	5 47 07·5	4 11 52·5	3·5
17th	8 03 00	3 51 05	4 11 55	2·5
18th	9 56 58	5 45 00	4 11 58	3·0
19th	9 43 00	5 30 59	4 12 01	3·0
20th	7 43 00	3 30 56	4 12 04	3·0

APPENDIX II.

TABLE, No. 2.

From Mittun to Dera Ghazee Khan. The Time-keepers were examined at Mittun, and again at Dera Ghazee Khan. The following Table shows the result of each rate, while for the Longitude it gives a Mean of both.*

| Stations. | Latitudes. | Diff. Longitude by | | Mean. | Longitude. |
		Mittun-kote.	Dera Ghazee Khan.		
No. 1	28·58·25 N.				
2	29·04·38	03·57	04·21	04·9	70·30·34 E.
3	29·04·49	10·45	11·10	10·37	37·22
4	29·23·44	12·54	13·31	13·12	39·37
5	29·31·53	25·36	26·20	25·58	52·23
6	29·42·00	25·15	26·01	25·38	52·3
7	29·53·00	28·34	29·20	28·57	55·22†
8	30·06·02	27·34	28·04	28·4	54·29

Dera Ghazee to Dera Ismail Khan. The Watches were examined at these places, and the following Table gives the Longitude of the intermediate stations, deduced from a mean of the old and new rates.

| Stations. | Latitudes. | Diff. of Longitude by rates. | | | Longitude. |
		Old.	New.	Mean.	
No. 1	30·33·19	02·00 E.	01·51 E.	01·55 E.	70·56·24 E.
2	30·56·49	01·00 W.	01·18 W.	01·09 W.	70·53·20
3	31·09·09	01·10 E.	00·39 E.	00·52 E.	70·55·24
4	31·24·55	04·42	04·24	04·33	70·59·02
5	31·37·16	09·57	09·21	09·39	71·04·08
6	31·42·30	05·03	04·24	04·43	70·59·12
7	31·47·54	06·30	05·50	06·10	71·00·39

* Mittun was fixed from Roree.   † Indifferent.

TABLES,

In which the Geographical Position of Points and Places in the Line of the Indus, as they stand in the published Maps, are compared with the Observations of the present Mission.

No. 3.
From the Sea to Mittun.

Places.	Latitude.		Longitude.	
	Map.	Mission.	Map.	Mission.
	° ′ ″	° ′ ″	° ′ ″	° ′ ″
Barree Gorah .	24·12·00 N.	24·13·20 N.	67·54·30 E.	67·36·00 E.
Efflux Hejamree . . .	24·08·42	24·16·42	67·57·00	67·47·03
Tatta Bunder .	24·44·00	24·44·30	68·19·00	68·01·06
Hyderabad do.	25·22·00	25·22·04	68·41·00	68·23·03
Schewan do. .	26·22·00	26·22·35	68·09·00	67·55·17
Roree do. .	27·43·29	27·41·59	68·56·00	68·55·39
Chatchur do. .	28·53·29	28·52·07	70·31·00	70·27·57
Mittun do. .	28 54·00	28·53·19	70·29·00	70·26·25

No. 4.
Mittun to Attock.

Places.	Latitude.		Longitude.	
	Map.	Mission.	Map.	Mission.
	° ′ ″	° ′ ″	° ′ ″	° ′ ″
Nowshaira .	29·11·00 N.	29·12·19 N.	70·38·00 E.	70·35·28 E.
Raick . . .	29·21·00	29·24·20	70·45·00	70·39·01
Sherroo . .	29·42·00	29·42·00	70·58·00	70·50·03
Dera Ghazee Khan . .	29·58·00	30·03·26	71·00·00	71·51·23
Dera Dean Pemah* . .	30·40·00	30·33·19	71·06·00	71·00·24
Ditto† . .	30·51·30	30·39·20	70·57·30	—
Leia . . .	31·08·00	30·58·01	71·05·00	70·59·23
Rajun . . .	31·14·00	31·08·39	71·06·00	70·57·42
Khahree . .	31·30·00	31·24·25	71·01·00	70·54·02
Bukkur . .	31·44·00	31·37·16	71·14·00	71·06·28
Dera Ismail Khan . .	31·57·00	31·48·39	71·07·00	70·59·30
Kalabagh .	33·07·00	32·57·36	71·40·00	71·35·23
Confluence of Schewan .	33·10·00	33·01·48	—	—
Attock . .	33·55·40	33·53·53	72·27·00	72·16·27

* East Bank. † West Bank.

TABLE, No. 5.

Sectional or Cross River Soundings. 1st, in the Delta, in the months of December and January.

Parallel of Latitude.	Soundings.	Widths.
24° 17′ N.	5.6.7.6.5½.5.4½.4.4.3.2.2.2.1¾.1½ 1.1½ fathoms	
19	¼.2.3½.4.4½.6.5½.5½ 6.4.3½.3½.3.3.2½. 2½. 2¼. 2. 2.2.2.2½.	734yds.
21	1½.1½.2.3.3½.3½.1½.1½.2.2.3.2½.2½.2½.1.2.2½.2.	631
26	1½ 1½.1½.1½.1½.1½.1½.1½.1.1½.1½.1½. 1½. 1½. 1½. 1¾.1¾.1¾.1¾.1¾.1¾.1¾.1½.	455
28	1.1.1.1¼.1½.1¼.2.2¼.2.2.2.2.2.1½.1½.1½.1.½.	1277
34	¾.¾.¾.¾.1.1¼.1¼.1½.1½.1¼.1¼.1½.1¾.2. 2. 2.2¼.2¼. 2¼.2¼.1.1.1.½.½.	——
37	1.1.1.1.1.1¼.1¼.1¼.1¼.1¼.1.1.1.1¼.1½.1.1.1.1.1¼. 1.1.1.1.1.1.1.1.1.1.1.1.1.1.1.1.1.¾.¾.½.½.	841
44	1.1.1.½.3.3.3.4½.3½.3.2.1½.1.1.1.1.¾.¾.½..	691
47	¼.½.½.¼.¼.½.½.¾.1.½.2.3.3½.3½.3½.3.	——
48	½.1.½.½.½.2.2¼.4.1.1.1.3.3.3.3.3½.3½.2½.2. 1¾. 1. 1 .½ (1007 dry.) 1.1.1.1.½.	1132
50	1.2.2½.2.2.1½.1½.1.2.2.1¼.2.2.2.1¾.1½.1½.2.1. 1. 1.1¼.2.¾.	——

Between the Delta and Sehwan, in the months of January and February.

Parallel of Latitude.	Soundings.	Widths.
54	1.1.1¼.1¾.2.1½.1.1.1.1¼.1.1¼.1¼.1½.1½.1½.1½.1½ 1¾.2.1½.1.	780yds.
58	1.1.1½.1¾.2.2.2.2.2.2.1¼.1.¾.¾.¾.¾.¾.1.¾.( ) 1.1¼.1.1.1.2.1¾.1¼.1¼.¾.½.	978

Between the Delta and Sehwan, in the months of January and February—(continued).

Parallel of Latitude.	Soundings.	Widths.
25° 00'	$\frac{3}{4}.\frac{1}{2}.\frac{1}{2}.1.1.1.1\frac{1}{4}.1\frac{1}{2}.2.2\frac{1}{2}.2.1\frac{1}{2}.1\frac{1}{4}.1.$	834 yds.
13	$1\frac{1}{2}.1\frac{1}{2}.3.3.2\frac{1}{2}.2.1\frac{3}{4}.1\frac{1}{2}.1\frac{1}{2}.1\frac{1}{4}.1\frac{1}{2}.1\frac{1}{2}.1.1.$	590
19	$3.3\frac{1}{2}.3\frac{1}{2}.3\frac{1}{2}.3.3.2\frac{1}{4}.1\frac{1}{2}.1\frac{1}{4}.1.\frac{1}{2}.\frac{1}{2}.\frac{1}{2}.$	400
22	$\frac{3}{4}.1\frac{1}{2}.1.1.1.1\frac{1}{4}.1.1\frac{1}{2}.1\frac{1}{2}.1\frac{1}{2}.1\frac{1}{2}.1.1.1.1.1\frac{1}{2}.\frac{3}{4}.1.1\frac{1}{2}.$ $1\frac{1}{4}.1\frac{3}{4}.1\frac{1}{2}.1\frac{1}{2}.1\frac{1}{2}.1.1\frac{3}{4}.$ ◯ $1\frac{1}{2}.2\frac{1}{2}.2.$	
25	$4\frac{1}{2}.3\frac{3}{4}.1\frac{1}{2}.2\frac{1}{4}.1\frac{1}{2}.1\frac{1}{2}.1.$	518
31	$1.1\frac{1}{2}.1\frac{3}{4}.1\frac{1}{2}.1\frac{1}{4}.1.1.1\frac{1}{4}.1\frac{3}{4}.1\frac{1}{2}.1\frac{3}{4}.1\frac{3}{4}.1\frac{3}{4}.1.\frac{1}{2}.1.\frac{3}{4}.\frac{1}{2}.$	460
35	$\frac{1}{2}.\frac{1}{2}.\frac{1}{2}.\frac{3}{4}.\frac{3}{4}.1.1.1.1\frac{1}{2}.1\frac{1}{2}.1\frac{1}{2}.1\frac{1}{2}.1\frac{3}{4}.2\frac{1}{4}.2\frac{1}{2}.2\frac{3}{4}.$	700
26° 00'	$1.1\frac{1}{2}.1\frac{3}{4}.2.2\frac{1}{4}.2.2.2.1\frac{3}{4}.1\frac{1}{2}.1\frac{1}{2}.1\frac{1}{2}.1\frac{1}{4}.1\frac{1}{4}.1.$	522
11	$1.1\frac{1}{2}.1\frac{1}{2}.1\frac{1}{2}.1.1.1.1\frac{1}{2}.1.2.1\frac{1}{2}.1\frac{1}{2}.2.2.2.1\frac{1}{2}.1\frac{1}{4}.\frac{1}{2}.\frac{1}{4}$	600
16	$3.4.4\frac{1}{4}.4\frac{1}{4}.3\frac{1}{2}.2\frac{1}{2}.2.\frac{3}{4}.\frac{3}{4}.\frac{3}{4}.1.1.1.1\frac{1}{2}.1\frac{1}{2}.2.2\frac{1}{2}.2\frac{1}{2}.2\frac{3}{4}.$ $1.1.1.1.\frac{3}{4}.\frac{1}{2}.\frac{3}{4}.\frac{3}{4}.\frac{1}{2}.1.1\frac{1}{4}.1\frac{1}{2}.1\frac{1}{2}.2.2.1.\frac{1}{2}.$	1000

Between Sehwan and Bukkur, in the months of February and March.

Parallel of Latitude.	Soundings.	Widths.
24	$\frac{3}{4}.\frac{3}{4}.\frac{3}{4}.1.1\frac{1}{4}.1\frac{1}{2}.1\frac{1}{2}.1\frac{1}{2}.1.\frac{1}{2}.1\frac{1}{2}.1\frac{1}{2}.1\frac{1}{2}.1\frac{1}{2}.1\frac{1}{2}.1\frac{3}{4}.1\frac{3}{4}.$ $1\frac{3}{4}.1\frac{1}{2}.1\frac{1}{2}.1\frac{1}{2}.1\frac{1}{2}.1\frac{1}{4}.1\frac{1}{4}.1\frac{1}{4}.1\frac{1}{4}.1.1\frac{1}{4}.\frac{1}{2}.$ ◯ $\frac{1}{2}.\frac{1}{2}.$ $\frac{1}{2}.\frac{1}{2}.\frac{1}{2}.\frac{3}{4}.\frac{3}{4}.\frac{3}{4}.\frac{1}{2}.\frac{1}{2}.$ ◯ $\frac{1}{2}.\frac{1}{2}.\frac{1}{2}.\frac{1}{2}.\frac{1}{2}.1.1\frac{1}{2}.1\frac{1}{4}.2\frac{1}{2}.$ $2\frac{1}{2}.2\frac{1}{2}.$	1684 yds.
28	$\frac{1}{2}.\frac{3}{4}.\frac{3}{4}.\frac{1}{2}.\frac{3}{4}.\frac{3}{4}.1.1.1.\frac{3}{4}.\frac{3}{4}.\frac{3}{4}.1.1.1.1.1\frac{1}{4}.1\frac{1}{4}.1\frac{1}{4}.\frac{3}{4}.\frac{3}{4}.1.$ $1.\frac{3}{4}.\frac{1}{2}.\frac{1}{2}.\frac{1}{2}.\frac{3}{4}.1\frac{1}{2}.2\frac{1}{4}.2\frac{1}{4}.1\frac{1}{2}.\frac{1}{4}.\frac{1}{2}.\frac{1}{2}.\frac{3}{4}.\frac{3}{4}.\frac{1}{2}.1.1\frac{1}{2}.$ $1\frac{1}{2}.1\frac{1}{2}.1\frac{1}{4}.1.\frac{3}{4}.\frac{3}{4}.\frac{1}{2}.$	1456
41	$2.2.2\frac{1}{4}.3\frac{1}{4}.2\frac{1}{4}.2\frac{1}{2}.2\frac{1}{2}.1\frac{1}{2}.2.2.2.1\frac{1}{2}.1\frac{1}{4}.1.\frac{3}{4}.\frac{3}{4}.\frac{3}{4}.1.$ $1.1\frac{1}{4}.\frac{3}{4}.\frac{3}{4}.\frac{3}{4}.1.1.1.\frac{3}{4}.1.1.\frac{3}{4}.$	763

Between Sehwan and Bukkur, in the months of February and March—(*continued.*)

Parallel of Latitude.	Soundings.	Widths.
42′	1. ½. ½. ¾. ◯ ¾. ¾. ¾. ¾. ¾. 1.1.1.1¼. 1¼.1¼.1.½. ½. ◯ ½. ½. ◯ ½.½.½.½.½. ◯ ½.½.½.1.1¼.2½.2½. 2½.2½.2½.2½.2½.2.3.2.2¼.2.2½.1¾.1¾.1½.1.	1600 yds.
44	½. ½.1¼.1¼. 2.1½.1½.1½.1¼.1¼.1½.1¾.1¾. 2. 2¼.2¼. 2.2¼.3.3.	658
45	½.1.2.2.2.2¼.2¼.2¼.2¼.2¼.2.2. 2¼.2¼.2¼.2¼.2¼.2. 1¾.1½.1½.1½.1¾.1¾.1¾.1½.	452
27° 10′	2.2.2.2.2.2.1½.1½.1½.1½. 1¼.1¼.1¼. 1¼. 1½.1½.1½. 1¼.1.1.1.¾.½ ½ ½.½.½.½.½.½.	622
18	½.¾.1¼.1¼.1½.1½.1½.1¾.2½.2½.2¼ 2½.2.2½.3¼.4½.4.	850
29	1½.2¾. 3.4.4.4.4½. 4.3.3.3. 2½. 2½. 2½.2.1½.1¼.1½. 1½.1½.1½.	690
40	1¾. 2.2¾.1½. 2. 2¼.1¾.1¾.1½.1¼.1½.1½.1½.¾.½.½.½. ¾.¾.¾.1.1¼.1¼.1½.1½.1¾.2¾.2¾.2¼.2.2¾.3.2¾.2. 1¼.1.	1896

Between Bukkur and Mittun, in the month of April.

Parallel of Latitude.	Soundings.	Widths.
27° 58′	2¼.4.4½.4.3½.3½.3¼.3.2¼. 2.1¾.1½. 1½.1½.1½.1½.1¼.1¼.1.1. 1.¾.½.	561 yds.
28 03	2.2.2¾.3¾.2¾.2½.2.1½.1.1. ¾.½.½.½.¼.½.¾.1½.1½. 2.2.1¾.2.2. 1½. 1½. 2.1½. 1.1. 1¾. 1½. 1.1¾. 2½.2¼.1½. 1¼. 1.¾. ½.½.½.½. ◯ ½.¾.½.	1067
08	1. ◯ ½.½.½.¾. ½.1.1.1.1¼.1¾.1½.1¼. 2. 2½. 2½.1¾.1¼.1.1.¾. ¾.½. ¼.½.½.¾.1.1¼.1½. 1½.1½.1½.1½.1½.1½.1½.1½.1½.1¾.1¾. 2.2.2.2.2.2¼.2¼.2¼.2.1¼.1½.1.1¾.2.2¼.2½.3.3¼.3.	1123

Between Bukkur and Mittun, in the month of April.

Parallel of Latitude.	Soundings.	Widths.
28° 15′	1¼.1½.1½.1¾.2.2¼.2½.3.2¼ 2.2¼.2¼.2¼.2.2.2.2 2¼.2.2.3.1¾. 1½.1¼.1¼.1.1¼.1½.1¾ 1¾.1¾.2.2.1¾.1¾.1½.1¾.1¾.1¼.1¼.1. 1.¾.1.1.1.1.1.½.½.½. (100 yds.) ½.½.½.¾.¾.¾.¾.1.1½. 1½.½.½.½.½.¾.¾.	1969 yds.
17	½.½.½.½.½.½.½.½.½.½.¼.¼.½.½.¾.¾.3.1.1.1.1.1.1.1.1.1.1.1.1.1.1. 1.1.1½.2½.2¾.3.3½.4.4.4½.4.4½.3½.½.2¾.1¾.3.3¼.1.1.1.1. ¾.½.	663
30	1.1.1.¾.¾.1.1.1.1.¾.¾.½.½.½.½.½.½.½.½.½.½.½.½. ( ) ½.½.¾. 1.¼.1½.½.½.½. ( ) ½.½.½. ( ) ½.½.¾.1¼.1¼.1.1.1½.1¼. 1½.2¼.1¼.1.1.1.1¼.1¼.1¼.1¼.1½.	1685
36	1¼.1.1¾.2.2.2.2½.2½.2½.2½.2½.2½.2½.2½.2¾.2¾.2¾.2½.2¼.2¼ 2¾.2¾.2½.2¼.2¼.2.2.2.1¾.1¾.1¾.2.2¼.2¼.1¾.1½.1.1.1.½.½. ½.½.½.½. ( ) ½.½.½. ( ) ½.½.½.½.½.¾.¾.1.1.1. 1¼.1¼. 1¾. 1½.1½.1¼.1¼.1.1.1.1. ( )	1859
43	2¼.2¼.2¼.1.1½.1½.1½.1½.2.2.2¼.2½.2½.2½.2¼.2¼ 2.1¾.1½.1. 1¼.1½. 2.2¼.1.1¼.1½. 1½.1¾. 2.2.2. 1¼.1.2¾.2½.2½. 2¼.1¾. 1¾.1¼.¾.½. ( )	1323
52	¾.1.1¼.1¼.1¼.1½.1¾.2.1½.1½.1½.1¼.1¼.1¼.1¼.1½.1½.1½.1¾.2. 2.2.1½.1¼.1.1.¾.¾.½.½.1¼.¼.¾.1.1.1¾.1.1¼.1¼.1½.1¾.1¾.2. 2¾.3¼.5.6½.7.5½.4¾.6.4¾.4½.4½.	995

Between Mittun and Kalabagh, in the months of May, June, and July.

Parallel of Latitude.	Soundings.	Widths.
58′	½.¾. 1.1¾.½.½.½.½.½.½.½.¾.¾.1.1.1.1.1.1.1.1.1. 1.1.1.1½.1½. 1¾.2.2¼.2½.2½.2½.2¾ 2½.	600 yds.
29° 04′	1.1.1.1.1½.1½.2.1½.1¾.2.2.2.2.2.2 4.7.2¼. . . .	635
12	1.1¾.2.2.2.2.1¾.1.1¼.1¼.1½.1½.1½.1½. ( ) ½.½.½.½.¼.1.½.¾. ¾.1.1.1.1.1.1.1.1.¼.2.2.2.2.2½.2½.2½.2½.2¾.2½.2¼.2.2.1¾. 1½.1½.1½.1¼.1¼.1.1.¾.½.½.½.½.½.	1132

Between Mittun and Kalabagh, in the months of May, June, and July—(continued.)

Parallel of Latitude.	Soundings.	Widths.
23′	1¼.1¾.1¾.1½.1½.1½.1½.1½.1½. ○ 1.1.¾. ○ 1.1.1.1.1.1. 1.1.1½.2.2.2½.4.2¼.1¾.1½.1.1.1.1.1.¾.1.1.1.1.1.1. . .	—
42	1.1.1.1.1.1.1.1¼.1.1.1.1.¾.¾.½.½.½.½ ½.½.½.½.½.½.½.½.½.½. ○ 1.1.¾.1.2¼.1¾.2¾.3.3.2½.2.2.2.2.1¾.1½.2¾.1½.1½.¾.	1071 yds.
30° 57′	1¼.1½.2.1½.1¾.2.2.2.2.1¾.1½.1½.1½.1½.1½.1½.1½.1½.1¼.1¼. 1¼.1¼ 1.1 1.2.2 2.2.1¾.1½.1½.1.1¾.1½.1½.1.1¾.1¾.1.¾.1. 1¼.1¼.1½.1½ 1¾.2½.2¼.2¼.	707
31° 47′	1½.2.1½.1¾.1.1.¾.½.½.½.1.1½.1.¾.2.2.2.2.1¼.1¾.1½.1½.1¼ 1¼.1½.1½.1½.1¼.2.2.2.2.2.2.2.2¼.2¼.2½.2½.2½.3½.2½.2.2. 1¾.1¾.2.2.2.2.2¼.2.1½.1¼.1¼.1¾.½.½. . . .	1551
32° 10′	2½.2½.2½.2¼.2.2.2.1¼.1¼.1½.1½.1½.1¼.1.1.1.1.1.1.¾.¾.¾.¾.1½. 2.1½.1.1¼.1.1.1.1.1.¾.¾.½.½ ½.¾.½.1.½.½ ½.¾.1.1.1.1¼.1½.1¾. 2.2¼.2¼.2¼.2¼.2¼.1¾.¾.1.¾.1.1.1.¾.¾.½.½.¾.¾.¾.¾.¾.1.1.1. ¾.¾.½.¾.¾.½.½.½.	1855

After advancing North of the Parallel of 29° the freshes were found strong and the river high: soundings, therefore, it is needless to multiply, since the increased discharge does not affect the depths so much as the current, and the general width of the river's bed.

TABLE, No. 6.

Irregularities in the Bed of the Indus Soundings.

Between Attock and Kalabagh, there is at some places a depth of (in the freshes) . . . . . 31 fathoms.
Ditto Kalabagh and Dera Ismail Khan, under the mountains on the west bank, do. . . . . 10 ditto.
Ditto Dera Ismail Khan and the Sea, influence of the tide never had a greater cast than . . . . 6 ditto.
The result of a register kept at Hyderabad gives the mean depth in the freshes at about . . . . 4 ditto.
But the common depth in the freshes . . . . 2½ ditto.

	Current.	Miles.	Yards.
The usual current in the freshes is		5	992
When the freshes are strong		6	1272
The greatest measured velocity		8	323
Between Attock and Kalabagh, where the river is hemmed in by mountains, it is estimated in the freshes		10	
In the dry season usual		2	1376
Ditto, ditto, strong		3	1248

In a channel 1855 yards wide, the current in the middle of July has been found to vary its strength in different depths as follows:—

$\frac{1}{2}$ fathom	. . . .	2·7 knots.
$\frac{3}{4}$ do.	. . . .	3·4 do.
1 do.	. . . .	4·7 do.
$1\frac{1}{2}$ do.	. . . .	2·9 do.
2 do.	. . . .	4·8 do.
$2\frac{1}{4}$ do.	. . . .	5·8 do.

By experiments with Massey's patent Log Machine, the ground-current of the Indus has been found equal in velocity to that of its surface.

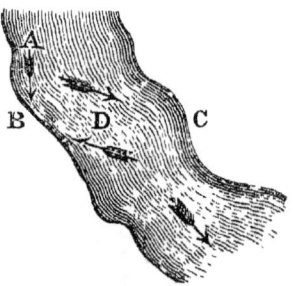

When the stream *A* encounters the bank at *B*, it is thrown off in the direction *C*: that part of the bed called *D* is thus cut off from a further supply. An irregularity in the level is the immediate consequence; to restore which, a surface-stream rushes up, as represented by the centre arrow in the figure: but as the water at the bottom of the surface *D* runs off by the declivity of the river's bed, no equilibrium can take place, while a rotatory motion, fatal to the bank, is given to a large body of water in its immediate vicinity.

APPENDIX II.

TABLE, No. 7.

Tonnage upon the Indus.

Boats	\	Kurwars from								No. of Boats.	Remarks.
	100	80/90	70/80	60/70	50/60	40/54	30/40	20/30	10/20		
Doondahs	7	33	47	50	70	70	100	100	150	627	Between the Sea and Bukkur.
Doondahs	0	0	0	0	0	0	0	11	0	11	Bukkur and Mittun.
Zohruks	0	0	0	0	0	0	60	0	0	60	
Zohruks	0	0	0	0	0	0	0	107	0	107	Mittun and Kalabagh.
Duggahs	0	0	0	0	0	0	10	0	0	10	
Duggahs	0	0	0	0	0	0	0	46	0	46	Kalabagh and Attock.
Total	7	33	47	50	70	70	170	264	150	861	

Abstract.

Upon the Lower Indus are 627 boats carrying 25,530 Kurwars.
  Do. Upper do. 188 do. do. 6,550 do.
  Do. Attock do. 46 do. do. 1,150 do.

       Total . . . 861   33,230
Deduct for old and worn-out 161   5,635

       Boats . . . 700 carrying 27,595 do.

Available between the Sea and Attock, in which neither fishing-craft nor the boats of the Punjaub rivers are included.

TABLE, No. 8.

Price of Boats at Pind Dadur Khan.

A Zohruk, cedar built, of 100 mds. costs 100 Nanukshakee Rupees.
    Do.   do.   200   do.   200—225   do.
    Do.   do.   300   do.   300   do.
    Do.   do.   400   do.   350   do.
    Do.   do.   500   do.   450   do.
    Do.   do.   600   do.   475   do.
    Do.   do.   700   do.   500   do
    Do.   do.   800   do.   500—600   do.
    Do.   do.   900   do.   600—700   do.
    Do.   do.   1,000   do.   700—800   do.

TABLE, No. 9.

Hire of Boats.

Per diem.

On the Lower Indus, Doondahs of 16 Kurwars $1\frac{3}{4}$ Korah Rupees.
    Do.   do.   35   do. $3\frac{1}{2}$ do.
    Do.   do.   40   do. $3\frac{1}{2}$ do.
    Do.   do.   38   do. $3\frac{1}{2}$ do.
    Do.   do.   60   do. $4\frac{1}{2}$ do.

Per month.

On the Upper Indus, Zohruks of 100 mds. at 10 Rupees Goondah.
    Do.   do.   700   do.   60   do.

And in the same proportion for boats of a greater or less burden.

Note.—The Nanukshakee and Bombay Rupee are all equal. Goondah is one anna short of the Nanukshakee.

    127 Korah = 100 Rupees Bombay.
    18 Mamads = 1 Kurwar.

APPENDIX III.

Notes on Cabool.

Cabool favourable for commerce—Its extent—Division of government—The Ameer's army—His position powerful—Relations with Koondooz, Bokhára, Candahar, Persia—The Sikhs—Internal affairs of Cabool—Character and policy of Dost Mahomed—Prices and supplies of the country—Value of land—Crippled resources—Amount of revenue—Moderate duties—Profit on English goods—Tribes of Cabool—Ghiljees.

In speaking of Cabool, I of course do not refer to the vast kingdom which once extended from Meshid to Delhi, and from the ocean to Cashmere. I treat only of the small and flourishing territory which surrounds the capital of that decayed monarchy. As a city, Cabool owes its importance more to its position, which is centrical for commerce, than to its being the seat of government; and it has therefore stemmed with success the various revolutions which have disturbed the general peace of Afghanistan. Invigorated as it is by this advantage of position, there are few places in the east better adapted for a metropolis. Its political, although inferior to its commercial advantages, are enhanced by them, since Cabool has a rapid and regular communication with the countries adjacent, and is consequently supplied with accurate information of what passes in them. And as to the abundant resources of foreign lands, it has not the wealth nor has it the exuberant productions of India, or even Bokhára, but it possesses a race of people far more hardy than the inhabitants of either of those regions, and who have, for the last eight or nine centuries, enabled the rulers of Cabool to overrun the surrounding countries. Chief after chief has issued from the mountains, and enjoyed in succession, as trophies of his valour and success, the riches and the revenues of the lands which he subdued.

The present ruler of Cabool, Dost Mahomed Khan, assumed a few years ago the title of Ameer. The chiefship comprehends the country extending from Hindoo Koosh to the southward of Ghuzni, and from Bámeeán to the mountains of Khyber. The eastern portion, or Julálábad, is a recent addition of territory, and has increased the chief's revenues from eighteen to twenty-four lacs of rupees per annum. This territory is apportioned in separate governments to the different sons of the Ameer—a policy which is more wise than popular. His brother, Ameer Khan, who ruled Ghuzni, is dead, and that district is also held by one of his own family. The distribution is as follows:—Meer Ufzul Khan, the eldest son, holds Zoormut, an agricultural district east of Ghuzni; Mahomed Akbar Khan Sirdár, the favourite son, has Julálábad, and is constituted chief of the Ghiljees; Akrom Khan has charge of Bámeeán, Besoot, and the Huzarás, tributary to Cabool; Hyder Khan has Ghuzni; and the son of Ameer Khan has charge of Kohistan, having lately been ejected from Ghuzni to make way for the Ameer's son; and when another of the sons shall be old enough, the nephew will probably be again removed. The Ameer himself governs Cabool, where he usually resides, having with him his brother, the Nuwáb Jubbár Khan. He has a park of forty-five guns, most of which are serviceable; about two thousand five hundred "Juzzálchees," or infantry, armed with a musket as large as a wall-piece, which is used with a rest; and twelve or thirteen thousand horse, one-twelfth of which are Kuzzilbáshes. About nine thousand of these are highly efficient. Three thousand ride the government horses, and receive pay, under a system of raising troops called "umlaee," which is new in Afghanistan, and in which Dost Mahomed Khan considers a great portion of his strength to lie. Such is a brief account of the means of offence and defence possessed by the chief of Cabool.

It is natural to suppose that the jealous attention of the surrounding nations would be directed towards a country holding so prominent a position as Cabool; but although too weak to pursue foreign conquests on a large scale, the chief of Cabool is strong enough to resist the attacks of all those around him, and the rugged nature of his country gives to his troops a power which frees him from every hazard. In his wars with the Sikhs, who are a very powerful nation, and will continue to be so as long as they are ruled by their present chief, this has been singularly exemplified; but similar success might not attend a campaign in any other direction, since religious animosity here inspirits the Mahomedan to war against the enemies of his faith. As it seems clear that no permanent impression could be made by the chief of Cabool on the conquests of the Sikhs in the plain of Pesháwur, the attention of the Afghans is probably turned in that direction, from some fear of the ruler of the Punjaub pursuing his conquests to Cabool; but there is still less chance of permanent success to Sikh arms in this quarter. The nature of Dost Mahomed Khan's position is hazardous, as it compels him to dissipate his resources in defensive preparations, which cripple his power, and augment the discontent of his followers, whom his revenues at no time enable him liberally to reward. A cessation of hostilities with the Sikhs would release him from this evil, though it would be attended with this disadvantage—that many of the Mahomedan tribes inhabiting the mountains of Eastern Afghanistan, stretching to the valley of the Indus, who now regard the ruler of Cabool as the champion of Islam, might then view him simply as an ambitious ruler seeking for personal aggrandisement, which would certainly diminish their ardour as his auxiliaries. From no direction but the east has Dost Mahomed Khan to fear an opponent.

The military position of Cabool is such that, if the governor of the city have any stability, a sum of money placed at his disposal can always command the presence of good troops, with every probability that the service performed will be to the advantage of the donor. In the time of the former monarchy the benefit of the money thus paid resulted to the state. In the present condition of the chiefship it would fall to the power that advanced it; and this gives the ruler of Cabool no small influence in this part of Asia.

To the north of Cabool the mountainous regions of Hindoo Koosh make it difficult for the chief to extend his power, or for others to invade him. The ruler of Koondooz, Meer Moorád Beg, has no feeling of cordiality towards Dost Mahomed Khan. This arises from fear of his power; for, if unemployed elsewhere, the chief of Cabool could no doubt make a successful inroad upon him. Moorád Beg excels more in a foray than in war. He might make a "chuppao" on Bámeeán, but the retaliation would be ruinous to himself. The independent Uzbek states, west of Koondooz and Balkh, such as Siripool, Shibberghan, and Maimuna, keep up little or no understanding or union with one another, and would fall a prey to the first power that attacked them. Bokhárá, to the north, is protected by its remote situation in the desert, and the character for commerce and religion which it possesses. The ruler of it lately sent an envoy to Cabool to congratulate the chief on the successful issue of his wars with the Sikhs. The Meer of Koondooz divined, and probably not erroneously, evils to himself from a league that places him between two powers, either of which separately might crush him, but whose ability to do so is undoubted when bound together by family ties. Moorád Beg therefore resented the formation of this alliance, first by threatening to seize the envoy, and next by shutting up the road of the caravan; but his suspicions have been removed, or at least lulled for a time, and an exchange of presents and friendly expressions has passed between the chiefs of Cabool and Koondooz.

Candahar, to the west, is still held by the brothers of the chief of Cabool, who profess homage to him, if they do not at all times exhibit it. Some years ago, Shah Shoojah ool Moolk sought to regain his lost empire near Candahar. The chief of Cabool forthwith quitted his own frontier, combined with his brothers, and, by a victory which he obtained, saved them and himself. Common interest dictated these proceedings; and on matters which relate to the general welfare of the family, the conduct and professions of the Candahar chiefs towards Cabool tally with one another. They address the Ameer as his inferiors: they seek his counsel as the head of their family, and they follow it when given. Such, however, is not altogether the case in matters in which their relationship with foreign states is concerned. Their advanced position to the west places them in jeopardy from Herat and Persia; and at this time their alarm led them, if not actually to slight their brother in Cabool, at least to court an alliance with Persia, contrary to his avowed wishes.

This, however, is a temporary inconvenience, which a settlement of the affairs of Herat may remedy: if not, Candahar itself may be overthrown, and, through it, the interests of Cabool most materially affected. Nor would the Kuzzilbásh, or Persian faction, resident in Cabool, with its present feelings, be a useless instrument in the hands of the Shah to sap the independence of the Afghans in their capital city. Dost Mahomed has lately reduced the pay of these men, and cast reflections on their courage in open court, observing that none of them were ever killed in his wars; but he may have mistaken a want of inclination, originating from disappointed hopes, for a want of courage. At all events he has lost sight of the great political maxim—that of putting it out of the power of these men to injure him before he insults them. On the south, the chief of Cabool has nothing to fear—the country, which is mountainous, and in many parts barren, being held by wild Afghan tribes, who are all independent of each other; and if they do not increase his strength, are certainly not to be numbered among his enemies.

When the great monarchies of Cabool and Persia adjoined each other, an intercourse usual among neighbouring nations existed between them. A desire to avert evil from Sikh encroachment lately led the chiefs of Afghanistan to sue for a renewal of this intercourse, but at no time were the feelings between Afghans and Persians cordial; and any approach to sympathy one with another, considering their difference of creed, must ever be forced and unnatural. Much more so is any connexion at the present time, when Persia exists as a monarchy and Afghanistan is dismembered into small principalities; yet the deeds of Nádir are held fresh in remembrance by the Afghans, and some vague ideas of Persian glory, at the beginning of a new reign, flitting before the chiefs of Afghanistan, contributed to the dread and hastened their anxiety to propitiate the monarch. The zeal of the chief of Cabool to effect this object was quickened by his solicitude, real or pretended, to war with his infidel adversaries, the Sikhs; but he seems to have forgotten that he sought to introduce among his countrymen those whom they considered to be still greater enemies. It was also equally certain that the power of Persia, being a consolidated one, would ultimately prove fatal to himself and all the reigning chiefs of Cabool. The Afghans would have been conquered in detail by those whom they sought as auxiliaries: for although each chiefship has a ruler, the country is without a head; and the natural jealousy and inveterate hatred to which divided power gives rise would have made it appear as an unoccupied land, and hastened its fall. Interested persons urged the Afghan chiefs to this line of policy. Persia saw the advantage with which she could enter the land; and, counselled by others, speedily responded to their call with abundance of promises, which the same advisers pronounced to be the signs of favour and condescension. The style of address, however, which was that of a master to a subject, first roused the suspicions of Dost Mahomed Khan.

To a point where so much attention is directed, nothing but a heathful rule can crush the aspirings of the ambitious and the intrigues of the discontented. For the last eleven years Dost Mahomed Khan has gathered strength; but the additions of his power bring with them cares and anxieties, which have of late been unfavourable to his popularity. The kings of Persia and Bokhárá may congratulate him, and perhaps sincerely, on his success against infidels; but he has purchased that success at an expensive price—a share of the good will both of the subject and the merchant, although both these classes readily admit the necessity under which he acted, and even point with exultation to his triumphs. Wars are not carried on without money and an increase of duties and taxes. A resumption of some lands assigned for charity (wugfea), which had no heirs, a lapse of the jagheers of Hajee Khan and some of those dissaffected to him, together with loans and fines, somewhat arbitrarily taken, and a reduction of allowances, are the means to which the Ameer has resorted for increasing his army, already too large for his country. The evidences of success in his campaign at Candahar and Peshawur have as yet borne him through his difficulties; but as reverses would have prostrated him, his experiment was hazardous in the extreme. To the vigilance which he has exercised over every branch of the administration his success is attributable. His sole aim is money; and he seeks for it from a full knowledge of what it can purchase. He expends his entire income, although his own household is maintained on the economical scale of 5000 rupees a month. Dost Mahomed's comprehension is quick; his knowledge of character very great; and he cannot be long deceived. He listens to every individual who complains, and with a forbearance and temper which are more highly praised than his equity and justice. In matters of a trifling nature he still follows the law (Shura); but in greater things his necessities have tarnished his decisions, although, as these affect only the wealthier and least numerous portion of his subjects, his doing so has not occasioned general dissatisfaction. Nothing marks the man's superiority more than the ability with which he manages all around him, as he does, with powers and resources so crippled. His patience and delays bespeak ambition; and as a rash act might be fatal to him, his caution is extreme, and his suspicion so easily excited as to amount almost to infirmity, although self-reflection brings back with it his self-confidence. A peace with his eastern neighbours would certainly render the power of the Ameer durable, and enable him to reduce his army and expenses; but as his fame has outstripped his power, he may rather covet the dominions of those western neighbours than their friendship. If he were less exacting, and such as he was before he came in contact with the Sikhs, he might consolidate his power. Whether his religious wars and government have resulted from a strong spirit of orthodoxy or from ambition is a question yet to be solved.

The state of parties and the policy pursued by the Ameer have had a singular effect on the prices and supplies of the country. The quantity of grain received in former times by a soldier as his pay or by a proprietor from his lands is unaltered; but such is the scarcity of money, that the value of grain is deteriorated by one-third, and often by one-half. It was at one time unusual, and even considered a disgrace, to part with land in Cabool; but it may now be had at from six to seven years' purchase, and is for sale everywhere. During the monarchy the Afghans went, in the course of their service, to Pesháwur, Sinde, Cashmere, and the other provinces, and brought back with them their savings. No such opportunities now present themselves: the Koh Dámun, Julálábad, and Lughmán are their Sinde and Cashmere; and the complaint of poverty and want is much more general than it formerly was, although provisions can now be purchased at a rate much more moderate than during the monarchy. In the time of the kings the inhabitants of the territories around the city set the government at defiance; and history makes honourable mention of the resistance that they offered to Baber, Nádir, and the other conquerors. But this independence has now been broken without a struggle, and three or four thousand families of the Kohistan have fled the country, and sought a home in Balkh and the valley of the Oxus. There is no evidence, however, that this migration has lessened the quantity of grain, although the Kohistan partly supplies the city, for greater industry now characterises the agriculturist than formerly. With a revenue of from eighty to ninety lacs of rupees, which I learn was the amount of receipts by the Sudozye princes, they were careless of the small sums that could be exacted from such troublesome subjects; but a revenue of twenty-four or twenty-five lacs of rupees, with foreign enemies to contend with, requires a greater vigour in the internal government, and has led to obedient, though not overwilling subjects. The effect of it would also seem to be, what is so much sought in every government, cheap provisions for the people. It may, however, be said that a scarcity of money, with low prices, indicates some irregularity in the state of affairs; yet the interest on money is but six per cent. per annum, being lower by one-half than is common among the native governments in India.

When state expediency renders it necessary to demand a greater amount of duties than usage has authorised commerce must receive a check. At this time the transit duty of this country still continues to increase; and it must have become greater even than it is, had it not been for the burthens which press upon it. Some grievances, however, have been got rid of by the custom-house being no longer formed and managed directly under the chief. Cabool can no longer boast of taking only one in forty, like Bokhárá; but as compared with Persia, Herat,

Candahar, and the Punjaub, Cabool is yet spoken of in terms of approbation by the trading community. A Jew from Bhawulpoor, whose authority ought to be good, declared to me that " The treatment of merchants in Cabool was as under the kings of Israel; that the Afghans were free from prejudices, behaved well, did not overtax them, and that the duties which the Ameer had lately demanded were such as any ruler who was under difficulties was justified in demanding." It strikes an European with surprise that any merchants should frequent marts where the duties are so liable to be changed; but there are certain broad lines which the ruler must never overstep, or the channel of commerce by his country would be deserted. This has not been lost sight of; and the custom-house duties of Cabool now yield two lacs and twenty-two thousand rupees per annum, while it was formerly but eighty-two thousand, nor can more than fifteen or twenty thousand of these receipts be attributed to increased duties. At the present time the profit on English goods brought from India to Cabool is rated at fifty per cent., and if they are pushed on to Bokhárá, they give a cent. per cent. return. The shawls of Cashmere, which are sent to Persia and Turkey, pass through Cabool and Bokhárá to Meshid, the merchants preferring this circuitous road to the exactions which they are sure to experience in Candahar and Herat.

The system of government among the Afghans is too well known to require any recapitulation from me. The republican genius which marks it is unchanged; and whatever power a Sudozye or a Barukzye may acquire, its preservation can only be ensured by not infringing the rights of the tribes, and the laws by which they are allowed to govern themselves. The ruler of Cabool has not erred in this point; and although he cannot reckon among his well-wishers those who were favoured by the dynasty which he succeeded, he has a large body of the community at least to applaud his administration. Nothing but his limited revenue prevents his being a popular ruler; and, even with this disadvantage, his name is seldom mentioned beyond the precincts of his court but with respect.

From the Ghiljees, or the race which ruled Cabool before the last kings, the Barukzyes have little to fear. They are a very numerous tribe in Afghanistan, being rated at two hundred thousand families, and extending from Candahar to Gundamuk, half-way to Pesháwur: but the tribes to the east and west of Cabool have little or no intercourse with one another; their ill-concerted plans of restoring themselves to power in Shah Mahmood's reign show how little probability there is of their being able again to obtain an important position in Afghan history. They might be used as a faction, but have been unable to make any head since they were ejected from power by Nádir, whose alleged cause of grievance, when attacking Hindoostan, was the protection given by the Moghul to his enemies the Ghiljees. The Ameer of Cabool has allied himself by marriage to both branches of this tribe, and so also has his son, Mahomed Akbar Khan, who, as I have said, is chief of the Eastern Ghiljees, in which government he succeeded the Nuwáb Jubbár Khan. Those to the west have more to do with the affairs of Candahar than Cabool, and this is the tribe which sometimes plunders the caravans between these two cities. They are a body of men distinguished for their fine appearance and physical strength, and still bear in lively remembrance that they were once the rulers of the land.

APPENDIX IV.

VOCABULARY OF THE KAFFIR LANGUAGE.

English.	Káffir.	English.	Káffir.
God	Yamrai, Doghum.	Cow	Istriki Gá.
Sky	Dillú.	Sheep	Váni.
Star	Tárah.	Goat	Vasrú.
Sun	Soe.	Dog	Tún.
Moon	Más.	Shepherd	Pashká.
World	Dúnyá, or Doonyá.	Herd	Icho.
Earth	Patál.	Tiger	Si.
Water	Aw.	House	Amá.
Wind	Dámu.	Door	Do.
Fire	Ai.	Window	Dan.
Lightning	Pulak.	Rope	Uterek.
Thunder	Trankyás.	Wheat	Gúm.
Clouds	Mayár.	Pin	Kakhchec.
Rain	Wásh.	Barley	Yú.
Snow	Zim.	Grass	Yús.
Ice	Achama.	Flour	Bre.
Moist	Ashai.	Bread	Eu.
Hot	Tapi.	Milk	Zor.
Cold	Yoz.	Cheese	Kilá.
Spring	Vastmik.	Jar	Shá.
Summer	Vasunt.	Pot	Siri.
Autumn	Shuri.	Salt	Yok.
Winter	Zuin.	Man	Nawistá.
Hill	Dá.	Woman	Mushi.
Plain	Gulúlá.	Son	Dablá.
Pond	Azá.	Daughter	Dablé.
River	Gulmulá.	Father	Tálá.
Canal	Shueláw.	Mother	Hai.
Tree	Ushtun.	Brother	Burá.
Desert	Chatadá.	Sister	Sosi.
Fruits	Deráz.	Uncle	Kenchtaulá.
Green	Yúz.	Priest	Deshtáu.
Horse	Goá.	Ink	Kachá.
Ass	Gudá.	Tongue	Jip.
Bullock	Gá.	Hair	Kech.

English.	Káffir.	English.	Káffir.
Forehead	Taluk.	Arrow	Kain.
Ear	Kár.	Sword	Tarvalé.
Eye	Acháu.	Shield	Karai.
Nose	Nású.	Spear	Shel.
Mouth	Ash.	Armour	Jirah.
Teeth	Dint.	Axe	Chavi.
Chin	Deti.	Knife	Katai.
Heart	Zundirwán.	Tobacco	Tamákú.
Hand	Chapál pain.	One	Ek.
Finger	Azun.	Two	Dú.
Nail	Nunchá.	Three	Tre.
Foot	Kur.	Four	Chatá.
Cotton	Poche.	Five	Pich.
Wool	Varak.	Six	Shú.
Cloth	Kamis.	Seven	Soti.
Shoe	Vachai.	Eight	Osht.
Quilt	Barastán.	Nine	Nú.
Iron	Chimá.	Ten	Dosh.
Silver	Chittá.	Twenty	Vashi.
Gold	Soné.	Thirty	(Not known, having only even tens.)
Soldier	Oatáh.		
Chief	Salmanash.		
Troop	Katki.	Forty	Dovashi.
Fort	Qila.	Sixty	Trewashi.
Wall	Barkán.	Eighty	Chatavashi.
King	Pachá.	Hundred	Chal.
Bow	Shindri.	Thousand	Hazár.

QUESTIONS IN THE KAFFIR LANGUAGE.

English.	Káffir.
What is your name?	Too ba nam Kussoora?
Where is your country?	Eema ba deshaki neora?
Where are you going?	Akeeny gayish?
In your country do they dance?	Eema ba deshukna natee chast?
Do you drink wine?	Chookrye piash?
I do not understand?	Yai ná piam?
Give me water?	Een aw áo?
Is the road bad?	Poont Awaiwa?
Are there bears in Káffiristan?	Eema ba deshukna broo wa?
How many days' journey is it from Wygal to Cumdesh?	Wygal oshtee kittee wass ká dunooá Cumdesh?
Who lives in Sháh Kuttore's country?	Sháh Kuttore ba deshukna Kinisheenustmom?
Mahomedans reside there?	Moosulman nisheenustmom?
Is there any king in Wygal?	Wygal Pachá waist a nu wair?
How many towns are there?	Kittee Shuhrwár?

APPENDIX IV.

SPECIMENS OF THE PUSHYE DIALECT.

English.	Pushye.	English.	Pushye.
Bread	A..	Foot	Payam.
Water	O...	Waist	Gainum.
M...	A..	Breast	Simoom.
Wife	Katookoom.	Belly	Koochum.
S..	P......	Thigh	Dawaram.
Forehead	T...	Knee	Kareem.
Eyebrows	Kash.	Fingers	Angorum.
Nose	Nost.	Ear	Kaiam.
Lip	Ooshame.	Hair	Loom.
M...	Gilanam.	Butter	Choost.
B..i	Darim.	Flour	Abooe.
Hand	Hustam.	Meat	Pe.

QUESTIONS.

English.	Pushye.
Are you hungry?	Awa toomá?
Are you thirsty?	Tanooma?
The Sun is hot!	Soora Gurma?
Have you fever?	Pare jech ke?
What is your name?	Name kera?
Where are you going?	Kuro shart ke?
When will you return?	Kema le yai?
Is it snowing?	Lange taro?

APPENDIX V.

Description of the Wild Sheep and Goats of Cabool, extracted from Dr. Lord's Rough Notes on Natural History, now in the Library of the Asiatic Society of Calcutta.

GOSFUND-I-KOH (mountain sheep); Booz-i-koh (mountain goat); Goch or Kock, Persian name. Argali—Ovis Argali—New Species: Male.—This fine animal, which has all the general appearance of a sheep, with the singular distinction of having large and well-marked lachrymal sinuses, is found in great numbers in the hills north of Cabool, which form part of the great Hindoo Koosh and its outliers. The dimensions are as follows:—

	Ft.	In.
From vertex to root of tail	3	11
From vertex to end of nose	0	11
Tail (bare underneath, no tuft at end)	0	$3\frac{1}{2}$
Total length	5	$1\frac{1}{2}$
Height to point of shoulder (wither)	3	$2\frac{1}{2}$
Height at highest point of loins	3	$0\frac{3}{4}$
Horn measured along its curve	2	8

The horn is of an irregular triangular form, with an angle in front; the longest side behind and shortest at top, thus . Towards its base it slightly approaches to a quadrilateral form, in consequence of its anterior side presenting a bulge (see section) a short distance below the angle, which, however, is soon smoothed off, leaving the triangular form distinct. The horn is transversely wrinkled to within about four inches of the tip; and in addition to these wrinkles, there occurs at intervals of about four or six inches a mark resembling a crack or flaw in the horn, and said to indicate one year of its growth. The horns spring up over the orbit and in front of the ears. At their origin the anterior angles are distant from each other three inches; the superior angles, where the horns rise at the top of the forehead, are so close, that the little finger can scarcely lie between them. They rise but a short way before they begin to bend backwards, and end by twisting round spirally towards the front.

The forehead is flat for some distance below the horns, but the nose is convex. The breadth between inferior angles of eyes about four inches. The colour of the eyes I was unable to ascertain, as the animal had been dead some time. Immediately under each eye is a large lachrymal sinus (larmiers), into which a finger can with ease be inserted. The ears are small and erect; the beard is white or greyish under the jaws, and continues almost black down the throat as far as the breast. There is no muzzle, the hair growing to the very tip of the nose.

The belly had been cut open by the "shikari," (hunter), and the intestines, with the parts of generation, removed. It was a male; but from its mutilated state it was impossible to say whether there had been any inguinal pouches or not. The fore-knees had callosities, no brushes, horns of a dirty white, light brown colour, shaded in the front. Hoofs black; no sinus at base of toes.

General colour fulvous, a slightly reddish brown. The shade is rather darker over the spine from the middle of the body to the tail, which is black, but there is no regular black stripe running along the back. On the haunches there is an intermixture of grey, and in their rear a disk of a dirty white, which is continued under the belly. The head is grey, as is also the beard under the jaws.

Mohun Lall saw this same animal, under the name Booz-i-koh, brought to Mr. M'Niel, near Mushed.

The Paychi (bezoar) is said occasionally to be found in its belly.

Markhor—Pazuhu—male, eight years old. The animal, to which the natives gave the above names indiscriminately, is undoubtedly a goat, and probably the Capra Ægagrus, though the length and shape of the horns seems not exactly to correspond with those of that animal. It was brought to me from the hills north of Cabool, and is said to be found also round towards the Sufued Koh. Its dimensions are as follow :—

	Ft.	In.
From vertex to root of tail	4	0
From vertex to tip of nose	0	$10\frac{1}{2}$
Length of tail (bare underneath, tuft of blackish hair)	0	9
Total length	5	$7\frac{1}{2}$
Height of shoulders	2	10
Height at loins	2	10
Length of horn along curve	2	$0\frac{1}{2}$
Circumference at base	0	9

Horn of a long oval form, rather flattened in front, on which side were twelve tubercles or knots (the last scarcely discernible), which were not continued round the horn.

Breadth of forehead between the eyes, $4\frac{3}{4}$ inches. The horns spring up anterior to the orbits; two fingers can with ease be placed between them on the top of the forehead. They are closer at their insertion than at any other part, as they curve a little outwards, upwards, and then backwards.

The profile, from the insertion of the horns to the tip of the nose, was perfectly straight.

It must be an extremely powerful animal; the depth of the chest immediately behind the shoulders was 1 foot 6 inches; the legs are strong and muscular, and the hoofs nearly as large as those of a small cow.

The beard is black, and confined to a tuft under the chin.

The fore-knees had the hair rubbed off, and slight callosities rather on their outer face.

The general colour of the head and body was a dull brownish grey, lighter under the belly, but becoming darker, and almost black, in the front of each leg. The back of the leg was shaded out with a dirty white or fawn colour. The hoofs were black. The horns were blackish towards the root, of a dirty yellow higher up, showing their annual growth by cracks or flaws. The tail had a tuft of black hair at its end. There was no lachrymal sinus. There was hair at the end of the nose, and a black bit on the posterior half of the spine.

The shikari had ripped up all the lower part of the belly.

Markhor.—The same animal brought to me at Koondooz, 14th December, from the hills near Baghlán, where it is said to be abundant.

This is the third of these ruminant animals which has been brought to me from the Cabool mountains, and its horns, erect and spiral, render it the most remarkable of the three. It is in all respects a goat. Its dimensions are as follow :—

	Ft.	In.
Length from vertex to root of tail	4	0
Length from vertex to tip of nose	0	$10\frac{1}{2}$

	Ft.	In.
Length of tail (bare underneath, tuft of black hair)	0	6
Total length	5	4½
Height at shoulders	3	1
Height at loins	2	10
Length of horn in straight line	2	1½
Length of horn along spiral	2	6
Circumference of horn at base	0	8½
Distance of tips	1	8

The horns touch at the base, and proceed in long spiral folds upwards, outwards, and a little backwards, forming two complete revolutions. Were it not for these revolutions, the shape would be distinctly triangular. There are no annulations or wrinkles, though the horn is rough. The breadth of the forehead between the eyes, 5 inches. The horns spring anterior to the orbits: in front there is room for a finger between their anterior angles; but on the back of the forehead their posterior angles may be said to touch.

The profile is quite straight; no lachrymal sinus. The beard is grey on the chin, and continued in long white shaggy hair down the whole neck. The fore-knees had large, well-marked callosities quite in front: there was a callosity on the breast.

General colour, dull rufus grey, blackish from between the horns to the tail; grey colour under the belly, on the back of the haunches, and below the knee of each leg. Hoofs black, tipped with white. Horns uniform, dirty yellowish colour, darker towards the root. Annual cracks or flaws distinct. The tail had a small tuft of black hair on its end.

The lower part of the belly had been ripped up, and intestines removed by the shikari.

APPENDIX VI.

AN EASTERN ESSAY ON PHYSIOGNOMY, &c.

BE it known to men of wisdom and understanding that this tract contains the science of physiognomy, and is copied from a book named "Nufuyus ul funoon." This is a science which shows the secret dispositions and hidden qualities of mankind by a sight of the face and limbs. For instance, you see a man, and immediately learn from his countenance whether he possesses good or evil habits, and what is suitable for him.

There is a sufficient reason to call this science most valuable and useful. A man who lives in the city is better in temper than the native of the desert. By the city is meant where a body of men reside together, and where a person is not seen alone, and cannot avoid the society of other people. Since wickedness and fraud are prevalent among men, the science in question stands as a security for teaching all the secrets of the heart, and is therefore very excellent.

They who train the horse, camel, hawk, falcon, &c., can find, from their appearance, their good or bad qualities, and thus tame them immediately. If this is advantageous for beasts, it must be extremely useful to mankind.

The wisest and most experienced individuals have said that good temper is found in company with a good face, and that bad habits are associated with a bad countenance.

Imám Shafái says that he endeavoured very much to acquire this science, and read many works on it. In his travels from Yemen to Medina he met a person at one of the stages. He was of ruddy complexion, had blue eyes, and a projecting forehead, which, according to the science of physiognomy, are very unlucky features. "He saw and saluted me," says the Imám, "and with an open face and sweet tongue inquired after my health, and conducted me to his own house. He set fresh jars of water before me, and spread a beautiful table-cloth, over which he placed the most delicious food. He also provided the cattle with grass, and pleased me by his delightful stories till I fell asleep. Every one with me was furnished with a good bed and a nice room. On receiving such kindness I lost all belief in the science of physiognomy, and did not sleep during the night from pondering over these contradictions to it. When I prepared to start in the morning, I informed the man that I was a native of Medina, residing in the street called 'Zoto,' and that if he had any commission to be executed in that city, he had only to ask for the house of Mahomed, son of Adrees Shafái, where he would find me ready to receive his commands.

"On hearing this the man burst into a fit of passion, asked whether he was the slave of my father, or I had deposited any money with him. I replied that I had done nothing of the kind. He then stated that it was impossible for him to let me go without paying for all the things which I had ate, and the services he had done me. I answered that he was right in telling me so, but before payment he should fix the sum. He replied, 'You are to pay me for the stable, and the kind inquiries which I made after your health (though he had never seen me before), and also for the new jar of fresh water with which I had made ablution; and for the bed, floor, and house, where I had passed the night comfortably. I should also pay him,' he added, 'for the food I got, as well as for the stable where I kept my horses, and the price of the grass he had given to them.' I ordered my slave to pay him what he wanted, and since that day my faith in the science of physiognomy has become fixed." They who love this science will have their wishes gratified in the two chapters I now write on it.

Chapter the first will describe the nature of the countenance, features, colour, shape, and limbs of man. The noblest part of man is the face, because the beauty of the body depends upon its handsome features, and its defects appear in a rude and ugly countenance, while the good and bad of other parts are not considered of such consequence. The marks and signs which appear on the face of man are a good index to the secrets of his heart, which the limbs do not present; and there are sound reasons for this remark. For instance, when a man is under the influence of anger, fear, pleasure, sorrow, or shame, the colour of his face is changed according to the passion; and by each colour you can read what is passing in the heart, and what causes the colour to appear. As the colour brought in the face by anger is quite different from that caused by fear, in the same way the colour of the face in fear varies from that in shame. Such evident changes in the face show the changes which take place at different times in the heart, and which are not to be learnt by other marks. I have fully investigated this, and I come to the conclusion that the appearance of such signs in the face is a proof of the secrets of the heart. I will write first a minute description of the reasons for this science.

If a man have a small forehead, it shows that he is

rude and foolish, because the place of the heart is smaller than that of the forehead, and therefore the difference thus shows itself. If it is neither small nor large, and has a frown, it shows the strength of anger, because when a person is in a passion he looks so. If the forehead is large enough, it shows the man is overpowered by passion, or is lazy; because if it is large, on account of the strength of stomach, it brings forth idleness—if in consequence of the heat of the stomach, it will open the veins, and thus anger takes place in the heart. If the forehead has successive lines, it teaches that the man is a boaster; if it has no lines, we should learn that the person is full of enmity. Abundance of hair is a proof of the existence of grief and worthless words. It is also probable that those having it have a mad temper, as madness causes grief.

If the eyebrows are long, and descend towards the ear, it shows that the man is selfish and boasting. If the eyebrows bend towards the nose, it shows the foolishness of the man. If the eyes are large, it is a proof of his being lazy. It affords reason also to believe that there is cold in his brain, which is really injurious to the senses. Eyes large and projecting show ignorance and foolishness. Eyes deep-seated hide the darkness of the heart and an evil disposition; for the monkey has such eyes, and possesses a cross temper. The lion has the same eyes, and therefore tears the belly of man. If the eyes be small and black, they show malice in the heart, because the blackness of the eyes is created by madness, and madness brings forth this bad disposition. If the eyes be red, like wine, it is a proof of wrathfulness and boldness, because anger makes the eyes red. Blue or light-coloured eyes bespeak a cold heart, as those colours come out of cold materials. Eyes that are open or staring give reason to believe that the possessor is quarrelsome, as the dog has similar eyes and habits. If eyes are yellow, and quick in movement, it shows a man easily alarmed; if mixed with blue and yellow, it shows a man of a perplexed mind. If there are moles inside the eyes, it indicates the heart is not pure. If there is a black line all round the eye, we should believe that the man always thinks ill of others. If yellow and black colours are united in the eyes, it is a proof that he is addicted to the murdering his species; if the moles are red, he is to be reckoned one of the faithless among men. If there is a green colour mixed with yellow in the eyes, we must learn that the individual is fond of mischief and theft. If the eyes are pure, white, and shining, it shows boldness, as the colour of the eyes of cocks is the same. The eye should be mixed with red, green, black, and yellow; and that description is said to be good, and is called "meshee," or buffalo eye. If the eyelids are warped, the man is fond of cheating and fighting. The people of Arabia praise eyes which are half closed. If a woman has such eyes, she is very much admired. Some say they prove the person to be mild-hearted, because women have such eyes. Those eyes show that a woman is fond of allurements.

If the nose is thin, it shows the man to be no stranger to disgrace, enmity, and fighting: these are the habits of a dog. If the tip of the nose is thick, and full of flesh, it is a proof of being destitute of understanding, because this is made known by the features and habits of a bullock. If the orifices of the nose are open, it shows anger. The length of a nose, if thick, shows a want of generosity: this is known by the hog's face. If the nose is like an arch where it meets with the eyebrows, the individual is quarrelsome and bad, because the crow has the same feature and habits.

If the mouth is open and broad, the man is avaricious, and fond of gluttony, because eating much causes heat, which opens the mouth and the passage to the stomach. The mouth of a lion is also open, and he eats much. If the lips are thick, the man is a fool, but bold. The lip which is thick, and hangs down, is a sure sign of the above. When the lip is thick, and the upper one comes over the lower to hide it, we should believe that the person is a hero, and generous, as the lion has such lips. If the lips are thin and open, and the teeth look out of the lips, the man is known to be powerful and strong, as the elephant has the same kind of lips and teeth. If the lips be thick, and the upper one hangs over the other, it shows that the man is ignorant: such lips are peculiar to an ass. If the teeth are thin and weak, and separated from each other, we should say that the man is feeble and lazy. If the teeth are numerous, the man is powerful: he is also avaricious, and a vagabond. He who has angry features is always full of wrath.

If the flesh is in abundance on the face, we should think the man destitute of wisdom, as a bullock. The veins of the brain, in consequence of the flesh over the face are obstructed in their rapid circulation, and thus deprived of sense. If there is not much flesh on the face we should think the person is always deliberating, because deliberation causes madness, and madness makes the flesh scant. If the face is hard, and covered over with lines, it shows sadness, and a broken heart. If it is hard, broad, and long, the man is considered of mean disposition, miserable, and quick in making his friendship, which however is like that of the fox. There are very few persons who are free from such defects, and have good features. A man with such is considered to be civil and mild, but sometimes an ugly face is attended by similar qualities, though this is very rare. If the ear and eye look swelling, and the veins be drawn up tight on the neck, these are the signs of an angry person. He who laughs very little is thinking of doing harm to others, and is also not pleased to see men happy and contented. A very loud speaker is sure to quarrel, and be of a long tongue. The man who coughs in laughing is rude.

If the ears are long, the man is destined to live long and have little sense, because the ears of an ass are large, and length of age is in consequence of the heat of the temper. If the neck is thick and strong, it shows rage. The neck of a male is stronger than that of a female. If it is thin, the man is of low heart; if it is of good form, we should say it exhibits generosity.

If the neck is hard and small, we should know the person is given to fraud and pretended civility. This is learnt by the wolf's habits. If the voice is thick and loud, it shows boldness and a hero. He who talks quickly has an evil disposition and anger. If a man speaks slowly, we should know that he is master of patience, and has a good heart. If any one has got a good voice it shows he is a fool, as a good voice and understanding are never found together. If there be plenty of hard flesh, it is proof of a want of understanding; if it is soft, the man is supposed to have a good temper and quick genius. If the throat-bone is thin, the man is powerful; if thick, the woman is virtuous.

If both hands are long and come down to the knees, it shows both greatness and selfishness; if they are small and hard, the individual is quarrelsome, full of fear, and with an evil heart. If the palm is soft and beautiful, the man has a good understanding and plenty of sense; if small, it is the reason for being proud and uncivil, as females are generally so, and thus proved. If the foot is long and hard and has plenty of flesh over it, the man is without wisdom; if small and neat, he is supposed to be great and honourable. If the lower part of the foot is thin, we should know that the person is given to evil deeds; if thick, and the veins appear over it, he is considered to be persevering, because many celebrated individuals have similar feet. If the foot is small and beautiful, we should know there is weakness in mind, because women shew this.

If the toes of the feet are placed over one another and the nails also in the same manner, it is proof of a bad and quarrelsome disposition, for this is the habit and feature of some birds. If the toes of both feet are joined on near to each other, the man is of ill heart. If the thigh is fat and fleshy, the man is a fool and shameless; if there are veins over it, he is wise: mules have such thighs.

If the bones of the arm be covered with numerous veins, it shows strength of heart; if the thighs are fat and fleshy, the heart is weak: females have generally such thighs.

Chapter the Second will contain the hints for ascertaining the two various secrets from the two different limbs, if, as sometimes happens, the circumstances do not fall out according to the appearance or order of the science: therefore this treats of these exceptions.

In this science we should keep a full faith on the secrets which we learn from the appearance of the limbs, as the temper is never changed but by the heat, cold, dryness, and softness in the heart. When young, the appearance and limbs are quite different from that in age. By features and appearance the female is distinguished from the male, and so on in animals.

You are to follow or adopt three cases if you command the secrets or believe in this science. First, if the appearance of such features, which I have already mentioned, should not command an immediate belief in the secrets, we should have a full discussion before any doubt takes place or the opinion is confirmed. Sometimes one appearance of the features creates numerous different circumstances, therefore we must discuss, and not satisfy ourselves by a single glance or idea.

Secondly, we should possess such a knowledge of the science as to know the true secrets by the external features, and not believe what is thought without reflection. It is told that when the learned Aklimoon was living, there was a king celebrated for religion, piety, and wisdom. This king ordered his picture to be drawn on paper, and sent it to the learned Aklimoon. On seeing the picture and examining all the features and limbs, he said that the king was very fond of the sex. People heard this with astonishment, lost all their faith in this science, and said that Aklimoon was an ignorant person. This news was conveyed to the king, who was astonished. He mounted his horse, and came to Aklimoon. The king treated him honourably, and said that what he had thought of him, from seeing the picture, was right and true; for I was formerly really given to women," said the king to Aklimoon, "but now, in consequence of my piety, wisdom, and science, I have abandoned all such pleasures."

Thirdly, as the above reasons are perfectly clear for knowing the dispositions of man, sometimes the features which exhibit boldness are at the same time connected with those which show cowardice. We should, then, compare them with each other; and if one feature predominates over the other, we should believe the habit so indicated has taken deep root. These remarks have been examined by, and met with the approval of many people; but to be fully acquainted with the science of physiognomy, men should also learn something of astronomy.

THE END.

London: Printed by W. Clowes and Sons, Stamford Street.

www.bookjungle.com *email: sales@bookjungle.com fax: 630-214-0564 mail: Book Jungle PO Box 2226 Champaign, IL 61825*

The Codes Of Hammurabi And Moses
W. W. Davies

QTY

The discovery of the Hammurabi Code is one of the greatest achievements of archaeology, and is of paramount interest, not only to the student of the Bible, but also to all those interested in ancient history...

Religion   **ISBN:** *1-59462-338-4*   **Pages:132**
MSRP *$12.95*

The Theory of Moral Sentiments
Adam Smith

QTY

This work from 1749. contains original theories of conscience amd moral judgment and it is the foundation for systemof morals.

Philosophy   ISBN: *1-59462-777-0*   **Pages:536**
MSRP *$19.95*

Jessica's First Prayer
Hesba Stretton

QTY

In a screened and secluded corner of one of the many railway-bridges which span the streets of London there could be seen a few years ago, from five o'clock every morning until half past eight, a tidily set-out coffee-stall, consisting of a trestle and board, upon which stood two large tin cans, with a small fire of charcoal burning under each so as to keep the coffee boiling during the early hours of the morning when the work-people were thronging into the city on their way to their daily toil...

Childrens   ISBN: *1-59462-373-2*   **Pages:84**
MSRP *$9.95*

My Life and Work
Henry Ford

QTY

Henry Ford revolutionized the world with his implementation of mass production for the Model T automobile. Gain valuable business insight into his life and work with his own auto-biography... "We have only started on our development of our country we have not as yet, with all our talk of wonderful progress, done more than scratch the surface. The progress has been wonderful enough but..."

Biographies/   ISBN: *1-59462-198-5*   **Pages:300**
MSRP *$21.95*

www.bookjungle.com email: sales@bookjungle.com fax: 630-214-0564 mail: Book Jungle PO Box 2226 Champaign, IL 61825

The Art of Cross-Examination
Francis Wellman

QTY

I presume it is the experience of every author, after his first book is published upon an important subject, to be almost overwhelmed with a wealth of ideas and illustrations which could readily have been included in his book, and which to his own mind, at least, seem to make a second edition inevitable. Such certainly was the case with me; and when the first edition had reached its sixth impression in five months, I rejoiced to learn that it seemed to my publishers that the book had met with a sufficiently favorable reception to justify a second and considerably enlarged edition. ...

Reference   ISBN: *1-59462-647-2*   **Pages:412**
MSRP $19.95

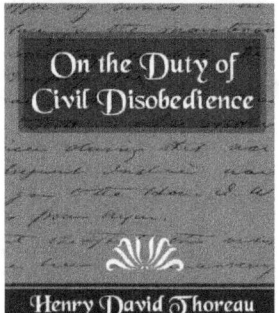

On the Duty of Civil Disobedience
Henry David Thoreau

QTY

Thoreau wrote his famous essay, On the Duty of Civil Disobedience, as a protest against an unjust but popular war and the immoral but popular institution of slave-owning. He did more than write—he declined to pay his taxes, and was hauled off to gaol in consequence. Who can say how much this refusal of his hastened the end of the war and of slavery ?

Law   ISBN: *1-59462-747-9*   **Pages:48**
MSRP $7.45

Dream Psychology Psychoanalysis for Beginners
Sigmund Freud

QTY

Sigmund Freud, born Sigismund Schlomo Freud (May 6, 1856 - September 23, 1939), was a Jewish-Austrian neurologist and psychiatrist who co-founded the psychoanalytic school of psychology. Freud is best known for his theories of the unconscious mind, especially involving the mechanism of repression; his redefinition of sexual desire as mobile and directed towards a wide variety of objects; and his therapeutic techniques, especially his understanding of transference in the therapeutic relationship and the presumed value of dreams as sources of insight into unconscious desires.

Psychology   ISBN: *1-59462-905-6*   **Pages:196**
MSRP $15.45

The Miracle of Right Thought
Orison Swett Marden

QTY

Believe with all of your heart that you will do what you were made to do. When the mind has once formed the habit of holding cheerful, happy, prosperous pictures, it will not be easy to form the opposite habit. It does not matter how improbable or how far away this realization may see, or how dark the prospects may be, if we visualize them as best we can, as vividly as possible, hold tenaciously to them and vigorously struggle to attain them, they will gradually become actualized, realized in the life. But a desire, a longing without endeavor, a yearning abandoned or held indifferently will vanish without realization.

Self Help   ISBN: *1-59462-644-8*   **Pages:360**
MSRP $25.45

www.bookjungle.com email: sales@bookjungle.com fax: 630-214-0564 mail: Book Jungle PO Box 2226 Champaign, IL 61825

QTY

	Title	ISBN	Price
☐	**The Rosicrucian Cosmo-Conception Mystic Christianity** *by Max Heindel*	ISBN: *1-59462-188-8*	**$38.95**
	The Rosicrucian Cosmo-conception is not dogmatic, neither does it appeal to any other authority than the reason of the student. It is: not controversial, but is: sent forth in the, hope that it may help to clear...		New Age/Religion Pages 646
☐	**Abandonment To Divine Providence** *by Jean-Pierre de Caussade*	ISBN: *1-59462-228-0*	**$25.95**
	"The Rev. Jean Pierre de Caussade was one of the most remarkable spiritual writers of the Society of Jesus in France in the 18th Century. His death took place at Toulouse in 1751. His works have gone through many editions and have been republished...		Inspirational/Religion Pages 400
☐	**Mental Chemistry** *by Charles Haanel*	ISBN: *1-59462-192-6*	**$23.95**
	Mental Chemistry allows the change of material conditions by combining and appropriately utilizing the power of the mind. Much like applied chemistry creates something new and unique out of careful combinations of chemicals the mastery of mental chemistry...		New Age Pages 354
☐	**The Letters of Robert Browning and Elizabeth Barret Barrett 1845-1846 vol II**	ISBN: *1-59462-193-4*	**$35.95**
	by Robert Browning and Elizabeth Barrett		Biographies Pages 596
☐	**Gleanings In Genesis (volume I)** *by Arthur W. Pink*	ISBN: *1-59462-130-6*	**$27.45**
	Appropriately has Genesis been termed "the seed plot of the Bible" for in it we have, in germ form, almost all of the great doctrines which are afterwards fully developed in the books of Scripture which follow...		Religion/Inspirational Pages 420
☐	**The Master Key** *by L. W. de Laurence*	ISBN: *1-59462-001-6*	**$30.95**
	In no branch of human knowledge has there been a more lively increase of the spirit of research during the past few years than in the study of Psychology, Concentration and Mental Discipline. The requests for authentic lessons in Thought Control, Mental Discipline and...		New Age/Business Pages 422
☐	**The Lesser Key Of Solomon Goetia** *by L. W. de Laurence*	ISBN: *1-59462-092-X*	**$9.95**
	This translation of the first book of the "Lernegton" which is now for the first time made accessible to students of Talismanic Magic was done, after careful collation and edition, from numerous Ancient Manuscripts in Hebrew, Latin, and French...		New Age/Occult Pages 92
☐	**Rubaiyat Of Omar Khayyam** *by Edward Fitzgerald*	ISBN:*1-59462-332-5*	**$13.95**
	Edward Fitzgerald, whom the world has already learned, in spite of his own efforts to remain within the shadow of anonymity, to look upon as one of the rarest poets of the century, was born at Bredfield, in Suffolk, on the 31st of March, 1809. He was the third son of John Purcell...		Music Pages 172
☐	**Ancient Law** *by Henry Maine*	ISBN: *1-59462-128-4*	**$29.95**
	The chief object of the following pages is to indicate some of the earliest ideas of mankind, as they are reflected in Ancient Law, and to point out the relation of those ideas to modern thought.		Religiom/History Pages 452
☐	**Far-Away Stories** *by William J. Locke*	ISBN: *1-59462-129-2*	**$19.45**
	"Good wine needs no bush, but a collection of mixed vintages does. And this book is just such a collection. Some of the stories I do not want to remain buried for ever in the museum files of dead magazine-numbers an author's not unpardonable vanity..."		Fiction Pages 272
☐	**Life of David Crockett** *by David Crockett*	ISBN: *1-59462-250-7*	**$27.45**
	"Colonel David Crockett was one of the most remarkable men of the times in which he lived. Born in humble life, but gifted with a strong will, an indomitable courage, and unremitting perseverance...		Biographies/New Age Pages 424
☐	**Lip-Reading** *by Edward Nitchie*	ISBN: *1-59462-206-X*	**$25.95**
	Edward B. Nitchie, founder of the New York School for the Hard of Hearing, now the Nitchie School of Lip-Reading, Inc, wrote "LIP-READING Principles and Practice". The development and perfecting of this meritorious work on lip-reading was an undertaking...		How-to Pages 400
☐	**A Handbook of Suggestive Therapeutics, Applied Hypnotism, Psychic Science**	ISBN: *1-59462-214-0*	**$24.95**
	by Henry Munro		Health/New Age/Health/Self-help Pages 376
☐	**A Doll's House: and Two Other Plays** *by Henrik Ibsen*	ISBN: *1-59462-112-8*	**$19.95**
	Henrik Ibsen created this classic when in revolutionary 1848 Rome. Introducing some striking concepts in playwriting for the realist genre, this play has been studied the world over.		Fiction/Classics/Plays 308
☐	**The Light of Asia** *by sir Edwin Arnold*	ISBN: *1-59462-204-3*	**$13.95**
	In this poetic masterpiece, Edwin Arnold describes the life and teachings of Buddha. The man who was to become known as Buddha to the world was born as Prince Gautama of India but he rejected the worldly riches and abandoned the reigns of power when...		Religion/History/Biographies Pages 170
☐	**The Complete Works of Guy de Maupassant** *by Guy de Maupassant*	ISBN: *1-59462-157-8*	**$16.95**
	"For days and days, nights and nights, I had dreamed of that first kiss which was to consecrate our engagement, and I knew not on what spot I should put my lips..."		Fiction/Classics Pages 240
☐	**The Art of Cross-Examination** *by Francis L. Wellman*	ISBN: *1-59462-309-0*	**$26.95**
	Written by a renowned trial lawyer, Wellman imparts his experience and uses case studies to explain how to use psychology to extract desired information through questioning.		How-to/Science/Reference Pages 408
☐	**Answered or Unanswered?** *by Louisa Vaughan*	ISBN: *1-59462-248-5*	**$10.95**
	Miracles of Faith in China		Religion Pages 112
☐	**The Edinburgh Lectures on Mental Science (1909)** *by Thomas*	ISBN: *1-59462-008-3*	**$11.95**
	This book contains the substance of a course of lectures recently given by the writer in the Queen Street Hall, Edinburgh. Its purpose is to indicate the Natural Principles governing the relation between Mental Action and Material Conditions...		New Age/Psychology Pages 148
☐	**Ayesha** *by H. Rider Haggard*	ISBN: *1-59462-301-5*	**$24.95**
	Verily and indeed it is the unexpected that happens! Probably if there was one person upon the earth from whom the Editor of this, and of a certain previous history, did not expect to hear again...		Classics Pages 380
☐	**Ayala's Angel** *by Anthony Trollope*	ISBN: *1-59462-352-X*	**$29.95**
	The two girls were both pretty, but Lucy who was twenty-one who supposed to be simple and comparatively unattractive, whereas Ayala was credited, as her Bombwhat romantic name might show, with poetic charm and a taste for romance. Ayala when her father died was nineteen...		Fiction Pages 484
☐	**The American Commonwealth** *by James Bryce*	ISBN: *1-59462-286-8*	**$34.45**
	An interpretation of American democratic political theory. It examines political mechanics and society from the perspective of Scotsman James Bryce		Politics Pages 572
☐	**Stories of the Pilgrims** *by Margaret P. Pumphrey*	ISBN: *1-59462-116-0*	**$17.95**
	This book explores pilgrims religious oppression in England as well as their escape to Holland and eventual crossing to America on the Mayflower, and their early days in New England...		History Pages 268

www.bookjungle.com email: sales@bookjungle.com fax: 630-214-0564 mail: Book Jungle PO Box 2226 Champaign, IL 61825

QTY

The Fasting Cure by **Sinclair Upton** ISBN: *1-59462-222-1* **$13.95**
In the Cosmopolitan Magazine for May, 1910, and in the Contemporary Review (London) for April, 1910, I published an article dealing with my experiences in fasting. I have written a great many magazine articles, but never one which attracted so much attention... *New Age/Self Help/Health Pages 164*

Hebrew Astrology by **Sepharial** ISBN: *1-59462-308-2* **$13.45**
In these days of advanced thinking it is a matter of common observation that we have left many of the old landmarks behind and that we are now pressing forward to greater heights and to a wider horizon than that which represented the mind-content of our progenitors... *Astrology Pages 144*

Thought Vibration or The Law of Attraction in the Thought World ISBN: *1-59462-127-6* **$12.95**
by **William Walker Atkinson** *Psychology/Religion Pages 144*

Optimism by **Helen Keller** ISBN: *1-59462-108-X* **$15.95**
Helen Keller was blind, deaf, and mute since 19 months old, yet famously learned how to overcome these handicaps, communicate with the world, and spread her lectures promoting optimism. An inspiring read for everyone... *Biographies/Inspirational Pages 84*

Sara Crewe by **Frances Burnett** ISBN: *1-59462-360-0* **$9.45**
In the first place, Miss Minchin lived in London. Her home was a large, dull, tall one, in a large, dull square, where all the houses were alike, and all the sparrows were alike, and where all the door-knockers made the same heavy sound... *Childrens/Classic Pages 88*

The Autobiography of Benjamin Franklin by **Benjamin Franklin** ISBN: *1-59462-135-7* **$24.95**
The Autobiography of Benjamin Franklin has probably been more extensively read than any other American historical work, and no other book of its kind has had such ups and downs of fortune. Franklin lived for many years in England, where he was agent... *Biographies/History Pages 332*

Name	
Email	
Telephone	
Address	
City, State ZIP	

☐ Credit Card   ☐ Check / Money Order

Credit Card Number	
Expiration Date	
Signature	

Please Mail to: Book Jungle
                  PO Box 2226
                  Champaign, IL 61825
or Fax to: 630-214-0564

ORDERING INFORMATION

web: *www.bookjungle.com*
email: *sales@bookjungle.com*
fax: *630-214-0564*
mail: *Book Jungle PO Box 2226 Champaign, IL 61825*
or PayPal *to sales@bookjungle.com*

Please contact us for bulk discounts

DIRECT-ORDER TERMS

**20% Discount if You Order
Two or More Books**
Free Domestic Shipping!
Accepted: Master Card, Visa,
Discover, American Express

www.ingramcontent.com/pod-product-compliance
Lightning Source LLC
Chambersburg PA
CBHW082103230426
43671CB00015B/2598